Y0-BSS-182

THE DECLINE OF THE TRADITIONAL PENSION

The traditional (final- or average-salary) pension that employers have provided their employees has suffered a huge decline in labor force coverage in the United Kingdom and the United States, and less severe declines in Canada and elsewhere. The traditional pension provides a precious measure of retirement security by paying retirees an annuity for life. This study compares developments in the countries just named and in Australia, Denmark, Germany, Japan, the Netherlands, Sweden, and Switzerland to explain the forces behind the decline of the traditional pension and to contrast the experience of public-sector employer-provided plans, where it remains dominant. Given the great value of the longevity insurance that the traditional plan provides, and the risks its diminished coverage entails, the book proposes a set of measures that either stem the decline or endow defined-contribution pensions with some of the attributes of the traditional plan.

George A. (Sandy) Mackenzie is Senior Strategic Policy Advisor in the Public Policy Institute of AARP in Washington, DC. A Rhodes Scholar, he spent 28 years with the International Monetary Fund (1978–2006) following a year of teaching and three years with the Canadian Department of Finance. Prior to joining the AARP Public Policy Institute, he was a lecturer at the University of California Washington Center. In addition to his book *Annuity Markets and Pension Reform* (2006, Cambridge University Press), Mr. Mackenzie has published articles in the *IMF Staff Papers*, *Public Finance/Finances Publiques*, *Finanzarchiv*, IMF Occasional Papers Series, *Public Budgeting and Finance*, and *Contingencies*, and studies with the Public Policy Institute of California and AARP PPI.

The Decline of the Traditional Pension

A Comparative Study of Threats to Retirement Security

GEORGE A. (SANDY) MACKENZIE

Public Policy Institute, AARP, Washington, DC

CAMBRIDGE UNIVERSITY PRESS
Cambridge, New York, Melbourne, Madrid, Cape Town, Singapore,
São Paulo, Delhi, Dubai, Tokyo, Mexico City

Cambridge University Press
32 Avenue of the Americas, New York, NY 10013-2473, USA

www.cambridge.org
Information on this title: www.cambridge.org/9780521518475

First published 2010

Printed in the United States of America

A catalog record for this publication is available from the British Library.

Library of Congress Cataloging in Publication data
Mackenzie, G. A. (George A.), 1950–
The decline of the traditional pension: a comparative study of threats to retirement
security / George A. (Sandy) Mackenzie.
p.   cm.
ISBN 978-0-521-51847-5 (hardback)
1. Pensions.   2. Investments.   3. Portfolio management.   I. Title.
HD7091.M16 2010
331.25′2–dc22   2010014784

ISBN 978-0-521-51847-5 Hardback

For Carolyn and Marjorie

Contents

Tables

Figures

Boxes

Acknowledgments

In writing this book, I have benefited immensely from the assistance of and useful comments from friends and colleagues around the world. In particular, I am grateful to David Blitzstein, Bruce Cain, Kevin Laughlin, Anna Rappaport, Doriana Ruffino, Allison Schrager, Gene Steuerle, and John Turner for comments on an early version of Chapter 6. I am also grateful to Rudy Penner, Eric Toder, and other former Urban Institute colleagues for their participation in a seminar on that version of the chapter. For comments on the treatment of specific countries (apart from the United States), I am indebted to Alan Borowski, Doug Andrews, Rob Brown, Klaus Blendstrup, Christina Wilke, Stephanie Siering, Junichi Sakamoto, and David Howdon.

My indebtedness to my colleagues in AARP is heavy indeed. Susan Reinhart and Janet McCubbin, the head of the Public Policy Institute and the Economics Team Director, respectively, have been strongly encouraging of my efforts to write this book. Without their support, finishing it might have presented an insuperable challenge. Matt Suntag of AARP International provided me with valuable advice on country experts. I should also thank Monica Ekman and Eunice Cash of AARP's Research Information Center for help with literature searches and requests, and Charlotte Nusberg for her tireless efforts to keep me informed of current international pension developments. I must note, however, that the views the book expresses do not necessarily represent those of AARP.

I hope that *The Decline of the Traditional Pension* will contribute to the enhancing of retirement security in the countries it surveys, and perhaps in other countries as well. Despite all the help I have received, I assume full responsibility for any errors that remain in it.

Introduction

Traditional Pensions in Trouble

The defined-benefit plan has been the preeminent pension form for over a century. Virtually all of the national pensions of industrial countries are defined-benefit plans, as are many of the national pensions in developing and emerging-market countries.[1] It remains the dominant second-tier plan for public-sector employees (i.e., civil servants, teachers, and other occupations working for governments at any level, and employees of public-sector enterprises and decentralized public agencies). Similarly, until recently it has been the dominant form in the private sector of those countries where the second tier covers a significant share of the workforce. Employer-provided defined-benefit plans are invariably average- or final-salary plans.

The labor force coverage of employer-provided plans varies greatly from one country to another, mainly because of variations in the coverage of private-sector employees. In some advanced economies, and notably in France and Italy, coverage is low.[2] However, in a group of ten advanced countries that includes five G-7 members (the United States,

---

[1] The book uses *national pension* to refer to the first tier of a country's pension system – the mandatory government-financed system that covers all or virtually all of a country's residents. It may be flat-rated, earnings-related, or a combination of both. The American equivalent is Social Security; the Canadian equivalent is the Canada/Quebec Pension Plan; and the Japanese equivalent is the National Pension (a flat rate scheme), plus the Employees' Pension Insurance (EPI) for private sector employees and Mutual Aid Associations (MAA) for public-sector employees. The EPI and MAA are earnings-related. The plans that governments and other public-sector employers provide their employees are referred to as *public-sector employer-provided plans*. They are part of the second tier.

[2] France has two economy-wide plans run by the private sector, one for blue-collar workers, and the other for white-collar workers and managers. However, these plans are PAYG, and in many respects they function more like a public than a private plan.

1

Table I.1. *Quantitative structural features of defined-benefit and defined-
contribution pension plans in ten countries (in percent except for column 5,
which is expressed in percentage points)*

	All employer plans		Role of defined-benefit plans			
	Assets in relation to GDP	Labor force coverage	Share of defined benefit in total as of date shown		Change in defined benefit share since date shown	
Australia	105.4	90.1	3.0	FY2007	…	…
Canada	55.3	34.2	79.6	2007	9	1995
Denmark	32.4	90.5	2.0	2005	…	…
Germany	4.1	59.0	100.0	2006	…	…
Japan	20.0	62.0	93.0	2008	−7	2001
Netherlands	132.2	100.0	97.0	2005	−3	1998
Sweden	8.7	90.0	14.0	2006	−30	2003
Switzerland	119.4	86.0	26.0	2005	−14	1990
United Kingdom	86.1	29.6	89.8	2007	2	2004
Open DB schemes only	…	…	36.0	2007	−36	2000
United States	74.3	50.0	17.0	2007	−16	1989

Sources: Column 1: OECD: Private Pension Outlook (2008b)
Column 2: National authorities and author's estimates; for Denmark, denominator is full-time employees; includes both public- and private-sector employees.
Columns 3 & 4: National authorities, country studies, and author's estimates.
Columns 5 & 6: National authorities, country studies and author's estimates.

Canada, Germany, the United Kingdom, and Japan), as well as Australia, the Netherlands, Denmark, Sweden, and Switzerland, employer-provided pensions cover a significant share of the labor force. The absolute number of employees covered by public- and private-sector plans in these countries is large, and private-sector plan assets amount to about 70 percent of the group's GDP (Table I.1).[3] The book's analysis of developments in employer-provided pensions concentrates on these ten countries.[4]

[3]   The combined GDP of these ten countries amounts to 70 percent of the combined GDP of OECD members and over half of global GDP. Their combined labor force exceeds 340 million.
[4]   There are not many countries in which employer-provided pensions cover a significant share of the labor force with assets that are large in relation to GDP. The ten countries that are the object of this study include all the industrial countries whose employer-provided pension plans have assets equivalent to at least 15 percent of GDP, apart from Finland, Iceland, and Ireland, which were excluded because of the small size of their economies

Until recently, defined-benefit plans held most of the assets of private-sector employer-provided plans in the ten countries, and the number of defined-benefit plan participants was much greater than the number of defined-contribution plan participants. These plans usually took the form of career-average or final-salary plans, and these are the *traditional* plans to which the book's title refers. However, the traditional pension's coverage of private-sector workers is falling, and in some countries, its future looks bleak.

In the United States and the United Kingdom, the decline in labor force coverage of plans that are still open has been precipitous, so much so that many observers believe that the defined-benefit plan cannot survive as an institution in the private sector. In 1989, defined-benefit plans in the United States covered 32 percent of the work force against 28 percent covered by defined-contribution plans. By 2007, coverage of defined-benefit plans had declined to 17 percent, and coverage of defined-contribution plans had increased to 41 percent.[5] In the United Kingdom, membership in open private-sector defined-benefit plans dropped from about 4 million in 2000 to 1.3 million (about 4 percent of the labor force) in 2007. In Australia, the demise of the defined-benefit plan is virtually complete, hastened by the pension reform of 1992, which introduced the Superannuation Guarantee, a compulsory employer-administered plan. Small- and medium-sized enterprises that had previously offered no pension plan to their workers now chose to offer defined-contribution plans, probably because they were cheaper to administer and less risky. They proved to be popular.

Defined-benefit plans may not have suffered so dramatic an erosion of membership in the other countries, but some declining trend is evident. In Canada in 1995, 87 percent of the members of private-sector employer-provided plans were covered by defined-benefit plans. By 2007, the share of defined-benefit membership in the private sector had fallen to less than 75 percent (Statistics Canada 2009). In Germany and Japan, a reform permitting defined-contribution or hybrid pensions was passed only eight years ago. Defined-benefit pensions remain preeminent, but defined-contribution plans have begun to spread.[6]

(OECD 2006). Germany, with externally invested assets of less than 15 percent of GDP, is also included because of its size and because it is an interesting case in light of its recent introduction of hybrid plans.

[5] These figures include participants covered by both types of plans, so there is some double counting.

[6] In Germany, the new plans have a guarantee on contributions and are classified legally as defined-benefit plans.

In the Netherlands, defined-contribution plans remain rare, but traditional pension plans now include a mechanism that changes the way risk is shared among the sponsor, workers, and pensioners to forestall the emergence of financial imbalances. In Sweden, the full implementation of a notional defined-contribution national pension system (NDC system) in 1999 prompted a wholesale move away from defined-benefit plans in the private sector. In Denmark and Switzerland, defined-contribution pensions, albeit with features that make them resemble defined-benefit plans, have been dominant for two decades.

In the realm of national pensions, the financial strains caused by increasing longevity have threatened to dislodge the defined-benefit plan from its prominent position. In countries like France and Germany, the effect of aging has been reinforced by the impact of declining labor force utilization on collections of the payroll taxes that finance the national pension plan. Aging has also affected the finances of the defined-benefit plans provided by public-sector employers.

Despite the financial pressures to which national pension plans have been subject, most countries have maintained the basic, typically earnings-related form of the plan, although some of them have enacted reforms that have raised average retirement ages and reduced accrual rates. Others have added an adjustment mechanism to offset the financial impact of aging. For example, Germany has added a "sustainability factor" to the adjustment formula for pensions that reduces pensions when the increase in the old-age dependency ratio increases (International Monetary Fund 2004a).

Sweden's reform of its first tier is more fundamental than Germany's. Sweden's NDC system was complemented by an individual account system. Of a total contribution rate of 18.5 percent, 16.0 percentage points finances the NDC system, leaving 2.5 percentage points for the individual account scheme, known as the premium pension. The premium pension may be invested in one or more of as many as 700 investment funds. In addition, the reform made the pension that members of a particular age cohort receive a function not only of members' earnings history, but also of the cohort's life expectancy, and incorporated an automatic balancing mechanism that suspends the indexation of pensions to restore balance (Könberg, Palmer, and Sundén 2006, 455–7; Turner 2009).

The United Kingdom is undertaking a major reform of its pension system. The current form of the first tier will be retained but made more generous, although starting pensions will be reduced over time to compensate for the fiscal impact of aging. The employer-provided system will be substantially changed by requiring employers to offer a pension to their employees. Employees not wishing to be covered will need to opt out (Department of Work and Pensions 2006a).

The Decline of the Traditional Pension is motivated by concerns over the consequences of the diminished standing of traditional pension plans. Despite certain shortcomings, these plans have served as a strong second pillar in pension systems that cover a large number of workers in some of the world's largest economies. Their diminished role may jeopardize retirement security for millions of workers around the world.

Working people who plan for a secure income in retirement confront three risks, apart from the risk that saving rates will fall when spells of unemployment, illness, or disability reduce earned income. First, they may save too little, either because of miscalculation or a failure or inability to stick to a saving plan. Second, even if they save enough, either underperforming financial markets or their own ill-considered investment decisions may prevent them from accumulating sufficient savings by the time they retire. Finally, even if workers skirt these perils and retire with an adequate nest egg, they may still suffer a needless diminishment of their welfare if they either neglect or are unable to purchase a life annuity, or some other form of longevity insurance.

Maintaining a traditional defined-benefit plan is not the only possible policy that employers can adopt to enhance the retirement security of their employees. However, it does provide protection against these three specific risks to a secure retirement. The capacity of other pension plans to do likewise is untested, and whether the arrangements that replace traditional defined-benefit pensions will be adequate in this respect is far from certain. A defined-contribution plan, if the contribution rate is high enough and if participation in the plan is a condition of employment, undoubtedly does achieve one important goal of a program of retirement income security: By forcing the participant to save, it mitigates the first risk.

Unfortunately, defined-contribution plans do not necessarily address the second and third risks. They may not even mitigate the first risk, that of inadequate saving, effectively. With 401(k) plans in the United States – now the dominant pension form in that country – the employee is free to decide whether or not to participate and what his or her contribution rate (up to a limit that the plan specifies) should be. These plans are also vulnerable to the second risk, because the investment decision is typically left to plan participants. The collapse of global equity markets in the fall of 2008 has brought home this risk as nothing else could to members of defined-contribution plans everywhere. Moreover, distributions from 401(k) plans are usually not annuitized, which increases the risk that the participant may outlive his or her resources in retirement. The failure of these and other alternatives to a defined-benefit plan to deal with all of the risks confronting retired people can, in principle, be addressed or at least mitigated. That they can does not mean they will, however.

Participation in a defined-benefits plan does entail risks of its own, notably the risk that the plan sponsor may not be able to honor its commitments to plan participants, and the risk that plan participants may need to relinquish their employment before they have become fully vested. However, a well-designed defined-benefit plan should substantially reduce the risks faced by plan members in saving for retirement and managing their finances once they have retired. As this book will explain, the pension plans that will replace them may not be capable of replicating the features that allow them to reduce effectively the risks to a secure income in retirement.

In light of these concerns, *The Decline of the Traditional Pension* has three main aims. The first is to explain as fully as possible the forces behind the decline in the traditional pension and account for the staying power of traditional pensions in the public sector, as well as assessing whether they can retain their dominant position given the pressures they are under. The second aim is to propose reforms that would reduce the risks to the retirement of private-sector workers and possibly public-sector workers that the erosion of the traditional pension's position has created. The private-sector reforms would aim to revive the traditional pension if possible, encourage variants of it that would provide a substantially similar degree of protection, or develop alternative forms that preserve its most valuable features should revival not be in the cards. The public-sector reforms would consider ways in which public-sector pensions might be put on a more sound financial footing. The third aim is to review some recent innovations in first-tier plans, notably the Swedish reform mentioned above.

The forces behind the decline of the traditional plan. Pension experts have identified many different causes of the decline of traditional plans, especially the decline of the traditional plan in the United States. Even before the collapse of global equity markets in the fall of 2008, some observers had fingered financial market volatility, and in particular the decline in long-term interest rates that has taken place in global markets since the late 1990s, coupled with the collapse of the high-tech stock market boom (the dot.com boom) in the early 2000s. Other experts have fingered complex and changeable regulatory frameworks, which have caused excessive increases in the cost of regulatory compliance.[7] Still others have pointed to increasing and unpredictable longevity, which has increased the cost of funding traditional defined-benefit plans. Yet another viewpoint holds that the costliness and inflexibility of the traditional plan have made it a financial albatross, given the uncertain environment with which corporations must cope. The natural corporate response is to shed an increasingly heavy burden. These are supply-side influences: They increase the cost to employers of sponsoring pension plans.

As subsequent chapters explain, demand-side influences have also been at work, which may have reduced the attractiveness to plan participants of defined-benefit plans relative to other pension-plan forms, or even relative to other employee benefits, like health insurance. These demand-side influences include declining employee tenure, a loss of attachment to particular companies, and a decrease in the value that plan participants attach to future benefits (an increase in the shortsightedness of plan participants), which would increase the attractiveness of plans that distribute their benefits earlier in retirement than defined-benefit plans do. Another possible demand-side influence is erosion in the faith of participants that defined-benefit plan sponsors will be able or willing to honor their commitments.

On both the supply and the demand sides, *The Decline of the Traditional Pension* will distinguish between those influences behind the decline of defined-benefit pensions that are reversible, and those that are not. Making this distinction will suggest ways in which the decline may be arrested, or partially reversed, and will make clear the need for measures to mitigate the consequences of a permanent decline in the role of traditional defined-benefit pension plans.

Pressures on public-sector employer-provided plans. Public-sector employer-provided plans have not suffered the same strains as some private-sector employer-provided plans. There are a number of reasons for this, including the lesser chances of public-sector bankruptcy and the lesser frequency and transparency of the reporting of plan balances. Nonetheless, underfunding was already an issue with some public-sector plans in the United States even before the collapse of the stock market, and many plans around the world have become seriously underfunded since then.

Reforms. The end result of the forces impinging on traditional private-sector plans can range from a phaseout or freeze – and the adoption of a

---

[7] Turner (2007) compares developments in the United States and Canada, and suggests that differences in regulatory complexity and tax treatment may explain why defined-benefit plans in Canada have held up better than they have in the United States. Brown and Liu (2001) argue along similar lines.

new type of plan – to relatively minor adjustments to plan parameters or a scaling back of the plan that leaves its structure unchanged. In between these extremes lie many alternatives. Adjustments to a plan's parameters could go beyond minor adjustments to include a substantial redefinition of the pensionable base, or a marked change in the pattern of accruals. Aggregate longevity risk – the risk that the life expectancies of entire cohorts could be misestimated – might, as many pension finance experts have suggested, be shared between sponsor and participant, or even borne entirely by the participant, instead of being borne entirely by the sponsor. This would mean that a plan would no longer guarantee a constant stream of income in retirement, although variations in that stream would not necessarily be substantial. Investment risk could also be shared; for example, by preserving a benefit in the form of an annuity, but making the payment a function not only of the employee's salary history but also of the financial performance of the plan, with a minimum payment guarantee.

Reform of the regulatory framework would certainly have to be considered (and is discussed further in the following text) and financial innovation and financial engineering may play a complementary role. In light of the inadequacy of the current menu of financial instruments to lay off some of the risks to which plan sponsors are subject, governments could consider broadening the range of the debt they issue to include such instruments as longevity or wage-indexed bonds. The right mix of reforms might enhance the welfare of retired people considerably, and reduce the risk of privation in old age.

Measures like these could reduce the cost of sponsoring defined-benefit plans. Nonetheless, many employees may still regard defined-contribution or hybrid plans as more attractive than defined-benefit plans, even after reforms along the lines just described. That part, if any, of the shift away from defined-benefit plans that reflects skepticism by employees as to the plan sponsor's ability or willingness to honor its commitments may be hard to reverse. Plan sponsors themselves could conclude that defined-benefit plans are too broken to be fixed. In these circumstances, it will be imperative that the successors to defined-benefit plans really do enhance retirement security as a well-designed defined-benefit plan would. These considerations apply to both public- and private-sector employer-provided plans.

The treatment of reform of public-sector plans considers the possible advantages of their adoption of the regulatory and accounting framework that applies to private-sector plans. This part of the analysis focuses on North American plans because information on them is more readily available than it is for other countries. Finally, the discussion of reform of national (first-tier) plans focuses on the consequences for retirement security of basic changes in plan design, like those enacted in Sweden.

Chapter Outline and Plan of the Book

The chapters that follow are grouped in two parts. Part one has five chapters, which provide basic background on the history of employer-provided pensions and basic structural characteristics of these pensions in the ten countries chosen for the study; review the economics of employer-provided pension plans; analyze recent controversies in pension-plan accounting, funding and investment; address key regulatory issues; and consider the special problems of public-sector employer-provided pensions. Part two has three chapters and begins with an analysis of recent trends in the role of defined-benefit pensions that aims to explain why their role has diminished so drastically in some countries and not in others. It then tackles the comprehensive reform agenda just described, and concludes with a summary of the book's main findings and recommendations.

Chapter 1 has two sections. The first is a brief review of the history of employer-provided pension plans that sets out the necessary conditions for private-sector employer-provided pensions to flourish. The second section turns to the more recent history of employer-provided pensions in the ten countries the book studies. It provides useful background for the discussion of later chapters, and covers basic topics like labor force coverage; the share in coverage of defined-benefit plans and recent trends in that share; vesting, portability, and other properties of the typical pension; and the basic regulatory framework and tax treatment of employer-provided pensions. This thematic treatment draws on Appendix 1, which concisely describes country by country the basic features of each country's employer-provided pension system.

Chapter 2 surveys the economics of employer-provided defined-benefit plans with four aims in mind. First, it explains that contractual saving plans like pensions can benefit plan participants because they compensate to some extent for capital market imperfections and impose discipline on saving decisions. Second, it analyzes how the design of these plans determines how risks are shared between plan sponsors and plan participants, and thus their cost to sponsors and their perceived attractiveness to participants. Third, it examines the incentives different plan designs entail for saving, job tenure, and the timing of retirement. Finally, it explains how employers have used pensions as a disciplining device and a tool of human resource management, and why the recent evolution of labor markets may have reduced the usefulness of traditional pensions as a motivational device to employers.

Chapter 3 is devoted to some basic issues in pension-plan accounting and investment. The first part of Chapter 3, which deals with accounting issues, addresses how to account for the cost of a plan's benefits, what discount rate should be applied to future liabilities, how assets should be valued, and what should be done when liabilities exceed assets. The second part addresses basic issues in investment. It begins by considering and rejecting the view of some pension economists that a pension plan's finances should not be viewed separately from the finances of its sponsor. It then reviews the traditional mean-variance model of investment, and explains why it cannot be applied to pension plans. The importance of asset-liability management (ALM) is then taken up. Perfect matching of a plan's liabilities with its assets, despite its desirability, is never possible, which means that pension-plan sponsors have to deal with investment, interest, and longevity risk. Liability-driven investment, which the chapter then considers, is a variant of ALM that tries to address these and other risks comprehensively. Risk budgeting is another.

Chapter 4 addresses regulatory issues. It begins by explaining why regulation is necessary, and distinguishes activist regulation, which is concerned with such issues as the coverage of the second tier and pension adequacy, from more traditional regulation that seeks to ensure that the implicit contracts a pension plan creates are honored. Chapter 4 then turns to describe the relatively recent development of risk-based supervision (RBS), which it contrasts with the more traditional approach based on the prudent person rule. The chapter describes and appraises the Dutch system of RBS, because it is considered to be very advanced. Chapter 4 ends by treating a key issue of governance: the potential for a conflict of interest when officials of the company sponsoring a plan sit on investment boards.

Chapter 5 has two sections: The first is devoted to public-sector second-tier plans, and the second to recent reforms at the first-tier level. The section on public-sector plans briefly sketches their basic features, concentrating on the United States and Canada, and addresses the question of their staying power, which contrasts markedly with the decline of their private sector counterparts. It then analyzes some special current issues, notably the justification for the use of a discount rate derived from average asset returns and the rationale of social investing. The second section of

Chapter 5 discusses some recent reforms of national pension systems, notably the Swedish reform. The chapter's emphasis is on how the new systems function and their role in correcting a plan's financial imbalances. (Chapter 7 considers the lessons these reforms may have for other countries.)

Chapter 6 draws on the preceding five chapters to analyze comprehensively the reasons for the decline in the traditional private-sector employer-provided defined-benefit plan in the large Anglo-Saxon countries, and its comparative resilience elsewhere. The book's analysis casts serious doubt on some of the explanations for the decline in the defined-benefit plan in the United States and the United Kingdom that experts have advanced. In particular, the so-called perfect storm of falling equity prices and interest rates in 2001–02 should not have had the impact that some observers claimed, and the effect of increasing aggregate longevity risk has been exaggerated. The financial collapse of the fall of 2008 will almost certainly lead to a further decline in the traditional pension's coverage, but the trend to decline was underway long before the crisis erupted. However, the combination of changes in the structure of labor markets – notably declining tenure and unionization – and heavy-handed regulation have undoubtedly had an influence. In addition, simple ignorance and shortsightedness may have unduly influenced employees' choices between defined-benefit and defined-contribution plans. The analysis presented in Chapter 6 identifies those factors behind the decline of defined-benefit plans that are reversible and those that are not, because this distinction has a critical bearing on the design of reform.

Chapter 7 is devoted to reform and has two parts. The first concentrates on reform of private-sector traditional defined-benefit plans. Reforms to level the regulatory and fiscal playing fields for traditional pensions might partially reverse their decline. In light of the conclusions reached in Chapter 6, however, any reversal is likely to be modest. Consequently, fewer workers in the private sector, if not the public sector, will be covered by traditional defined-benefit plans.

Chapter 7 runs through a range of options with a view to preserving the best features of traditional pension plans, beginning with downsizing, and relatively minor changes to their structure that would alter the distribution of risks between sponsor and plan members in an acceptable way. The chapter then considers the merits of hybrid plans and some recent innovations that make defined-contribution plans more like defined-benefit plans.

In the second part, Chapter 7 considers reform options for public-sector employer-provided plans, and the lessons that the Swedish reform may hold for reform of the first tier in other countries. Chapter 8 concludes the book with a summing up of the book's main findings and recommendations.

The Decline of the Traditional Pension has two appendices. Appendix 1 provides a summary of the main features of the ten employer-provided pension systems with which the book is concerned. Appendix 2 develops some of the analytical aspects presented in Chapter 3 of the economics of defined-benefit plans and the treatment of reform options given in Chapter 7. The appendices are followed by a glossary, which defines terms that may not be familiar to all readers.

PART ONE

1

The Development of Employer-Provided Pensions

Introduction

Employer-provided pensions have a venerable pedigree. In England, the first employer to offer a pension is thought to have been King Henry III, who in 1269 awarded an aging and infirm retainer a pension of four pence per day (Lewin 2003, 32). For more than a millennium, monastic communities throughout Europe provided a pension in kind to those of their members who were no longer capable of toiling in the fields or in the monastic workshops. Perhaps the most famous pension arrangement in European history is *Les Invalides* in Paris, established by Louis XIV for the benefit of soldiers disabled by fighting his wars.

The development of banking and the monetization of European economies meant that pensions eventually came to be paid in currency rather than in kind. Even in the late nineteenth century, however, the pension remained an *ex gratia* benefit bestowed by established family businesses or governments on long-serving employees. It was not funded, either on the books of the business paying it or externally.[1] In the United Kingdom, Hannah (1986, 13) notes that friendly societies that were organized around a trade or occupation and trade unions provided some limited support for old age, albeit to a lesser extent. "For almost all of the working

---

[1] A famous literary example of such a pension is the one paid to Charles Lamb's alter ego Elia by the countinghouse where he had clerked for many years. His pension is to replace two-thirds of his income, which is in line with the rule of thumb that many U.S. retirement planners use today (Lamb 1980). What is striking to twenty-first-century sensibility is Elia's surprise when his employers tell him that he will receive a pension, and his lack of foreknowledge of what would presumably be the lion's share of his postemployment income. Speaking of the United Kingdom in the late nineteenth century, Hannah (1986) states that "*ex gratia* provision was widespread, but its extent is unknown" (p. 13).

classes, [however] working life continued until incapacity prevented it" (Hannah 1986, 13).

The modern pension is a much more complex social institution than its antecedents, and did not really become widespread in industrialized countries until well into the twentieth century. American Express established the first private, employer-provided pension plan in the United States in 1875, but Costa (1998) notes that as of the turn of the century there were only a dozen such plans in that country. In the United Kingdom, the companies that pioneered employer-provided pensions in the late nineteenth century were among the country's largest employers. This was also the case in Germany, where the first private-sector employer to offer a pension was the manufacturing company Siemens (Siemens AG 2009). The first employer-provided pension plans in the United Kingdom were offered to civil service managers in 1859 (Sass 2006, 79). Typically, the coverage of pensions was limited to the better-paid employees.

The emergence of employer-provided pension plans coincided with the ascendancy of large corporations, growing sophistication of financial markets, rising standards of living, and increasing life expectancies at all ages, but notably at more advanced ages. The tax code's treatment of contractual saving was a catalyst to their spread throughout the economy. In the United Kingdom, the Finance Act of 1921 exempted both employer and employee contributions, as well as investment income from tax. Tax was due on pensions only if they exceeded the exemption threshold established by the law (Hannah 1986, 19–20). This is an early example of the *exempt-exempt-taxed* (EET) method of taxing pension funds, discussed later. In the United States, favorable tax treatment of employer-provided pensions dates from 1913.

The first section of this chapter reviews the conditions under which private-sector employer-provided pensions can be expected to develop. Apart from its historical interest, the discussion may shed some light on the recent declines in coverage that have occurred in some countries. The second section of the chapter covers the main structural features of contemporary employer-provided plans in the ten countries the book surveys. The book's main subject is the traditional pension, not the employer-provided pension system as a whole. Nonetheless, an understanding of the second tier of a country's pension system as a whole is necessary to understand the forces acting on the traditional pension. In addition, the experiences of countries where alternatives to traditional pensions have proven to be viable or have shown some promise are worth studying.

General Conditions for the Development of Employer-Provided Pensions

Pensions are usually paid to people who are leaving a long-standing employment, and who are leaving the labor force, or planning to work only part time or occasionally. If people never retired, there would be no need for employer-provided pensions. In other words, retirement, or reduced labor-force participation, is a necessary but not a sufficient condition for the institution of employer-provided pensions to develop.

As many writers have emphasized, mass retirement is a recent phenomenon, about as recent an institution as the institution of pensions itself. The standard economic model of the decision to work assumes that leisure time is a good – making working time a "bad" – and the consumption that the income from work makes possible is also a good. When working incomes are very low, accumulating an adequate nest egg for retirement is very difficult, and stopping work in later life entails severe privation. However, as working incomes rise, retirement becomes more affordable. The extra leisure a retired person enjoys, complemented by consumption in retirement, outweighs the loss in income from work. To enjoy this greater leisure, a retired person must have some combination of a pension or savings to draw on.

Conventional economic theory predicts that increasing life expectancy would lead to some combination of an increase in the rate of personal saving during working life, a longer career, and a longer life postwork, assuming that there were no impediments to extending working life. The increase in the saving rate would be facilitated by an increase in living standards. Without the increase in living standards, consumption during working life would have to decline to finance the increase in consumption entailed by a longer postworking life.

What has happened in the last 50–60 years, which were the heyday of the traditional employer-provided pension in the industrial world? First, working lifetimes have not increased – they have, if anything, decreased at both ends, as people stayed in school longer and often retired earlier. This pattern has been reflected in the design of the early retirement provisions of employer-provided plans, and together with increasing longevity at later ages means that provision for retirement would have to increase. Second, income per capita has grown at a historically unprecedented rate, which has undoubtedly facilitated the tendency for many workers to exit the labor market in their sixties. These conditions imply that saving during working life must increase to finance additional consumption in retirement.[2] A large part of that increase in consumption has been financed by the first-tier pension, mainly on a pay-as-you-go basis. However, much of the rest has been financed by contractual saving. Chapter 2 explores further why employed people might want to rely on a contractual arrangement for their retirement saving rather than rely entirely on voluntary personal saving.

For the institution of employer-provided pensions to flourish, employers must be willing to establish and fund them, and the employee must find the deferred income that a pension provides to be an acceptable substitute for current income. In most countries today, as Chapter 2 explains, the favorable tax treatment of pensions makes them an attractive form of compensation to both employer and employee. When employer-provided pensions were just beginning to take root, however, the income tax itself had yet to become an institution.

An employer-provided pension could be attractive even without tax advantages to a civil servant or to an employee of a private business if it offered a less risky way of saving for retirement than placing money in a bank or another financial institution. Even in the late nineteenth century, opportunities for saving at a positive real rate of return would have been more limited than they are now in all the industrial countries, as would the opportunities for diversification of personal investments. Mutual funds and many other mainstays of personal finance in some of the industrial countries are comparatively recent developments. Bank runs would have been more frequent in the nineteenth century – although they are not a thing of the past – and the institution of deposit insurance had not yet been invented.

Those pensions that existed would have been mostly noncontributory and defined benefit. That they were noncontributory may have made the trade-off between the deferred compensation of a pension and current compensation less obvious. The lack of portability of a pension would not have been especially unattractive to committed career employees, and this feature of a pension could have increased the career employees' share of the company's workforce. The annuity provided under a traditional pension would not have had any competition until the middle of the twentieth century from Social Security, National Insurance, and other national

---

[2] If a worker wants to achieve a certain replacement rate when he or she retires without increasing years worked, the saving rate during working life has to vary with the expected length of the retirement period. If the saving rate does not go up as the expected length of life in retirement increases, the desired replacement rate will not be achieved.

pension schemes – although private annuity markets were developing in the United Kingdom and other countries – and would, as a result, have been more attractive than it otherwise would have been.

We take the dominant role of large corporations in the contemporary economy for granted, but small enterprises were the norm until well into the nineteenth century. Chandler (1977), in his classic study of business organization, argued that the growth of the large modern corporation meant that authority had to be substantially delegated to cadres of highly skilled subordinates with expertise in all the various facets of a large business. Delegation was necessary because the head of the business or a family member could no longer oversee everything. This need placed a premium on devices that would instill loyalty and devotion to duty among a firm's employees. The employer-provided pension and the practice of filling important vacancies from within were two such devices. The complications and cost of plan administration would be less daunting to the large corporation than it would be to a small one.

An even more important reason for employers to offer a pension was the role the pension played in bringing about the separation from the firm of employees who were considered too old to be up to the job.[3] The pension could be designed in such a way that most employees would choose to retire at a particular age. By providing their long-serving employees with a pension, the firm demonstrated a paternalistic concern for more senior employees' well-being in retirement, and encouraged younger employees to believe that they would be similarly provided for when they had reached retirement age. The pensions offered by U.S. railroads in the early 1900s had this goal in mind. The physically taxing work that was demanded of railroad employees meant that as employees aged they would lose their ability to carry out their responsibilities (McGill et al. 2005, 5–6).

For employer-provided pensions to become an accepted and viable institution, plan members must believe that they can count on the terms of the plan being observed. This requirement means that the modern employer-provided pension can no longer be a mere *ex gratia* payment. Instead, it must be based on a contractual arrangement that the employer cannot arbitrarily change.[4] This requires a body of laws or established rules to

---

[3] Costa (1998, 11) speaking of the United States notes that "… [at] the beginning of the twentieth century, aging was associated with a loss of productivity."

[4] In other words, the employer sponsoring a pension plan for its employees normally has a legal responsibility to fund the benefits that have already been accrued. The terms on which future benefits accrue may normally be altered, although the ability of the employer to do this unilaterally varies from country to country.

ensure that acquired rights are respected. It also requires some basic trust by the employee in his or her employer. Unionization of the workforce may promote this sense of trust in both the employer and the institution of pensions, if union representatives are in favor of pensions and command the support of the rank and file. As Chapter 6 will explain, the declining role of unionization in the United States in particular may be, in part, behind the declining role played by the traditional pension.

Another basic condition is economic stability. Financial market instability, high and varying rates of inflation, and large and prolonged swings in the level of economic activity can wreak havoc on a pension plan's finances. Two other conditions are the development of a large, organized economic sector and the growth in the average size of enterprises. Economies of scale are important in pension-plan administration, particularly with regard to the traditional plan. Large plan size also mitigates the select or individual *longevity risk* entailed by pensions taking the form of life annuities, and makes the pension benefits paid to retirees more predictable. The development of actuarial science in the course of the nineteenth century and the growth of the related statistical infrastructure allowed pension plans to make reasonably accurate projections of life expectancies, which reduced the risk to employers of offering pensions.

The risk to the employer is also reduced when financial markets offer a range of instruments sufficient for a plan portfolio to be well diversified. Government bonds should be available over a long range of maturities to fund adequately a plan's obligations to its members. Finally, although life expectancy after retirement has to be long enough to make the institution of pensions worthwhile, the cost of pension plans is more manageable if it is not especially long. Life expectancies at retirement in the early to mid-twentieth century, despite having improved significantly since the nineteenth century, were considerably shorter than they are now.[5] In sum, by the early years of the twentieth century, the preconditions for employer-provided pensions were in place in a number of industrialized countries, notably in the United Kingdom and the United States.

Main Features and Recent Trends: A Ten-Country Comparison

Coverage of the Working-Age Population
The coverage ratio – usually defined as the ratio of the number of active plan members to the number of employed persons or labor-force participants – is

---

[5] The increase in life expectancies that has occurred in the course of the twentieth century may also have been accompanied by an increase in aggregate longevity risk. As a result, retirement at a given age like 65 is more costly socially, and the costs are harder to predict. See Chapter 6.

a basic indicator of the contribution of employer-provided pensions to retirement security. Unless the first tier is very generous, a working person without second-tier coverage must rely heavily on his or her own voluntary saving. This may prove to be more difficult for an employed person earning a modest income and struggling to make ends meet than it would for a highly remunerated professional, but it could challenge anyone's resolve to defer present gratification for income security in retirement.

Coverage in the ten countries discussed in this volume runs the gamut from low to near universal. They fall quite readily into three groups: low- or narrow-coverage countries (Canada, the United States, and the United Kingdom); medium-coverage countries (Germany and Japan, although Germany straddles low and medium); and high- or broad-coverage countries (Australia, Denmark, the Netherlands, Switzerland, and Sweden). The United Kingdom's coverage is the lowest of the ten countries at about 30 percent. Although the coverage of the labor force in the United States is noticeably higher at 50 percent than coverage in Canada or the United Kingdom, it is convenient to include the United States in the low-coverage group because of the decline in the role of the defined-benefit plan. The Netherlands is the highest of the high-coverage group at almost 100 percent. Australia demonstrates that being a former British colony is no impediment to broad coverage.

The huge spread between the highest and lowest coverage rates is not a great puzzle. In the low-coverage (Anglo-Saxon) countries, employers can choose not to offer an employer-provided plan (and if they do, plan membership is not necessarily a condition of employment).[6] In the high-coverage countries, coverage is either mandatory or effectively so. In Australia and Switzerland, employers are required to offer nearly all of their employees a pension plan, which their employees automatically join. In Denmark and the Netherlands, participation in an employer-provided pension is not, strictly speaking, mandatory, but collective bargaining and other labor contracts normally include a pension plan. Many industries have an industry-wide plan. In the Netherlands, an employer's association employing at least 60 percent of the workforce and supported by a labor association may petition the government to include the rest of the workforce under the terms of its plan. In Sweden, pension plans are the product of nationwide collective bargaining; the private sector is covered by two plans. In none of the three countries must the employees whose working conditions are covered by a collective agreement be members of a labor

---

[6] Without meaning to slight Australia, the book refers to the trio of low-coverage countries as the Anglo-Saxon countries.

union, but the role of collective agreements is much more important in those countries than it is in the Anglo-Saxon countries. The share of the labor force that is unionized does not vary closely with the rate of coverage of the second tier.

The two routes to broad coverage taken by the five countries are quite different. The transferability of the Danish–Dutch–Swedish model to other countries aspiring to a second tier with broad coverage is quite limited. Unless a country has similar labor market and collective-bargaining institutions, this route to broad, second-tier coverage is barred. The Australian–Swiss route to broad coverage does not require the development of a corporatist labor-market model. It does, however, require political consensus as to the importance of a sturdy second tier. In Australia's case, the increase in coverage that began in the mid-1980s and preceded the formal act establishing the new system in 1992 owed a great deal to acceptance by the country's trade unions of deferred rather than current compensation, and the perceived inadequacy of that country's first-tier pension (see Appendix 1, Australia).

In the three narrow-coverage countries, pension provision by the employer is voluntary, although becoming a member of an employer-sponsored plan is often a condition of employment at certain companies or for certain occupational groups. This is truer of the public than the private sector. Public-sector pensions in the three countries would normally cover all or nearly all full-time employment categories. In the United States, the dominant employer-provided pension in the private sector is now the 401(k) plan, membership in which is voluntary. Some 20 percent of workers whose employers offer a 401(k) plan do not join.[7] Equally important, the contribution rates of 401(k) plans are chosen by the plan member within a range that the employer specifies, and a large share of plan members do not take full advantage of the "match" that many employers offer (see Appendix 1, United States). Provision of a pension by the employer is also voluntary in Germany and Japan.

In addition to these cross-country differences in the coverage of second-tier plans, its trend also differs from country to country. In Canada

---

[7]   In 2006, some 56 percent of the U.S. workforce aged 21 to 64 were estimated to be eligible for an employer-provided plan (Employee Benefits Research Institute 2007). The actual participation rate was about 46 percent. An estimated 40 percent of the workforce is believed to participate in 401(k) plans (Mackenzie and Wu 2009). Because most of the difference between the percentage eligible and the percentage who participate reflects workers who choose not to participate in a 401(k) plan, and not a defined-benefit plan, it is likely that about four in five workers who are eligible to participate in 401(k) do so.

and the United Kingdom, the rate of coverage has been declining for some time. The decline is precipitous in the United Kingdom, where most defined-benefit plans are closed to new members if not also to old ones. Membership in defined-contribution plans has also fallen, although not as much. In Canada, the decline in membership of defined-benefit plans has been more gradual.

When participation in the second tier is voluntary and coverage is declining, the reasons for the decline in coverage should be found in some combination of the diminished willingness of employers to offer a pension, be it defined benefit or defined contribution, and a waning interest by their employees to join a plan. Distinguishing the question of why *overall* coverage is declining from the question of why the *shares* of coverage of the two major plan types are changing is very important.

The first part of this chapter noted the role that pensions have been thought to play in maintaining the loyalty and effectiveness of long-time employees. As Chapter 2 discusses, the traditional pension, the design of which favors long tenures, is better suited to that purpose than a defined-contribution plan. The demise of lifetime employment weakens the rationale for the traditional pension plan, as Chapter 6 discusses. What is not clear is whether the decline of the traditional pension would lead to a decline in the overall coverage of employer-provided plans, or whether the coverage of defined-contribution plans would expand to offset the shedding of members by defined-benefit plans.

In the United States, a more or less constant rate of coverage of about 50 percent masks an ongoing shift from traditional defined-benefit plans to cash-balance plans and defined-contribution plans, usually 401(k) plans. The relative constancy of overall coverage coupled with the spread of the 401(k) plan suggests that one set of economic and social forces determines the demand for pensions, and another set of forces – the relative advantages of the two types of plans – determines the mix of plans. In the United Kingdom, the spread of defined-contribution plans has been too slow to offset the pell-mell decline of the traditional pension.

Germany and Australia have bucked the declining trend in coverage. In Germany, coverage has been increasing since the reforms in 2001–02, which introduced a type of tax-favored hybrid plan. Reforms in both Australia and Switzerland beginning in the mid-1980s resulted in a very big increase in coverage in both countries, particularly in Australia. In the other four countries, coverage has generally remained constant over the past decade.

Disparities in Coverage

When labor-force coverage is significantly less than 100 percent, it is important to know how it varies by income, status of work (part time versus full time), and other societal and demographic markers. Studies of the United States find a pronounced relationship between both income and age and coverage (see Appendix 1, United States). Well-paid, older workers have high rates of coverage, and low-paid, younger workers have low rates of coverage. This does not necessarily mean that the older a worker is, other things being equal, the greater the likelihood of coverage. The older a person is, up to a certain age, the more he or she tends to earn, and the easier it may be to save. Coverage of the second tier in the United States is also correlated positively with educational attainment, and varies by ethnic group and employer size. It also varies by employment status: The coverage of part-time workers is much lower than that of full-time workers. Similar disparities in coverage are found in Canada and the United Kingdom. In both countries, rates of coverage vary noticeably with age and income.

Another feature common to low-coverage countries is unequal coverage of the public and private sectors. Coverage is always much higher in the former than in the latter, a feature that reflects the weight of history (as we have already discussed, the pension as an organized institution really began in the public sector), the economies of scale in plan administration that the large scale of public-sector employment makes possible, and other influences explored further in Chapter 5. In the United Kingdom and to a lesser extent in Canada, the near-universal coverage and steady employment growth in the public sector have partially masked a disturbingly large decline of second-tier coverage in private-sector employment.

Adequacy

The demographic, economic, and sectoral differences in coverage have potentially serious consequences, but these cannot be adequately considered without a sense of the contribution of the other two tiers to retirement security, particularly the first tier (e.g., Social Security in the United States). It is not easy to characterize the adequacy of an entire pension system, because the assessment depends on much more than the system's structure. The standard yardstick for such an assessment, which is used in a 2008 Organization for Economic Cooperation and Development (OECD) study (OECD 2008b) is the replacement ratio that the system generates. The study adopted the standard criterion that the replacement rate – a measure of

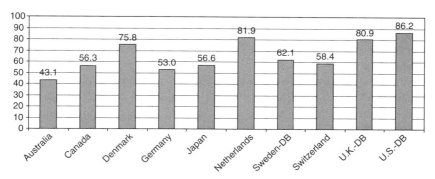

Figure 1.1. Replacement ratios in percent.
Source: OECD. See text for assumptions

income generated by *all* tiers of the pension system – should equal at least 70 percent of final salary. To ensure comparability across countries, the study derives its measure assuming that an average salary is paid in each country, and that the pensioner has worked continuously from age 20 to retirement age. The calculations are done for "representative" defined-contribution and defined-benefit plans in the United Kingdom and the United States. For smaller countries, the predominant form of pension is modeled.

How do the ten countries fare by this metric? Australia comes out at the bottom with a replacement rate less than 45 percent, because the first tier replaces less than 20 percent of an average worker's salary compared to 30 to 40 percent in most of the other countries (see Figure 1.1).[8] Germany has the second-lowest rate, which reflects the low average accrual rate of occupational pensions. Canada, Japan, and Switzerland have replacement ratios between 55 and 60 percent. Both of the U.S. pension forms score well, as does the defined-benefit form in the Netherlands and United Kingdom.

There is no obvious correlation between the relative country rankings by replacement ratio and coverage. Judging from these calculations, Australia has an obvious problem of adequacy, although the way in which the life annuity that the defined-contribution plans finance has been calculated may exaggerate it.[9] Germany may have a problem as well, albeit one that is

[8]   Actual rates of replacement of the current cohort of retirees could be less than the OECD's estimates, because the current system has not been in place for a whole working lifetime.
[9]   The OECD study calculates the replacement ratio in Australia and other countries where defined contributions predominate by assuming that accumulated balances are used to buy an indexed life annuity. Because the replacement ratio is calculated at the outset of retirement, this method depresses the ratio when compared to a standard defined-benefit pension. That said, first-tier defined-benefit pensions are invariably indexed.

less acute. In Germany's case, however, the second and third tiers will have to increase their contribution to the overall replacement ratio simply to make up for the decline in the contribution of the first tier (see Appendix 1, Germany).

These calculations, valuable though they are, must be viewed with some reserve. The fact that a country where a defined-benefit plan predominates can bestow a pension that is high relative to final salary on a worker who has been a lifelong plan member is not really relevant to the situation of a worker who has contributed intermittently or not at all. In the United Kingdom, for example, comparatively few workers draw a traditional pension that replaces as high a share of income as Figure 1.1 portrays. The same is true of the United States, albeit to a lesser extent.

The Predominant Pension Form

The ten countries may also be classified by the prominent form of pension. Canada, Germany, Japan, the Netherlands, and the United Kingdom are defined-benefit countries; the United States is a mix of defined-benefit and defined-contribution [mainly 401(k)] pensions, although defined-contribution plans now predominate. Australia is a defined-contribution country; Denmark and Switzerland are effectively hybrids, and Sweden is a mix. The countries with the broadest coverage are either defined contribution or hybrid. The Netherlands is an exception, but its defined-benefit plans differ in a basic way from those of the other countries.

Regulatory Issues – Legal Forms

In the four countries with a common law tradition, pensions that are offered by the employer are organized as trusts. A trust is or can be a very flexible legal arrangement. In the case of pensions, the underlying principle is that the employer has a fiduciary responsibility to its employees to manage the plan's resources for the employees' exclusive benefit. In the United States, the Employee Retirement Income Security Act of 1974 (ERISA) created two classes of trustees: named trustees and trustees by virtue of their role in the management or administration of the plan. Named trustees are normally those trustees who are assigned their role by the plan document. ERISA defines the term fiduciary very broadly to include any person exercising discretionary authority with respect to the plan's management, or any person advising on the plan's investments for a fee [ERISA, §3(21)]. Officers of the company can be trustees, but there is no obligation to include labor representatives in any administrative body or board.

ERISA requires, in the Anglo-Saxon tradition, that plan trustees adhere to a "prudent-man" standard in all decisions pertaining to the plan. The language of the law is worth quoting: "... a fiduciary shall discharge his duties with respect to a plan solely in the interests of the participants and beneficiaries and ... for the exclusive purpose of: (i) providing benefits to participants and their beneficiaries; and (ii) defraying reasonable expenses of administering the plan ... with the care, skill, prudence and diligence under the circumstances then prevailing that a prudent man acting in a like capacity and familiar with such matters would use in the conduct of an enterprise of a like character and with like aims" (ERISA §404(a)1). The application of the prudent-man or prudent-person principle to the investment activities of a pension plan is addressed in Chapter 4. The prudent-person standard is, as Chapter 4 explains, a social standard. Prudent investing is what investment advisors who are deemed to be prudent do. The same applies to the general management and administration of a plan.

Two other models of pension management are also found in the ten countries: pension foundation and insurance company models. Under the insurance company model, the sponsoring employer contracts with an insurance company, in return for an agreed premium for each employee, to provide a pension according to the terms of the pension arrangement. The premium the sponsoring company pays is normally fixed, making the insurance company responsible for the extra costs it will incur if the company's employees live longer than expected or if the investment experience is unfavorable. The insurance model applies in a number of countries, but its role is most important in Denmark, Germany, the Netherlands, and Switzerland. In the Netherlands, pension insurance is a feature of small plans that serves as a means of pooling risk, and one to which small employers would not normally have access. A similar function is played by multiemployer pension plans in Canada and the United States.

Under the pension company or pension foundation model, the pension plan is managed by an entity that is legally independent of the employer. Labor typically has a stronger representation in the governing or administrative bodies of the plan than it does in a trust; however, one important similarity with the trust model is that, in the foundation model, the employer is responsible for making up funding shortfalls. However, the employer is not directly responsible for ill-advised investment decisions. The foundation model is particularly important in the Netherlands, Sweden, and Switzerland.

A discussion of the legal implications of these three models would itself require an entire book (and a lawyer, not an economist, to write it). From the plan sponsor's point of view, the two critical features of a plan are probably the degree of risk the sponsor bears, and the extent of its control over investment decisions and interpretation of the plan's rules. The trust arrangement entails the most risk for the sponsor and bestows the most control on it. The risk in the trust arrangement is not simply the risk of losses stemming from unfavorable market conditions and inappropriate actuarial assumptions, but liability risk from a breach of fiduciary duty. Plan trustees are legally responsible for their decisions. The insurance model is at the other end of the spectrum with least risk, and the foundation model lies in between. The foundation model is best for giving labor a voice. With the trust model, the role of labor in plan decisions will normally depend on the grantor of the trust. In some countries including the United Kingdom, the law provides for a minimum representation of plan participants on the board of trustees.

Regulatory Issues – Accounting and Funding

Formerly, pension accounting rules varied considerably across countries. Recently, national accounting standards began converging, with European countries adopting International Accounting Standard 19 (IAS 19), and with a concerted effort to bridge the gap between the American and European standards.[10] Convergence has been significant on such basic issues as the valuation of assets (a fair-value standard, or marking to market when assets are actively traded) and the choice of discount rate used to calculate the present value of the stream of future pension obligations (use of a high-quality corporate bond rate if not a risk-free rate). Convergence has also been achieved among the standard-setters regarding the valuation of accrued pension rights of the current workforce despite disagreements within the accounting profession. Official differences remain regarding the consequences of a shortfall in funding (or plan assets from liabilities), which Chapter 3 addresses. In addition, public-sector plans are not necessarily subject to the same accounting and funding standards as private-sector plans.

---

[10] The American standard-setter in accounting is the Federal Accounting Standards Board (FASB). The British equivalent is the Accounting Standards Board. The International Accounting Standards Board (IASB) is the international standard-setter. IAS 19 is the IAS's statement of accounting principles for employee benefits, and FRS 17 is the British equivalent. The equivalent statement from FASB is FASB 158 – Employers' Accounting for Defined Benefit Pensions and Other Postretirement Plans.

The practice of fair-value accounting was controversial even before the collapse of financial markets in the fall of 2008, with some commentators (who did not have pension funds specifically in mind) claiming that fair-value accounting contributed to the crisis by encouraging procyclical behavior. In the specific case of pension funds, the practice is alleged to have obliged plan sponsors to increase their contributions in periods of low profitability and encouraged them to take a contribution holiday when they were most able to afford making one, that is, when market valuations were high. Criticism of the use of high-quality corporate rates to discount plan liabilities has also intensified as the gap between these rates and government bonds has increased. Chapter 3 addresses both issues.

A basic issue in pension-plan regulation is how to determine when a plan is seriously underfunded and what to do about it. The ten countries differ considerably in the approaches that plans are expected to follow in addressing and resolving a funding shortfall. In Europe, the current emphasis is on preventive measures and the use of stress testing and simulations of the impact of financial market fluctuations and variations in other risks that impinge on the balance of a plan's assets and liabilities to detect a plan's vulnerabilities to changes in the financial or economic environment. The Netherlands is in the vanguard of this approach.

In Canada and the United States, the approach remains static in the sense that plans are expected to measure their asset-liability ratio under current conditions. They are not required to test the robustness of plan finances to interest rate, investment, and other risks, although many plans conduct their own tests. In these two countries, an adjustment (to eliminate a shortfall of assets from liabilities) is triggered when an actuarial valuation concludes that a shortfall exists. In the Netherlands, an adjustment can be triggered – even if a plan has a funding ratio greater than 100 percent – if the plan fails either a stress test or a test simulating shocks to interest rates, equity values, and other determinants of the ratio of assets to liabilities. The rules that determine the speed of a plan's adjustment to a funding shortfall are addressed in Chapters 3 and 4.

Portability, Vesting, and Benefit Preservation

A pension is portable when its benefits accompany a plan member from one job to another. A plan member's benefits vest when the member does not lose them when he or she separates from the plan sponsor. Benefits are preserved, even if they are not portable, when they are ultimately paid to the plan member upon reaching retirement age. There are degrees of portability, vesting, and preservation, and complete portability can offset incomplete preservation to some degree.[11]

Portability, timely vesting, and benefit preservation are critically important attributes of a pension plan, especially in economies where workers change jobs frequently and job tenures are short. The law usually establishes a maximum vesting period for a pension plan and usually differentiates by type of plan. If this period is long and employers generally take advantage of it, employees with comparatively short tenures will be shortchanged, and in effect will subsidize the pensions of their colleagues with longer tenures.[12] Limited portability can be a serious matter unless the benefits accrued by a plan member prior to separation are properly preserved. However, as Chapter 2 explains, full preservation in nominal terms usually entails only partial preservation in real terms.

As a general rule, for most countries, not just the ten countries surveyed, defined-contribution plans vest earlier and are more portable than defined-benefit plans. Typically, even the employer contribution to defined-contribution plans vests shortly after the contribution is made if not immediately (see Table 1.1). Defined-benefit plans are portable in several European countries, in Australia, and to some extent in Canada, but not in the United Kingdom and the United States.

Vesting rules differ substantially across countries. Germany and the United States have the most onerous requirements from the plan member's perspective apart from Japan, where for most plans, there is no formal vesting as such, although it is customary for departing employees to receive a pension of some amount. Vesting periods for defined-benefit plans in the United States have not changed since the passage of ERISA in 1974.

For defined-contribution plans, full preservation of benefits should be relatively easy to arrange, and is common.[13] That is not the case with the traditional pension. Complete preservation would require that accrued benefits as of the date of a plan member's separation earn a market-related

---

[11] In the case of a defined-contribution plan, portability means that account balances of plans sponsored by the former employer can be transferred to the plan of the new employer. In these circumstances, preservation of benefits is automatic (although there is no guarantee that the rate of return applying to the assets invested in the new plan will equal or exceed the rate of inflation).

[12] In some countries, the typical vesting period embodied in plan documents can be a good deal less than the statutory maximum. In Denmark, for example, the prescribed maximum vesting period for employer contributions is five years. In practice, immediate vesting is common (OECD 2008a, 221).

[13] Even if contributions to defined-contribution plans were not portable, they would normally earn interest over the period between a plan member's separation and the date at which they could be withdrawn.

Table 1.1. *Portability, vesting, and benefit preservation in ten countries*

	Portability		Legal vesting requirement[a]		Preservation
	DB	DC	DB[b]	DC	DB
Australia	Total	Total	Immediate	Immediate	Total
Canada	Limited	Total	2 years in most provinces		Partial
Denmark	Total[c]	Total[c]	5 years by statute but immediate common; 5 years or 30 years of age for insurance company pensions		Total
Germany	Total with conditions	NA	5 years and 30 years of age	NA	Total
Japan	Limited	DC-C transferable to plan of new employer	Depends upon plan	DC-C 3 years	Limited
Netherlands	Total	Total	Immediate	Immediate	Total (if plan indexes fully)
Sweden	Depends[d]	Depends[d]	Immediate or nearly		Total
Switzerland	Total	Total	Immediate	Immediate	Total
United Kingdom	Limited	Limited	2 years	Immediate	Near total
United States	Limited	Total (most plans)	5 years[e]	3 years	Limited

Notes: DB, defined benefit; DC, defined contribution.
[a] Employee contributions generally vest immediately.
[b] Takes no account of waiting period.
[c] With plans managed by insurance companies, former employer must give consent.
[d] Totally portable if employee transfers without changing job classification; otherwise, preserved.
[e] With cliff vesting (see Appendix 1, United States).
Sources: OECD (2008a) and various country sources.

rate of interest between that date and the date at which the former plan member reaches retirement age. Complete or near complete preservation applies in seven of the ten countries; the exceptions are Canada, Japan, and the United States (see Table 1.1).

Taxation
In general, the ten countries have applied the EET model of taxation of pension plans. Under the EET model, employee contributions are exempt

from personal income tax and employer contributions are deductible from taxable profits, both up to a specified limit in most countries; earnings of plan investments are tax exempt; and payouts are taxed. (Table 1.2)

The most faithful adherents to the model are the three Anglo-Saxon countries, where tax preferences play a major role in encouraging participation in second-tier plans. Germany is a partial exception to this pattern, because the EET rule applies to some plan forms but not others. The major difference in taxation at the accumulation stage among the ten countries is the applicability of limits on the deductibility of contributions. Specified ceilings apply to contributions by both employer and employee in Canada, the Netherlands, the United Kingdom, and the United States. Some countries have no limits on deductibility.

The tax treatment of employer-provided pension plans is almost invariably more favorable than the treatment of other forms of saving, including third-tier retirement saving. This is particularly obvious in the United States, where limits on contributions to the 401(k) plan, an employer-provided defined-contribution plan, are much higher than limits on contributions to the individual retirement account (IRA), a personal pension plan offered by financial institutions. The tax code can also be used as a device to favor one type of plan over another.

The tax treatment of employer and employee contributions sometimes differs. In Australia, employee contributions are not deductible, which simply reflects the law's assignment of responsibility for the 9 percent of salary contribution to the employer. Voluntary employee contributions are after tax. In Sweden, employee contributions are not deductible because they are not allowed. In the United States, defined-benefit plans are treated differently from defined-contribution plans – in the former, only the employer's contribution is tax favored. The consequences of this differential treatment are uncertain. In evaluating the incidence of payroll taxes, economists usually assume that the real take-home wage is not affected by the share of the payroll tax that the employer pays. A similar logic could apply to pension-plan contributions. The favorable tax treatment of contractual saving is, however, more obvious to plan members when their own contributions are tax favored. Consequently, membership in a 401(k) plan might seem like a better deal than membership in a traditional plan.

Australia, Denmark, Sweden and Germany are the only countries that tax investment income (the first three apply a rate of 15 percent).[14] This

---

[14] Japan could be said to tax investment income indirectly (see Appendix 1, Japan). In Germany, investment income is taxed in the case of book reserve plans and support funds, but not the others (see Appendix 1, Germany).

Table 1.2. *Taxation of employer-provided pensions in ten industrial countries*

	Contributions		Investment income	Benefits (lump sum and annuity)
	Employer	Employee		
Australia	The fund is taxed at 15%; also applies to voluntary employee contributions	N/A	Taxed at 15%	Benefits at age 60+ are exempt; earlier ages are taxed favorably – see Appendix 1, Australia
Canada	Deductible with ceilings		Exempt	Taxed as ordinary income
Denmark	Deductible with ceiling on part financing lump sum		Taxed at 15%	Annuities: taxed as personal income. Lump sum: taxed at 40%
Germany	EET for three of five plan types – see Appendix 1, Germany			
Japan	Varies by plan – see Appendix 1, Japan			
Netherlands	EET, with a limit on contributions for DB plans determined by a maximum accrual rate, and an age-varying limit on contributions to DC plans. These limits apply to both employer and employee contributions.			
Sweden	Deductible if plan replacement rate ≤70%	N/A	Taxed at 15% with a notional measure of the rate of return	Taxed as earned income
Switzerland	Deductible	Deductible	Exempt	Taxed; rates vary by level of government and by canton; lump sums are taxed more favorably than annuities
United Kingdom	Deductible with ceilings		Exempt	Amounts exceeding an initial exemption are taxed as ordinary income
United States	Deductible with ceiling	DB: not deductible. DC: deductible with ceiling	Exempt	Taxed as ordinary income

Notes: DB, defined benefit; DC, defined contribution.
Sources: See Appendix 1.

practice is an important deviation from the EET model, because other things being equal, it means that the after-tax return to saving will not equal the before-tax return, as the discussion in Chapter 2 will show. It is probably no coincidence that in all four countries, second-tier participation is either mandatory or effectively mandatory. Finally, all countries tax distributions, but they tax them differently. In Canada, the United Kingdom, and the United States, distributions exceeding initial exemptions are taxed as ordinary income (apart from tax-free lump sums in the U.K.). In some of the other countries, pensions are taxed at special rates. Australia exempts benefits received after age 60.

All the countries, even those that have deviated from the EET rule, treat contractual saving and income more favorably than their income tax would treat it. However, the benefits of this favorable taxation are definitely greater for plan members in the higher income brackets. In the Anglo-Saxon countries, the emphasis on tax preferences as the instrument of choice to encourage plan participation partly explains the low participation rates of low-income workers.

The Form of the Benefit

In most countries, at least part – and sometimes all – of the pension benefit may be taken as a lump sum. In the United States, most 401(k) plans do not even offer an annuity option. Defined-benefit plans typically offer a lump-sum option, and must offer an annuity option. In the United Kingdom, those pensioners who had contracted out of the State Second Pension (S2P) scheme (see Appendix 1, United Kingdom) were required to annuitize their remaining balance by age 75, but that is no longer the case. Australia has been described as "a lump-sum culture" (Rein and Turner 2001), despite the fact that the annuity option is tax favored, a feature of the culture that may reflect the limited coverage in the past of the traditional pension and the income test that applies to the first-tier pension.

The move away from defined-benefit plans in the United Kingdom and the United States (and the prevalence of the lump-sum option in the latter) may be reducing significantly the share of wealth at retirement that is annuitized, and thus depriving many people of needed longevity insurance.[15] In some of the other countries, annuities are a more common choice. In Switzerland, lump-sum payments are possible when account balances are small, but otherwise 75 percent of the balance must be annuitized at a

---

[15] A U.S. survey of a group of employers offering 401(k) plans found that only 15 percent offered an annuity option, and only 6 percent of retirees offered the option chose to take it (Employee Benefits Research Institute, 2008b).

government-established premium per Swiss franc. In Japan, a majority of retirees choose a lump sum.

Outside the public sector, automatic indexation is largely a thing of the past. The Netherlands has recently adopted a policy of conditional indexation (see Appendix 1, the Netherlands), under which pensions are fully indexed when the finances of the plan permit it. In Denmark, the pensions being paid to existing retirees are increased on an ad hoc basis depending on the performance of the fund. For most workers in industrialized countries, however, the only indexed pension they will ever receive will be the public pension.

The treatment of widows/widowers and other survivors is another area where country practices differ. Canada, the United States, the United Kingdom, and Switzerland all have laws that protect the surviving spouses of deceased pensioners. In the other six countries, the law does not protect the pensioner's survivors, but in Denmark, Germany, and the Netherlands, custom apparently does. In Australia, the account holder is free to name one or more dependents as his or her beneficiaries, or to name a legal representative. However, a court order can divide an account balance between two ex-spouses upon the dissolution of a marriage. In Japan, in the case of the Employee Benefit Funds (EPFs), the eligible survivors should be the same as those who would be eligible if the pensioner's company had not contracted out of the EPI (see Appendix 1, Japan).

2

The Economics of Employer-Provided
Pension Plans

An Overview of the Life-Cycle Model of Saving

The life-cycle model of saving is the foundation of the economics of saving, and hence the starting point of modern pension economics. Its basic premise is that people will plan to spend all of their income in the course of their lifetimes, apart from the income that may be set aside to fund a bequest. As Keynes put it: "Consumption is the end of all economic activity" (Keynes 1973, 107).[1]

Unlike the most basic versions of the consumption function model, which are still found in macroeconomics textbooks, the life-cycle model does not assume that people mindlessly spend a fixed share of any additional income they earn. Instead, people are assumed to want to maintain a fairly constant level of consumption over time. The object of saving is to smooth consumption – that is, to transfer purchasing power from periods when income is typically high to periods when it is low. Saving can fluctuate over the course of a person's working life as his or her earned income rises and falls. However, even if income is completely smooth, saving is still necessary to ensure that consumption can be maintained at adequate levels once a person is no longer earning an income.

---

[1] John Maynard Keynes included a lengthy discussion of the motives for saving in the *General Theory of Employment, Interest and Money*. It is fascinating to revisit it in the light of the 70 subsequent years of work by economists on the consumption function. Keynes refers to eight subjective determining motives and four institutional motives of the level of consumption (and hence saving). Saving for retirement is the second of the subjective motives (the motive of foresight): "To provide for an anticipated future relation between the income and the needs of the individual or his family different from that which exists in the present, as, for example, *in relation to old age* (italics added), family education, or the maintenance of dependents ... (Keynes 1973, 107)." Saving to invest in human capital is also part of the second subjective factor. The seventh subjective factor, to bequeath a fortune, is now referred to as the bequest motive.

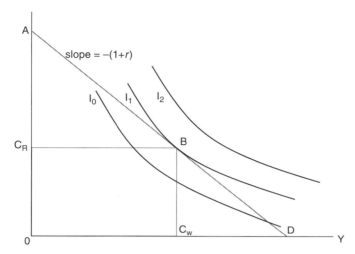

Figure 2.1. Consumption over the life cycle. *Source*: Author's model.

The role of saving in providing for retirement can be illustrated by a simple model with two time periods: period one, working life, and period two, postworking life or retirement. In Figure 2.1, an individual's income in period one (working life) is shown on the x-axis as D. He (or she)[2] is assumed to have no income from work in period two, and must save part of his income in period one to finance his consumption expenditure in period two when he is retired. The line ABD depicts all the combinations of consumption in the two periods that the individual may choose, assuming he spends his whole income during his lifetime. It is known as the intertemporal budget constraint (ITBC), and its slope is equal to $-(1+r)$, where r is the return to saving measured in real terms. It is normally assumed that financial intervention is costless, so that the cost of borrowing also equals r.[3]

The greater the value of r, the less is the amount of consumption that must be given up in period one to finance a given amount of consumption in period two. Moving up the ITBC from where it intersects the x-axis, we move from a state when all income is consumed in period one toward a state at the intersection of the ITBC with the y-axis where all income is consumed in period two.

[2] We are using the male pronoun for convenience throughout the book.
[3] If the rate of return to saving during working life is 50 percent (0.5), then the ITBC could be expressed as $C_R = 1.5^* (Y-C_W)$, where C_R stands for consumption in retirement, C_W for consumption in working life, and Y for working period income. Every dollar, pound, euro, or yen of consumption foregone during working life increases consumption in retirement by 50 percent.

The individual is assumed to have distinct and fixed preferences as to how much consumption he is willing to give up in period one. Such preferences are captured by indifference curves, three of which, I_0, I_1, and I_2, are illustrated and depict those combinations of working-life consumption and postworking-life consumption that are equally preferred. The preferred point will be at a point of tangency of an indifference curve and the ITBC, which is B on I_1. To the extent that our individual has a strong desire to smooth consumption, he would pick a point not far from the midpoint of the ITBC. At point B, an amount C_W is consumed during working life, and an amount C_R is to be consumed during retirement. The amount of saving undertaken in working life is $D - C_W$. If consumption in each period is assumed to be a *normal good* – that is, if an increase in income Y (an outward shift of the ITBC) will cause an increase in consumption in both periods – then an increase in the rate of return to saving would increase consumption in period two. Its effect on period-one consumption is uncertain.[4]

The life-cycle model makes strong assumptions about human behavior, and this very simplified version of the model makes strong assumptions about the world as well. In particular, it assumes away uncertainty: People live for two periods, each of a fixed length, and then die. There is no uncertainty about the date of death – and hence, no risk of outliving one's income in retirement (longevity risk) – and no uncertainty about either income from work or the rate of return to saving.

Both these assumptions can be discarded without compromising the basic predictions of the life-cycle theory. We can introduce longevity risk into the model by assuming that the probability of surviving into period two, p_S, is less than one. We can now introduce a simple annuity, which pays off in period two only if the individual survives to period two. When there are no annuities, the price in period one of a dollar in period two will be $\frac{1}{1+r}$, because this is the amount that must be put aside in period one to obtain one dollar's worth of period two consumption. However, when annuities are introduced, and because annuities are purchased rather than conventional saving instruments, the price of a dollar of period two income will be $\frac{p_S}{1+r}$. The lower the chance of survival, the cheaper is income in period two.[5] Given the rarified assumptions of the model, there can be no

---

[4]   An increase in the rate of return to saving generates a positive income effect, but also cheapens period-two consumption relative to period-one consumption. The former (income) effect would tend to increase period-one consumption, and the latter (the substitution effect) to reduce it.

[5]   As an example of how survival probability affects the price of an annuity: Assuming an interest rate of zero and a survival probability of 50 percent, the price per dollar of an

bequest motive, so the individual would only invest in annuities.[6] Uncertainty regarding rates of return requires a more complicated model. However, if consumption in each period is a normal good, then an increase in average rates of return should increase consumption in retirement. As is the case when the rate of return is certain, its effect on consumption in working life will be uncertain.

Apart from its assumptions about the external world, the life-cycle model in its pure form makes, in light of the recent advances in behavioral economies, startlingly implausible assumptions about the way people behave. The model portrays people as strong willed – although a textbook exposition would not use such a modifier – and able to make and to stick to rational decisions about their future well-being.[7] The fact that the consequences of these decisions may not be apparent for decades is irrelevant. In effect, the decision to save – to choose between jam today and jam tomorrow – is portrayed as essentially the same as the decision to choose between jam today and marmalade today. In fact, the diagram that economics texts (and this book) use to illustrate the first choice is no different from the one used to portray the quotidian choice of breakfast spreads.

Important Qualifications

In the simple world that Figure 2.1 portrays, there is no reason for an employer-provided pension plan of any kind. However, human frailty, market imperfections, and other institutional factors such as the treatment of saving by tax systems can make an employer-provided pension a more efficient way to save and a more reliable way of achieving financial security in retirement than voluntary saving.

There are good reasons and mounting evidence for thinking that, left to their own devices, many people would have difficulty achieving financial security in retirement. As the introduction noted, there are three risks that anyone aiming at security in retirement must confront in financing retirement: the risk of saving too little, the risk of poorly performing financial

---

annuity would be only 50 cents. For every two investors, only one would survive, so with costless financial intermediation, the survivor would receive one dollar for every 50 cents invested in annuities.

[6] See Mackenzie (2006, especially chap. 1), for a treatment of the demand for annuities that goes beyond the assumptions of this chapter's model. Milevsky (2006) is an authoritative treatment of annuities and insurance.

[7] Thaler and Sunstein (2008, 2009) make this point in memorable language: "If you look at economics textbooks, you will learn that homo economicus can think like Albert Einstein, store as much memory as IBM's Big Blue, and exercise the willpower of Mahatma Gandhi" (p. 6).

markets or ill-advised investment choices, and the risk of outliving one's resources in old age.

Several obstacles stand in the way of adequate saving. First, simply calculating the required rate of saving is not straightforward, even if income from work and the rates of return to saving may be predicted with certainty. Although this problem may be mitigated by the use of so-called retirement calculators or by seeking financial advice, not everyone uses, understands, or (in the case of the advice) can afford these remedies. In any event, retirement calculators are notorious for the conflicting answers they give (Rappaport and Turner 2009). Second, when saving involves a choice among many competing investments, the decision may be deferred. In contrast to the assumption of the standard economic model, decision making can involve considerable cost. The need to choose among many alternatives – even among varieties of jam or jelly – results in a paralysis of the chooser's will (Schwartz 2004,19–20).

Third, there is ample evidence that people tend to employ hyperbolic rates of discount when comparing current and future income.[8] Effectively, consumption today receives a much heavier weight in people's plans than consumption at some future date. Sociobiologists argue that human beings are much the same as they were when they lived on the savanna. Evolution has programmed us to worry about present dangers – beasts of prey and enemies – and not about distant contingencies like aging, which was a rare event in prehistory and even for most of history.

Fourth but probably related, saving is like going on a diet – it entails deferring gratification, and can always be put off a little longer. As Blake (2006b, 224) points out [following Mitchell and Utkus (2004)], there is no real sense of urgency about the saving decision, and certainly no sense of impending catastrophe. In this respect, personal retirement security is like Social Security (public pension) reform. The consequences of inaction are not real enough for the electorate to push politicians to take action, regardless of the number of studies of the problem that think tanks churn out. Conceivably, if people who were normally not too badly off were to experience real privation for a time, the abstract awareness of the need to save for retirement would take on concrete meaning and lead to action.

---

[8]   Income received at a distant date will be discounted at a rate well above the government bond yield for the same maturity; however, the extra discount applied to income received at a somewhat more distant date will be closer to the bond yield. For example, I may insist on receiving $400 ten years from now to give up $100 today, but will be content with $450 15 years from today.

As for investment of the funds that are saved, the model of rational behavior that economists employ implies that the investor chooses a portfolio allocation that maximizes the expected return subject to a given degree of risk, and selects that combination of risk and reward with which the investor is most comfortable (or in more technical language, of all the efficient combinations of risk and return, the investor picks the one that just touches on his highest indifference curve).

The actual behavior of investors diverges considerably from this norm. First, investors have difficulty determining the risk-return characteristics of a set of investment options. As Benartzi and Thaler (2001) found, given a choice of N funds, investors tend to invest their money in each fund in equal proportion (and thus following what has been called a $1/N$ rule). Consequently, if two of every five funds in a plan's menu of funds are aggressive-growth funds, a plan member could unwittingly choose a very risky portfolio. The choice of funds may also depend on the order or combination in which they are presented. For example, of a choice of three funds, the tendency will be to pick the one listed second. (Retailers and retail manufacturers are taking advantage of this tendency when they produce and market three similar versions of the same product.) Second, there is both excessive loss aversion and an aversion to recognition of loss. The life-cycle model, being based on the rational-choice theory that underlies neoclassical economics, assumes that when it comes to investment losses, bygone are bygones: What should matter is the *expected* return of an investment. In practice, however, loss-making investments are retained – losses create a lock-in effect – while profitable investments are sold to realize gains. Third, the tendency to take risks varies with the frequency of reporting of investment performance. Frequent reporting leads to more conservative investing, possibly because the variance of high-frequency data is greater than that of low-frequency data. Fourth, and of particular application to the United States, corporate employees do not realize the danger entailed by large holdings of company stock (Thaler and Sunstein 2008, 2009, 122–30). Because their future earnings depend on their employer's fortunes, holding company stock is tantamount to putting too many of one's eggs in one basket.

Finally, there is the decision of how to manage assets during retirement. Here, too, behavioral economics shines a light on tendencies that can reduce welfare significantly. In particular, there is little understanding of the longevity insurance that annuities provide. When the share of a retired person's assets that is annuitized is low, the risk that the nest egg will be depleted will be heightened. Combined with a tendency to underestimate longevity and the same problems of self-control that may have interfered with saving earlier in life, this is a recipe for privation in old age. Excessive discount rates can be a problem in retirement just as they were during working life, only in retirement they cause excessive dissaving rather than insufficient saving.

Excessive spending is not the only problem to result from keeping the retirement nest egg in a lump sum. People who are very afraid of exhausting their resources but unwilling to purchase an annuity may self-insure by choosing a very conservative drawdown rate. This practice may benefit their heirs, but subjects them to unnecessary want.[9]

A human being who recognizes his or her own frailty may, like Odysseus tieing himself to the mast to avoid succumbing to the Sirens' song, want to enter into a contractual arrangement, or a commitment device, that reduces the scope for destructive shortsightedness or other irrational behavior.[10] Certain types of employer-provided pension plans serve this purpose well; others, less so.

The Rationale for Employer-Provided Pension Plans

Shortsightedness and other human frailties can make a strong case for employer-provided pension plans or other institutions that constrain shortsighted saving decisions and reduce the likelihood of ill-considered investment choices. While recognition of the need for institutions that force us to save has played a role in promoting the development of employer-provided pensions, other influences have also been at work. In particular, the tax system treats employer-provided pensions very generously, particularly when the pensions are those of better-paid workers. In addition, employer-provided plans can handle the distribution of the retirement nest egg more efficiently than individuals can. Employer-provided pensions also serve as a device for increasing the motivation and productivity of the workforce, and for easing long-term employees' separation from their employers. This subsection will consider how these various influences have encouraged the spread of employer-provided plans in general. It is followed by a discussion of the impact of contractual saving on the saving rate, and in turn by a treatment of the rationale for particular types of pension plans, and their economic effects.

---

[9] See Mackenzie (2006, 28–30) and Blake (2006b, 238–39) for further discussion of this point.

[10] A very American example of such a device is the Christmas club, which is intended to ensure that people save enough to buy Christmas presents for their families. Members

Tax Issues

As Chapter 1 explains, the typical employer-provided pension scheme allows employer contributions as a deductible business expense, exempts employee contributions from income tax when they are made, exempts the plan's accrued earnings, and only taxes the distributions from the plan as they occur. In contrast, a pure income tax system taxes the initial saving, may tax accrued earnings, and definitely taxes earnings when they are distributed. As is shown below with the two-period model, contractual saving effectively shelters the plan's income from tax. For the same amount of gross saving (GS), and a constant tax rate t and interest rate r, the after-tax distribution with contractual saving in period two (DCS_2) is higher than the after-tax distribution through personal saving (DPS_2), as may be seen by comparing equations (2.1) and (2.2):

$$DPS_2 = GS(1-t)(1+r(1-t)) \tag{2.1}$$

$$DCS_2 = GS(1+r)(1-t) \tag{2.2}$$

The difference between the after-tax distributions is given by equation (2.3):

$$DCS_2 - DPS_2 = GS(1-t) \cdot t \cdot r \tag{2.3}$$

The difference between the two after-tax distributions equals the tax on the income from the personal saving plan.[11]

An example may make the impact of tax-favored contractual saving clearer. Suppose that a taxpayer who earns \$1,000 with a marginal tax rate of 30 percent and a before-tax interest rate on savings of 10 percent saves his after-tax income of \$700. One year later, after paying tax on the interest earned, he has (\$1,000 − \$300 + \$49) = \$749 in after-tax income. If the same \$1,000 had gone into a pension plan, tax would initially be zero, and the following year a pension of \$1,100 could be paid. If the income from the pension is treated as ordinary income for tax purposes, after-tax income would equal \$770. The difference of \$21 equals 0.1 times 0.3 times \$700, or the tax on the income from the personal saving plan as equation (2.3) implies.

---

make a payment once a month to the bank running the club. They earn no interest, and may not withdraw the money until close to Christmas (Surowiecki 2006).

[11] Dividing the difference between the after-tax distributions by net of tax saving [$GS\,(1-t)$] we obtain $r \cdot t$, which is a measure of the extra rate of return produced by the employer-provided pension.

The advantage that this favorable treatment bestows on an employer-provided pension plan is reduced when similar treatment is accorded certain personal saving plans. However, if the limits imposed on plan contributions are much higher than the limits imposed on personal saving plans, then an employer-provided, defined-contribution (DC) plan should retain its advantages for the better paid. This is the case in the United States, as already noted. However, a move from an income tax to a full-fledged tax on consumption would in practice significantly reduce the attractiveness of employer-provided pension plans.

Financial Intermediation Costs

The typical employer-provided pension plan should be able to reduce the costs associated with the buying and selling of financial assets and related activities to well below the costs that an individual investor would incur. This would be especially true of pension funds that pursue an active investment strategy. In the United States, where the costs that an individual investor incurs in investing in broad-market index funds is very low, this cost advantage would be less significant. The broad range and variability of these index funds by risk class means that an individual investor with some financial acumen should be able, in principle, to design an efficient portfolio.

The Annuity Market: Individual Versus Group Annuities

Another advantage enjoyed by employer-provided plans results not from fiscal conventions but from the economics of the annuity market. Individuals who want more longevity insurance than their first-tier pension provides, and who have not participated in an employer-provided plan must purchase an annuity in the individual market. These annuities are more expensive than annuities purchased on a group basis because adverse selection is a much more serious problem with individual than with group annuities. Group annuities also benefit from the economies of wholesale purchasing.[12] These advantages, which should apply in the case of traditional pension plans, hold whether the employer purchases annuities for

---

[12] Annuitants who voluntarily purchase their annuities live longer than nonannuitants, so that premiums will be higher than they would be if the population of annuitants had life expectancies similar to those of the general population. Pension plan members are unlikely to have joined their plans because they expect to live longer than the average. In the case of the traditional pension plan, participation is normally a condition of employment. Hence, adverse selection is not an issue.

retiring employees from an insurance company, or takes on all the longevity risk entailed by an obligation to pay a pension for life itself.[13]

Pension Plans and Human Resource Management

As Chapter 1 explained, the institution of employer-provided pensions began as a means of providing a dignified exit from work for employees who were no longer up to the demands – usually physical – of their jobs. Some economists have also argued that the typical employer-provided pension, because of its back-loaded benefits, can also serve as a way of ensuring that an employer recoups the costs of training and apprenticeship (Blake 2006b, 55–8). The deferral of pay discourages an employee from leaving before the employer has recouped the initial investment in the employee, and encourages an investment in knowledge that is specific to the firm as the employee matures.

Another rationale for a back-loaded pension (or any arrangement that defers pay) is that it increases the cost to a worker of the loss of job or promotion prospects from poor performance or shirking. The promise of a pension – and the threat of the loss of pension benefits, either in whole or in part – will spur workers to greater efforts. If workers share in the resulting increase in productivity, the sum of their current and deferred compensation (pensions) will be greater than the wages they would earn were there no pension plan, and it will be in their interest to participate in a plan (and in their employer's interest to offer one). The likelihood of a pension plan having these kinds of motivational effects will depend on its design, which should ensure that the plan remains actuarially fair or better than fair as a plan member's period of service lengthens.

The Impact of Contractual Saving on Personal Saving

The impact of contractual saving on the personal saving rate depends mainly on two influences: the tax regime – how favorably contractual saving is treated relative to voluntary saving – and how high the rate of contractual saving is relative to the rate of saving that would be undertaken voluntarily were there no pension plan. However, the fact that the amount of saving the participant does is not in his or her control does not necessarily mean that being a participant will increase saving.

---

[13] A pension plan with many members that funds its own annuities will benefit from the law of large numbers, just as an insurance company with many annuitants would. This practice leaves the plan exposed to aggregate longevity risk.

In approaching this issue it is not a bad idea to sidestep initially the complications posed by shortsighted behavior. The life-cycle model implies that participation in an employer-provided plan could be expected to reduce the amount of private voluntary saving that a participant would do. This follows from the fact that, if we abstract from the difference in the tax treatment of contractual and voluntary saving, the establishment of an employer-provided plan should not affect the amount of consumption a person would want to have in the postretirement period. Hence, provided that contractual saving is less than the amount of saving that would be undertaken voluntarily, private saving will simply decline by enough to keep the sum of private and contractual saving unchanged.

In the case of a 401(k) plan, the fact that plan sponsors will match a part of a participant's contribution might lead to an increase in contractual saving, but here again the effect on total saving will depend on what a participant's rate of saving would have been in the absence of a plan. A matching scheme effectively increases a participant's income, and so could lead to a decline in his or her own saving. Even if a participant takes full advantage of the match the employer offers, we may not infer that the participant's saving rate has increased.

If contractual saving exceeds what would be undertaken voluntarily, the effect on consumption during working life will depend on whether the participant can borrow or run down his or her asset holdings. The basic model implies that if borrowing is possible at the same rate of interest earned by plan contributions, there will be no effect on overall saving.

In practice, borrowing on the strength of pension wealth is difficult, even in countries with well-developed financial markets. Pension wealth may not be accessible until the plan member nears retirement, and even when financial markets are comparatively liberal, financial institutions may be reluctant to lend on the strength of the expected benefits a pension will pay.

This reluctance will not be affected much by the type of pension plan. With a traditional pension plan, valuing pension wealth requires estimating the path of future salary and interest rates as well as employee tenure. With a defined-contribution plan, the account balance may be directly measured, but its future value will depend not only on future contributions, but the realized rate of return on the plan member's investment portfolio. With either type of plan, any estimate of the effective collateral that pension wealth creates will be highly uncertain. A typical cash-balance plan, as found in the United States and described later in the chapter, will reduce the margin of uncertainty somewhat if the interest credit that applies to a plan member's hypothetical balance is either a constant or varies little.

Turning to the implications of the tax regime, the favorable tax treatment of contractual saving entails an income effect, because it increases the after-tax rate of return to contractual saving, although plan participants cannot normally increase their contractual saving in response to that increase. Economists assume that this increase in income would increase consumption in both periods one and two, and hence reduce period one saving.

In sum, favorable tax treatment of contractual saving can undoubtedly make contractual saving through pension-plan participation a superior option to total reliance on private voluntary saving, but the life-cycle model does not predict that it must increase the amount of saving for retirement. If people under-save in the absence of a contractual saving plan, pension-plan membership can increase the total amount of saving they do and can enhance welfare. Although under-savers may try to compensate for the effect of contractual saving by reducing their voluntary saving, it may be low already, and, as we have seen, borrowing on the strength of pension wealth to sustain consumption will be difficult.

The Economic Effects of Different Employer-Provided Pension Plans

The term defined-benefit (DB) plan is often used to refer only to what the book has termed traditional pension plans, where the benefit is determined by some measure of salary and the number of years of plan participation. However, the family of defined-benefit plans is far broader than that definition implies. This section of the chapter will first describe the structure of these traditional plans, and then turn to describe other defined-benefit plans – notably cash-balance plans and other hybrid plans – and finally to defined-contribution plans. These descriptions are the basis of an analysis of how the various plans distribute risk between plan sponsor and participant, and of their impact on voluntary saving, timing of retirement, and job tenure.

Traditional Pension Plans – Financing and Other Aspects of Design
The final-salary and the career-average pension are the two basic forms that the traditional pension takes. This type of defined-benefit pension can, in principle, take on an infinite number of forms. The pension is determined by applying an accrual factor to some measure of salary. In principle, the pensionable salary could be calculated in countless ways, and accrual factors can differ for different periods of service and change over time. In practice, limits will apply to both the number of years of service (i.e., active plan

membership) that may be counted toward the calculation of the pension, and to the number of years of service and age at retirement that make a contributor eligible for a pension.[14]

Final-salary and career-average salary plans are the same in many respects, but the differences in their design can cause big differences in the pensions received by employees whose salaries have grown on average at substantially different rates. Assuming that a plan contributor has satisfied the service and age requirements for a pension but has not reached the point at which pension rights stop accruing, and that the accrual factor, α, is constant, the formula for the pension under the career-average plan (PCA) will be, where pay_t stands for salary in year t, H for the year of hire, and R for the year of retirement (i.e., the first postwork year):

$$PCA = \alpha(R-H)\left[\frac{\sum\limits_{t=H}^{R-1} pay_t}{R-H}\right] = \alpha\sum_{t=H}^{R-1} pay_t \qquad (2.4)$$

The formula for the pension under a final-salary plan (PFS) is given by equation (2.5), where Y is the number of years at the end of career taken account of in calculating the average and w_t are the weights applied to each year.

$$PFS = \alpha(R-H)\sum_{t=R-Y}^{R-1} w_t \cdot pay_t \qquad (2.5)$$

Both of these plans can be described as making the pension a fraction of a weighted average of salary over a plan member's career. With the career-average plan, every year gets an equal weight. With the final-salary plan, the yearly salaries during the last few years – often the last three, but this depends on the design of the plan – are given weights than sum to one. Earlier years are not given any weight.

Even a small difference in average salary growth rates can result in a big difference in the pension payable under the two schemes. For example, an increase in average salary growth from 2.5 percent to 3.5 percent over 35 years increases the pension payable by a final-pension scheme by about 40 percent. The increase under a career-average plan is 21 percent.

Final-salary pension plans were conceived with more than retirement security in mind. They create a powerful incentive for strong (or at least

---

[14] A common formulation with U.S. and Canadian plans is that the number of years of service plus age at retirement must at least equal some stipulated figure, like 80.

promotion-achieving) performance on the job and loyalty to the firm, and reward the build-up of know-how that is specific to the firm. It is less clear, however, that they are superior to career-average plans as a form of contractual saving.

Traditional Pension Plans – Replacement Rates

Both the career-average and the final-salary pensions rely on the concept of the replacement ratio, which is the ratio of the pension to the plan's measure of income. In equations (2.4) and (2.5) for the two types of plans, the replacement ratio is the same, and is equal to $\alpha(R - H)$. For example, for a career of 30 years and an accrual factor of 0.015, the replacement ratio will be 45 percent. However, the value of a pension with these parameters will typically be much higher if the measure of income used is final salary than if it is career-average salary.

In practice, pension planners have a target replacement ratio in mind. In the United States, the value for the ratio often used by financial planners, taking account of all sources of income in retirement, is in the range of 70 to 80 percent. There is, however, considerable disagreement among economists as to what the target replacement ratio should be. Kotlikoff (2008) has emphasized the undeniable theoretical truth that the replacement ratio must be endogenously determined, and contends that the standard ratio of 70 percent that American retirement planners use is far too high.[15] Other economists, who have U.S. pensioners in mind, point to the increasing costs of health care as just one reason to assume a higher value (VanDerhei 2006.)[16]

Whatever target is chosen for the replacement ratio, an issue of at least as much importance is the measure of income to which it is applied. A measure of income that gives a heavy weight to the last few years of income effectively says that what counts is not smoothing consumption over one's lifetime, but basing consumption on the highest level of income attained during one's career. A pure career-average measure, on the other hand, is more in line with the life-cycle hypothesis.

Which measure of income is the best? Is either correct? Basing the pension on lifetime income means that, assuming income rose substantially

---

[15] The endogeneity of the replacement ratio can be demonstrated with the simple two-period model; in particular, consumption in retirement should depend on the rate of return to saving.

[16] If the aim of a retirement plan (pension and personal saving) is to maintain consumption in retirement at its level in working life, then the replacement ratio will depend on, among other influences, the saving rate pre-retirement, and the tax treatment of pension and other retirement income relative to earned income.

over working life, the pension will be related to income levels surpassed years ago. The life-cycle theory does allow for revisions to estimated lifetime income. Consumption undoubtedly adjusts with increases in income, when those are expected to persist; therefore, counting all the years of a career in determining a pension could mean that the pension replaces too low a share of income. Basing the pension on the final years of work, however, could mean that the replacement ratio is unnecessarily high if the pensioner has been given very large salary increases in the last years of work. A measure of income that averaged income over less than a lifetime but more than just the final years of work might strike the right balance.

The Traditional Pension Plan – Other Issues

The choice between a career-average and final-salary plan has implications for pension-plan financing, because the future obligations of a final-salary plan might be less predictable than a career-average plan. Whether this is so will depend on how salary increases and promotions in an organization are determined. If the distribution of salary increases is fixed – so that, for example, in a given year only x percent of the staff in a given occupation and salary range get an increase of b percent, y percent get an increase of c percent, and z percent get an increase of d percent ($x + y + z = 100$), then the distribution of salaries in the aggregate would be more predictable than the salaries of individual employees. Nonetheless, the longer the period over which salary was averaged, the more predictable would pension liabilities be.

In part because traditional pension plans have been used as a device to inculcate loyalty to a firm and in part because of their basic design, pension-plan vesting provisions usually penalize employees whose tenure with the sponsoring employer is short. As Chapter 1 noted, in both Germany and the United States it is possible to work for up to five years at a company and separate without any benefits. The period of employment before vesting can actually be longer than this, because qualifying for plan membership may require a preliminary period of employment.

The survey presented in Chapter 1 made clear that traditional pension plans are the least portable of plans, which means that, in most countries, someone who separates from a firm cannot take his benefits with him, either to place in the balance of a defined-contribution plan or to add to the benefits that will accrue under another defined-benefit plan. If no interest is applied to the benefits accrued under a traditional plan, and if they are not indexed, their real value can decline drastically between the date of separation and the time they are payable.

As a result, a worker who takes a series of jobs can substantially reduce his pension, even if he is vested under each of the plans in which he participates (see Box 2.1 for a more detailed explanation). Blake (2006b, 188–91) summarizes a study by Blake and Orszag (1997) of portability losses under U.K. defined-benefit plans. These losses are particularly severe when a worker separates from a firm at midcareer and establishes a personal pension plan because of the resulting loss of employer contributions.

Box 2.1. The cost of short tenures

The loss that an employee suffers by leaving early can be illustrated as follows. Assume that he or she started work in year 1 with an annual salary equal to W_1, which grows at an annual rate of g percent. If he had stayed at his employer for N years, with a final salary scheme with an accrual rate of α, his pension (P_{stay}) would be:

$$P_{stay} = \alpha \cdot N \cdot W_1 (1+g)^{N-1} \qquad (2.6)$$

If he leaves after M years and goes to a firm with an identical scheme, his pension (P_{quit}) will be:

$$P_{quit} = \alpha \cdot M \cdot W_1 (1+g)^{M-1} + \alpha (N-M) W_1 (1+g)^{N-1} \qquad (2.7)$$

The difference (P) between them is:

$$P_\Delta = \alpha \cdot M \cdot W_1 \{(1+g)^{N-1} - (1+g)^{M-1}\} \qquad (2.8)$$

The difference between the two outcomes expressed as a ratio of the pension enjoyed when the worker stays is:

$$P_\Delta / P_{stay} = (M/N)\{1 - (1/(1+g)^{N-M-2})\} \qquad (2.9)$$

The higher the value of g, the closer this ratio approaches M/N. For example, if g, which is a nominal magnitude, equals 5 percent, M is 10 years, and N is 30 years, then the loss in pension from quitting and not staying is 19 percent. Equation (2.9) can be solved for that value of M that will maximize the loss in the value of the pension that results from quitting the job. The precise value will depend on the values of g and N, but will be somewhere in the middle of the range (0–N). Leaving a job either early or toward the end of working life will be less costly than leaving it in the middle.

Source: Author's model and calculations.

There is nothing inherent in the basic structure of a traditional plan that requires that the accrued benefits of separated plan members not be adjusted for inflation over the interval between the date of separation and the date of eligibility for payment of benefits, or that vesting periods be long. The strength of the incentive to stay with an employer depends on the specific design of a plan, and, in addition to its vesting requirements, on the value or values of the accrual factor and the age at which early retirement is first possible.

In addition to creating a strong incentive to stay with an employer through the prime earning period, a pension can be designed to give employees reaching a certain age a strong nudge toward the door. Specifically, pensions can be designed so that the increase in the annual pension once a participant has reached a certain combination of age and years of service no longer compensates him for the loss of pension income when he works an additional year. The pension can simply be capped after the employee achieves some combination of years of service and age. If the gains to continued plan participation (and employment) are substantial prior to this point, and if the replacement rate is fairly high, the age at which participants retire will be concentrated within a narrow range. A pension design like this serves the same function as a mandatory retirement rule, but because it is voluntary, it cannot be challenged by the courts in countries where mandatory retirement is proscribed.

A traditional pension plan need not create such incentives. It can, for example, be designed so that additional years of work always result in an actuarially fair increase in the pension, at least up to some relatively advanced age.[17] An actuarially neutral design would not precipitate the mass exodus that occurs in late middle age with many plans. Plan participants would be less likely to hang on to employment just to boost their pension. The pension plan's design would be less of a factor in an employee's decision to stay on or leave the company.

The fact that the traditional pension has usually been designed to encourage the separation of employees from their employer over a relatively narrow age range in late middle age suggests that employers have viewed it more as a motivational device and a means of easing the departure of older workers, who have been presumed to be less productive than their younger colleagues, than as an instrument to promote saving for retirement. The

---

[17] An increase in the regular payment of a pension is actuarially fair when the additional expected benefit an employee earns by delaying retirement is exactly compensated by the effects of the decline in the expected payout period and the additional contributions that the participant makes.

move away from traditional plans to defined-contribution plans suggests that the motivational role of pensions may be less important than it used to be. In particular, a decline in long tenure may have reduced the perceived need for a means of encouraging retirement over a narrow age range.

Risks with Final-Salary Plans

The discussion has highlighted three risks faced by a participant in a final-salary plan that are specific to the plan. First, an unexpectedly flat trajectory for the salary can substantially reduce the final pension. Second, and to the extent that vesting periods are longer with such plans than they are with other plans, a participant may be obliged to quit before he or she is vested. Finally, there is the loss in the value of benefits from early separation described above, which occurs even with vested participants.

These risks are far from trivial, especially in a country like the United States, where maximum vesting requirements exceed average tenure. For very long-tenured employees, a traditional plan is of great value, because it addresses so effectively the three risks of retirement that the book has highlighted. The contractual saving entailed by a traditional plan takes place whether the participant wishes to save or not. The pension is not dependent on the performance of financial markets, apart from periods when performance is so poor as to threaten the plan sponsor's solvency. In addition, the pension is normally paid in the form of an annuity, although usually a nominal and not an indexed annuity. The plan sponsor bears both investment and longevity risk.

This leaves the risk that the plan sponsor is unable to meet its obligations to the plan, and pension insurance, if there is any, is insufficient to make up the loss. Most countries have regulatory regimes that are designed to make this a highly unlikely occurrence, but pension plans do become insolvent. Several countries partially insure their plan members against this eventuality.

Defined-Contribution Plans

Defined-contribution plans, like traditional pension plans, come in many varieties. The typical defined-contribution plan establishes an individual account for each participant, in which it deposits some specified percentage of the participant's wage or salary, usually up to some ceiling that the plan specifies. One critical feature of a defined-contribution plan is the scope for access to funds pre-retirement. Another is how much autonomy the participant has in investing the amount in his or her account. At one extreme, the assets of the plan may be invested collectively, and individual participants have no say (except perhaps through their representative on the investment committee, if there is one) in the allocation of the plan's assets. At the other extreme, investments may be self-directed, and participants may be able to choose among many different investment funds, or even among individual stocks and other instruments.

The 401(k) plan in the United States and the Superannuation Guarantee (SG) in Australia are examples of the latter, although they differ in other respects. The contribution rate (paid by employers) for the SG is currently fixed at 9 percent. The 401(k) plan participant is free to pick a rate of contribution between zero and a maximum rate stipulated by the plan sponsor. A dollar maximum applies to tax-favored contributions, which is adjusted every year in line with inflation. The difference in design reflects in large part the greater role played by U.S. Social Security than the role played by the Age Pension down under.

As Chapter 1 explains, the defined-contribution plans of the ten survey countries generally vest more quickly and are much more portable than traditional plans. As a result, participants in defined-contribution plans are much less likely to suffer the same loss of benefits from changing jobs that participants in a traditional plan suffer. Even if the account balance in a defined-contribution plan is not available to the account holder, it can be transferred to another employer's plan or, in some countries, to a personal saving plan where it can earn a return. The same is true of cash-balance plans, discussed in the following. Consequently, the risk that accrued benefits will be lost or eroded over time is much less with defined-contribution plans than it is with traditional plans. Although it is, in principle, possible to devise a defined-contribution plan that will retain employees until they have reached a certain age, this is not common practice.

Depending on their design, defined-contribution plans can leave their participants ill protected against at least one if not all three of the basic risks of retirement finance. If a plan's contribution rate is too low, the risk of under saving is heightened. If investments are self-directed, the specter of ill-considered investment decisions arises, and even if they are not, the typical defined-contribution plan places all of the risk of poor investment returns on contributors. Finally, the risk of inadequate longevity insurance is aggravated by the common practice of distributing the accumulated balances in the individual accounts of defined-contribution plans as a lump sum. These risks have been mitigated in countries like Switzerland and Denmark by guaranteeing a minimum rate of return on account balances and a maximum premium for annuities.

In other countries, these limitations on participants' choices might not be palatable, notably in the United States with respect to the 401(k) plan. There is an obvious appeal to a plan that allows participants to set their own contribution rate, as there is to the option of self-directed investments.[18] What is effectively a default setting of lump sum distribution has obvious appeal as well. As we have seen, however, there is reason to be concerned about under saving and poor investment choices. Simply proscribing freedom of choice is neither desirable nor workable, but less drastic policies that would at least move people in the right direction are available. This is one of the themes of Chapter 7.

Hybrid Pensions

Hybrid pension forms are found in about half of the ten survey countries. In the United States, the most prevalent form of hybrid pension is the cash-balance plan. The cash-balance plan has been aptly described by McGill et al. (2005) as "… a DB plan that looks and feels like a DC plan." Unlike defined-contribution plans, the balance in a cash-balance plan grows according to a formula, in which a notional or hypothetical account balance is fed by "pay credits" – usually a fixed percentage of salary – to which interest is credited. The applicable interest rate may be constant, or may be linked to the rate on Treasury bills or a similar financial instrument.

To understand the mechanics and the dynamics of a cash-balance plan, it is helpful to think of the balance at retirement as a sum of the pay credits made each year of a plan participant's career, accumulated forward at the plan's rate of interest to the last year of work. The pay credit for a given year will reach a sum by retirement that is determined by the number of years that have elapsed since that year and the average interest rate applied to the balance. The formula for the amount accumulated (AA_t) by the first year of retirement (R) that is attributable to participation in the plan in year t is given below, with PAY_t standing for the salary paid in the year t, c_t for the pay credit percentage, and i_t for the interest rate, which is assumed to be applied to the balance of year $t-1$:

$$AA_t = c_t \cdot PAY_t \cdot \prod_{S=t+1}^{R} (1 + i_s) \qquad (2.10)$$

---

[18] To the extent that employer-provided pensions are negotiated between workers and employers (or are designed to reflect to some degree employees' preferences) then short-sightedness on the part of employees could tend to push down the contribution rate that is set for defined-contribution plans.

The total accumulation over the worker's career (CA) is given by the following formula, where H stands for the year of hire:

$$CA = \sum_{t=H}^{R-1} AA_t = \sum_{t=H}^{R-1} \left(c_t \cdot PAY_t \cdot \prod_{S=t+1}^{R} (1+i_s) \right)$$ (2.11)

Note that the formula for the cumulative balance is exactly the same as the formula that would apply in the case of a defined-contribution plan with a contribution rate of c_t and a rate of return to contributions of i_t in each year t.

One feature that distinguishes the cash-balance plan from the typical 401(k) plan or another defined-contribution plan is that the implicit return to contributions is often fixed, or at any rate is less variable than the rate of return of a 401(k) plan with a large allocation to equities. The other key difference is that the plan sponsor is ultimately responsible for funding the plan. The degree of risk this responsibility imposes on the sponsor depends on how the interest rate is set. In principle, the plan sponsor assumes no investment risk if the rate of interest is set less than or equal to some short-term, market-determined rate, because the sponsor can hedge any risk by investing all of the plan's balance in short-term securities. When the rate of interest is fixed, then the sponsor has, in principle, exposed itself to some investment risk, although in practice this can be contained by setting the rate relatively low.

In the United States, a cash-balance plan is required to offer an annuity as a distribution option. In practice, distributions from cash-balance plans are normally paid out in a lump sum. Nonetheless, transforming the formula for the accumulated balance into the equivalent formula for an annuity helps illustrate the kinship between cash-balance plans and more conventional defined-benefit plans. Dividing both sides of equation (2.11) by an annuity factor ä, – the cost of one dollar of lifetime income as of the date the plan member retires – with P_{CB} standing for the value of the pension and assuming that the pay credit percentage is fixed:

$$P_{CB} = \sum_{t=H}^{R-1} \left(\frac{c}{\text{ä}} \cdot PAY_t \cdot \prod_{S=t+1}^{R} (1+i_t) \right)$$ (2.12)

As McGill et al. point out, the resulting formula is that of an indexed career-average plan, with the index being the accumulated rate of interest on past pay credits, and the accrual factor being $c/\text{ä}$.

Nonetheless, the apparent similarity with the traditional final-salary or average-salary plan is deceiving in several respects. First, cash-balance plans can be designed to strictly limit the degree of investment risk that the sponsor assumes, as noted. Second, and just as important, the sponsor of a cash-balance plan assumes no longevity risk, which is borne entirely by the plan's participants. Third, the liabilities of a cash-balance plan should be more predictable than those of a traditional pension, in that they are not as influenced by the age and length of service of the workforce.[19] Fourth, the likelihood that a significant degree of underfunding will develop with a cash-balance plan should be small, provided again that the plan's interest rate has not been set too high. Fifth, even if the balance accumulated in a cash-balance plan is not transferable to the plan of another employer when an employee separates, the balance continues to accrue interest, unlike the typical defined-benefit plan, where the accrued benefit is frozen at its value at the separation date (see Figure 2.2).[20] In all these respects, the cash-balance plan is more like a defined-contribution plan than a traditional pension plan. Traditional plans assign key risks to the plan sponsor, but this is not an *inherent* feature of a defined-benefit plan, particularly when the benefit assumes the form of a lump-sum upon retirement or separation.

The pension equity plan (PEP) is a cousin of the cash-balance plan. The main difference between them is the much greater weight that the PEP gives to end-career salary. The PEP applies an accrual coefficient to the participant's final salary averaged over a period that usually ranges from three to five years. The benefit paid is a lump sum, but is determined by the accrual factor (or average accrual factor), number of years worked, and final salary. There is no interest rate to produce a compounding effect.

Consequently, if the accrual factor is d, the number of years worked is $(R - H)$, and the average final salary is PAY, then the accumulated balance (AC_{PEP}) at career's end will be:

$$AC_{PEP} = d \cdot (R - H) \cdot PAY \qquad (2.13)$$

---

[19] Strictly, speaking, this depends on whether the pay credit increases with years of service. If it does not, the departure of one worker and his or her replacement by another at the same salary should have no effect on plan liabilities provided that a former employee's balance continues to be credited with interest after his separation. The present value of the accrued liabilities for past service is not altered by unexpected increases in average service time in these circumstances.

[20] With the typical final salary plan, the accrued benefit of a worker who separates before retirement remains fixed, and neither earns interest nor is indexed. The two plans shown have been set to produce the same benefit at retirement, assuming the worker does not separate before retirement. Salary grows by 2 percent per year, the pay credit percentage is 7.45 percent and the rate of accrual of the final salary plan is 1.25 percent. The interest rate that applies for the cash-balance plan is 5 percent.

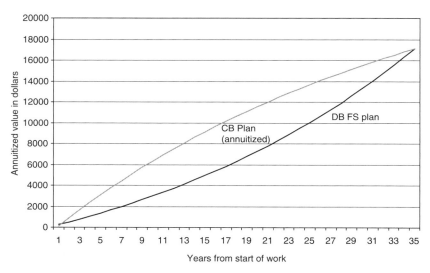

Figure 2.2. Comparison of value of pension benefit at retirement with value at early separation of a cash-balance and a traditional DB plan. *Source*: Author's calculations.

Because it places no weight on the early and middle segments of a participant's working life, the PEP treats the more rapidly promoted plan member more favorably than does the cash-balance plan. In this respect, it is like the traditional final-salary plan.[21]

It is straightforward to transform the expression for the accumulated balance into an expression for the pension annuity (P_{PEP}) as we did for the cash-balance plan:

$$P_{PEP} = \frac{d}{\ddot{a}} \cdot (R - H) \cdot PAY \tag{2.14}$$

If the annuity factor were a predetermined by the plan itself, and participants were required to annuitize, then a PEP would be indistinguishable from a final-salary plan. This is not the case, however, and so plan

[21] More formally, if we compare a cash-balance plan and a PEP assuming that the participant earns the same salary every year, and setting the parameters so that the two plans produce the same benefit, any shift of income from early years to the final years of the participant's career increases the benefit from the PEP above that of the cash-balance plan. The shift lowers the benefit of the cash-balance plan because income is shifted from years when it has a heavy weight to years when its weight is lighter. An increase in final salary, other things equal, must have a much larger effect on the benefit of a PEP than it does on a cash-balance plan, because it has a weight of 100 percent, much more than its weight in a cash-balance plan.

participants shoulder longevity risk with the PEP as well. The main difference between the cash-balance and the PEP lies in the consequences of an unpredictable salary path. This follows from the PEP's emphasis on the final salary. Comparing two employees, one with a flat and the other with a steep salary profile, the difference in the benefits they obtain from a PEP will be substantially greater than the difference in the benefits they would obtain from a cash-balance plan.

Other Hybrids

The second tier pensions of Denmark and Switzerland look like defined-contribution plans. However, the plans of both countries, particularly Swiss plans, have "add-ons" that give them a more than passing likeness to a traditional plan. Specifically, a minimum rate of return is guaranteed on account balances, and a maximum premium is set for converting the accumulated balance at retirement into an annuity. (See Appendix 1, Denmark and Switzerland.)

The Do-It-Yourself Approach to Steady Income and Longevity Insurance

Recent trends in the Anglo-Saxon and some other countries mean that self-insurance against longevity risk is likely to become considerably more common than it is now. The declining role of the traditional pension will increase the number of those retirees without an annuity from an employer-provided pension. A retired person in this position whose first-tier pension does not provide an adequate replacement rate may well lack adequate longevity insurance.

He or she must then deal with two different problems. First, he must manage his capital to generate a reasonably steady income over time. Second, he must try to ensure that his capital will not run out before he dies and leave him destitute. In other words, he must self-insure against longevity risk. In this section we consider the pitfalls that arise with efforts to generate sustained income in retirement when annuitization of a substantial share of the balance is not feasible. In Chapter 7 we consider ways in which a defined-contribution plan can be augmented to deal with longevity risk.

Even if the retirement lifespan were completely predictable, maintaining a steady income would be no mean feat. A retired person needs to employ a strategy, or at least apply a rule of thumb, that determines the rate at which he or she makes withdrawals to finance expenditure. Although most people might not draw up a formal withdrawal plan, this section will evaluate four different phased-withdrawal rules using Monte Carlo–simulation experiments to capture the effect of the uncertain rates of return on the assets in which a retired person's capital is held.[22] All experiments assume that the retiree, who is 65 years old, starts with $500,000. Under the first rule, withdrawals are initially set at a particular level ($25,000 annually) and maintained at that level in real terms until the end of the retirement period or asset exhaustion, whichever comes first.[23] Under the second, withdrawals are maintained at a constant proportion of the value of the portfolio. Under the third rule, withdrawals are determined by the remaining life expectancy of the participant assumed to be male, as explained below. Under the fourth and final rule, the rate of withdrawal is adjusted when the balance diverges from a specified benchmark balance, increasing when the actual account balance exceeds the benchmark, and vice versa (see Box 2.2). Rule 4 is a more sophisticated version of Rule 2. Note that all monetary values are expressed in real terms (2009 dollars).

Box 2.2.   Four rules for phased withdrawal

Rule 1 – Constant real withdrawals until assets are exhausted.
Rule 2 – Withdrawals set to equal a predetermined share of the account value.
Rule 3 – Withdrawals determined by remaining life expectancy.
Rule 4 – A version of Rule 2 modified to allow higher withdrawals when account balances exceed a specified benchmark, and require lower withdrawals when they fall short of that benchmark.

Source: Author's assumptions.

Problems with the Phased-Withdrawal Approach

The retired person's assets are invested in two funds, one composed of large capitalization stocks and the other composed of long-term government bonds, and the initial proportion of stocks and bonds is maintained by rebalancing the portfolio each year. Portfolio management fees amount to 1 percent of capital. We assume that retirees live until the age of 90 – by

---

[22] There is a large literature on the problem of making the nest egg last (achieving sustainable withdrawals). To give just two examples, Guyton and Klinger (2006) report on simulation experiments conducted to determine what asset allocation strategy yields the largest sustainable flow, while Ameriks et al. (2001) assess the role of partial annuitization of the nest egg in achieving sustainable income flows.

[23] The value of the initial balance and the initial withdrawal are chosen for the sake of illustration only.

no means so advanced an age these days – with no probability of dying before then. This allows us to focus on investment risk. The Monte Carlo experiments simulate real rates of return. Other assumptions are set out in Box 2.3.

Box 2.3.   Assumptions used in Monte Carlo simulations of four phased-withdrawal strategies

Financial parameters[a]	
Rates of return (in percent in real terms)	
Large-cap	9.0
Long-term bonds	2.8
Standard deviation (in percent)	
Large-cap	20.1
Long-term bonds	10.3
Initial balance	$500,000
Equity-bond mix	50–50
Initial withdrawal rate	5.0% of capital
Marginal and average tax rate	20%
Fees	1.0% of capital

[a] The distribution of returns is assumed to be lognormal [i.e., with the return denoted by r, log $(1+r)$ is a normally distributed random variable]. The rates of return and standard deviations are based on the performance of U.S. stocks and long-term government bonds over 1929 to 2007.
Source: Morningstar (2008). Life expectancies are derived from Social Security Administration (2002).

None of the four of the do-it-yourself phased-withdrawal strategies can consistently generate both a steady or guaranteed minimum income and a predictable final balance, which could be greater than zero if the retiree wanted to leave a bequest. If income is to be kept steady, or a minimum level is guaranteed, the final balance will vary hugely. Rule 4 is, however, more successful than the others in avoiding the extremes of a high final balance and plummeting standard of living in later years.[24]

---

[24] The conventional way of comparing and evaluating different withdrawal or decumulation strategies is to posit an intertemporal utility function and determine which strategy would maximize expected discounted utility. The book's approach was chosen on the grounds that it allows a comparison that is more intuitively appealing, and assumes that retirees attach great importance to a stable and durable stream of income.

Table 2.1. *Comparative performance of the phased withdrawal rules (in thousands of 2009 dollars except where noted)*

	Rule 1	Rule 2	Rule 3	Rule 4
Average withdrawal				
Mean	24.2	21.8	29.1	29.5
Standard deviation	1.9	5.6	7.5	6.6
Average final five years' withdrawal				
Mean	21.4	19.2	17.8	26.7
Standard deviation	7.7	8.4	8.3	6.1
Final balance				
Mean	281.3	369.6	41.9	64.1
Standard deviation	338.0	176.0	22.0	10.2
Probability of exhaustion (in percent)	25	0	0	0

Source: Author's simulation model.

Rule 1 achieves the smallest variance in withdrawals and thus expenditure of the four rules, and will achieve constant withdrawals throughout the 25 years (i.e., age 66 to age 90) 75 percent of the time. It will exhaust the account before the 25 years are up 25 percent of the time, however, and leave the retiree destitute or severely deprived (see Table 2.1). At the same time, however, the chances that a retiree dies with a large positive balance are substantial, because the mean final balance exceeds $280,000. The reason for this is that withdrawals are not increased when asset returns are above average. Under Rule 2, average withdrawals are lower than they are under Rule 1, because declining account balances drastically reduce withdrawals. For example, if the balance falls to $100,000, withdrawals under Rule 1 stay at $25,000, while they fall to $5,000 under Rule 2. The balance at age 90 does not climb as high as it does when asset returns are high under Rule 1, because withdrawals eat into part of the appreciation in asset values that takes place during rising markets. The standard deviation of the average withdrawal under Rule 2 is much larger than it is under Rule 1.

Dropping the withdrawal rate to 4 percent of the initial balance under Rule 1 reduces the risk of total penury but increases the likelihood of large residual account holdings. With this lower withdrawal rate under Rule 2, the retiree merely suffers a further decline in average withdrawals, which remain highly variable.

Rule 3 allows participants to withdraw funds at a rate that would exhaust the current balance (ignoring returns on investment) over the period of the participant's remaining life expectancy. For example, someone in his late seventies with a life expectancy of 10 years could withdraw 10 percent of the current account balance. The withdrawal rate is adjusted every year to reflect the age-specific decline in life expectancy. Compared with either Rule 1 or Rule 2, average withdrawals under Rule 3 are much higher, and end-period balances much lower. This reflects the fact that the initial withdrawal under a life expectancy rule is higher than 5 percent (because a 65-year-old man's life expectancy is estimated to be about 15 years), and continues to grow. When financial returns are above average, the withdrawal is substantially larger than it would be with Rules 1 or 2. However, the price that is paid for these initial fat years is lower withdrawals in the lean years and a substantial drop as the retiree ages.

Rule 4 addresses some of the shortcomings of the first three rules by adjusting the withdrawal by a fraction of the difference between the actual account balance and a target or benchmark balance that declines as the retiree ages. This rule allows a retiree to spend more when the account is comparatively flush, and requires him or her to make economies when the balance is comparatively low. This strategy succeeds in raising the average withdrawal. The decline in withdrawals late in life is less than it is with Rules 1 to 3 (Table 2.1). Rule 4 also substantially reduces the balance outstanding at age 90, although withdrawals can still fluctuate substantially.

The lack of stability, which is pronounced with Rules 1–3, is an unavoidable consequence of the randomness of investment returns. Further experimentation with the phased withdrawal rules would yield better performing rules, but the impact of unpredictable investment returns cannot be effectively neutralized.

A more predictable income stream and final balance are possible if the retiree is allowed to invest most of his assets in a risk-free asset, which the simulation experiments did not allow. Even a risk-free asset is not a guarantee of a completely stable income stream, however.[25] That would require the retiree to invest in financial instruments like zero-coupon bonds, although they would need to be indexed. The retiree buys a set of indexed "zeros," which do not have coupons and mature in successive years. He or she would have some bonds that mature in the first year of retirement, some

---

[25] If a retiree invests his or her portfolio entirely in risk-free bonds, he will still encounter investment risk (when bond prices are down and he needs to sell some of his holdings before they mature) and interest rate risk (when a bond matures, interest rates have fallen, and the proceeds of the redemption have to be invested in instruments with lower yields).

that mature in the second, some in the third, and so on until the last year. The retiree then knows precisely what income he can look forward to in each year of his post-working life, and can choose to hold zeros with the same real value at maturity. However, the steady income stream they provide normally comes at a cost of a low rate of return. For example, if the rate of return were equal to 1 percent in real terms, the $500,000 nest egg would sustain an annual income of about $22,700 over 25 years, but leave no inheritance.

The exposition must now take account of uncertain lifetimes. Longevity risk poses an intractable problem for a phased withdrawal strategy. Apart from annuities, there is no instrument that retirees or financial planners can use to hedge it, and there is no phased withdrawal strategy that can substitute for annuitization in the provision of longevity insurance. Even if the life expectancy of different cohorts of a population were known with certainty, average life expectancy is not much help as a planning tool, because there is so much variation around the mean.

Notwithstanding the limitations of averages, it is not unheard of for financial advisors to assume, for planning purposes, that a client will live as long as the average member of his age cohort will live. This assumption guarantees that the client has about an even chance of living past that date. At the other extreme, a planner might assume that a client will live to be 95 or 100 just to be on the safe side. The chances the client will surpass so advanced an age are small, but now the nest egg must be made to last even longer, and annual income will be even less.

Phased withdrawals may well remain the dominant strategy for most retirees in the Anglo-Saxon countries and Australia and for many retirees in some of the other countries. It is not certain whether more sophisticated approaches (see Chapter 7) will become commercially viable, and many retirees may prefer to have the option of access to more of their capital and to invest some of it in risky assets. If so, they will need to follow a strategy similar to Rule 4, so that withdrawals will have to be quite elastic with respect to the deviation of the actual path of account balances from some norm. This will require vigilance, a considerable measure of self-control, and some financial expertise.

Short of investing in low-yielding, risk-free assets, and quite apart from the risks posed by an uncertain lifetime, a retired person will not be able to stabilize both withdrawals and the bequest he or she will leave to any heirs. By reacting when asset returns are abnormally high or low, however, he should be able to damp down the fluctuations in the stream of withdrawals and its final balance.

3

Issues in Funding and Investing

Four Issues in Funding

Introduction

Employer-provided pension plans – traditional, hybrid, or defined contribution – all have balance sheets, and the aim of plan funding (at least in the case of traditional and hybrid plans) is to ensure that a plan will always have enough assets to honor its pension promises. A successful funding strategy will prevent a shortfall, or at least an excessive shortfall, of plan assets from liabilities and will require that a plan's sponsor take steps to close any gap that emerges between liabilities and assets in an appropriately short period of time. As Whittington (2006) points out, the adoption of the balance-sheet method of pension fund accounting, which is a necessary but not a sufficient condition for adequate funding, is relatively recent. He dates it from the issue by the Financial Accounting Standards Board (FASB) of Statement No. 87 in 1985.[1]

With the balance-sheet approach, the net cost that the plan incurs in a particular period is the increase in the plan's net liabilities. Net cost in period t (NC_t) can be represented by the following expression [equation (3.1)]:

$$NC_t = L_{t-1} \cdot r_t + B_t + BPS_t - A_{t-1} \cdot r_t + EXADJ_t \qquad (3.1)$$

The variable r stands again for the rate of interest, L stands for the stock of plan liabilities, B for benefits earned by plan members during the current period, BPS for the benefits earned from past service, A for assets, and

[1] Two earlier methods were: (i) reckoning the cost of the pension to the sponsor by the cash flow cost to the sponsor (which in practice meant ignoring any build-up in liabilities from increased service) and (ii) measuring the cost by starting with an estimate of the cost per plan member derived from an estimate of the pension that would ultimately be paid spread over the remaining working life of the member (Whittington 2006, 523–24).

EXADJ for what are called experience adjustments.[2] The first term on the right-hand side, $L_{t-1}r_t$, is the interest-carrying cost of the liabilities accumulated as of the previous period; $A_{t-1}r_t$ is the return on the plan's assets, and the last term, *EXADJ* is made up of the adjustments to assets and liabilities that are made necessary by either changes in the accounting assumptions, or deviations of actual experience with respect to wage growth, mortality, rates of separation, and so on, from their projected values. We have assumed for convenience that the rate of interest on liabilities equals the return on assets.

The components of equation (3.1) could be split into many parts. For example, the experience adjustment factor could be divided into one part reflecting the impact of revised accounting assumptions, and another part reflecting deviations of actual experience from projected. The last of these terms could, in turn, be divided into the deviations entailed by differences between actual and projected rates of mortality, separation from the firm, wage growth, and so on. Even in its aggregate form, however, equation (3.1) illustrates the extent to which projections of pension costs are at the mercy of forces beyond the plan's control.

Rather than attempt a comprehensive coverage of pension-plan accounting issues, this chapter will focus on four issues of particular relevance to this study: (1) how to account for the costs entailed by plan service, in particular the merits of projecting future wages as opposed to relying on current wages; (2) the choice of discount rate [r in equation (3.1)] and how it is affected by the risk of default by the plan sponsor and the correlation between asset and liability values; (3) how to value plan assets; and (4) how quickly to close any gap that emerges between liabilities and assets. A fifth topic, the problems entailed by aggregate longevity risk, is tackled in Chapters 6 and 7.

All four of these issues have inspired debate in the past. With the severe deterioration in the global financial climate since fall of 2008, the last three issues have become particularly important. How the issues are resolved can affect substantially the cost of funding a pension plan. As Chapter 6 discusses, some observers have blamed changes in accounting practices for contributing to the troubles of the traditional pension.

The second half of this chapter is devoted to investment issues, and concentrates mainly on traditional defined-benefit plans. We discuss asset-liability management (ALM), risk budgeting and liability-driven investing (LDI),

---

[2]   Benefits earned from past service would include benefits from past service that were recognized in the current period.

approaches that have gained popularity since the so-called perfect financial storm of 2002, as well as some related issues. It ends with a brief discussion of investing for defined-contribution plans.

The Cost of Plan Benefits[3]

The traditional pension plan promises to pay a stream of benefits, the amounts of which depend upon the behavior over decades of economic and financial variables over which the plan sponsor may have little or no control. In the case of a final-salary plan, the benefit that a plan member receives is particularly sensitive to his or her length of service (tenure) and the rate at which his salary increases during his career with the company sponsoring the plan. Even career-average plans are susceptible to unpredictable changes in wage and salary trends. The sponsor of a traditional pension plan must fund obligations that will stretch many years into the future; consequently, their value is highly uncertain.

To pinpoint the basic issues to be addressed in determining the cost of a plan's benefits, and allocating that cost to particular years, it is helpful to begin by assuming away all of the uncertainties involved in determining a pension plan's benefit obligations. In other words, assume that the size of the work force, the salary awards it will receive, and rate of turnover can be predicted with perfect accuracy. This means that the plan's sponsor knows the exact value of the benefits payable in any given year far into the future. How should these obligations be funded?

Suppose that these completely predictable long-term benefit obligations are equal from year to year, or alternatively, are a fixed fraction of the sponsoring company's wage bill. A pattern of benefits like this would arise if the number of retired employees were a stable fraction of the number of active ones, if life expectancy in retirement were constant, and if average pensions were a stable fraction of average salaries. In these uncomplicated circumstances – like those of a national pay-as-you-go (PAYG) pension system in a steady state – it would be enough for the sponsor to adopt pay-as-you-go financing. Given these admittedly unrealistic assumptions, there is no need to build up a reserve.

What makes the real world different from this conjectural one is that the ratio of retired employees to active ones can vary substantially over time, as

---

[3] This section of the chapter aims to illustrate the basic issues that arise with estimating and funding the cost of pension plan benefits. It is not a detailed guide to the various methods that actuaries in any of the countries surveyed employ. McGill et al. (2005) is an authoritative source on this topic for U.S. plans. European Financial Reporting Advisory Group (2008) discusses the conceptual aspects of accounting for the cost of current service in some detail.

the fortunes of companies wax and wane. When a pension plan starts up, it pays little or no benefits for many years. Similarly, if a company undergoes a growth spurt, the average age of its employees can decline, and with it the ratio of retired to active employees. Conversely, a company in decline may experience a marked rise in this ratio. A pay-as-you-go approach to financing could, therefore, either jeopardize the servicing of pension obligations, or require swingeing increases in the plan's costs from one accounting period to the next. Consequently, an approach that takes account of the temporal pattern of accumulation of obligations is necessary.

Two Approaches to Estimating the Cost to a Pension Plan of Member Service

Broadly speaking, there are two methods by which the cost of pension-plan service may be measured. The first is known as the accrued-benefits funding method and the second as the prospective-benefits funding method.[4] Each has variants that reflect different ways of measuring both accrued and prospective benefits under a plan.

The basic difference between the two methods is that the first method, as its name suggests, calculates the cost to the plan of the service of plan members as the service accrues, while the second makes a prospective estimate of the present value of the expected benefits that plan members will earn from their service, and spreads that cost evenly over the plan participant's entire period of service. The two major variants of the first method are the projected-unit method and the current-unit method.[5] Both measure plan service as it accrues, but the projected-unit method projects salaries to the assumed date of retirement, while the current-unit method uses current salaries (see Box 3.1).

Prospective accounting methods, by spreading funding costs evenly over a worker's service, avoid the escalating pattern of the current-unit method. One method that is used more often in Europe than in North America is the *entry-age normal method*. The entry-age normal method determines normal costs by estimating the present value of a worker's future benefits as of his or her entry age. The normal cost and contribution are determined by finding that contribution level at which the present value of future normal costs at entry age equal the present value of future benefits (PVFB).

---

[4] This is British terminology. In the United States, the two methods are known as the benefits-allocation method and the cost-allocation method. The British terminology is somewhat more descriptive than the American.

[5] Also known in the United States as the unit-credit cost method.

Box 3.1   Two examples of the accrued-benefit method

A plan member, aged 45, has a constant annual pensionable salary of $60,000. Her plan is a final-salary plan, with a constant accrual rate of 0.02. The *current-unit method* calculates the increment to her pension that is attributable to the current year by taking 2 percent of her current salary, or $1200. Assuming she will retire at age 65, the plan will have to provide a sum for the additional year of service that would pay for a life annuity of $1200 that begins in 20 years. Assuming further that the cost 20 years hence of a life annuity of $1 per year is $12, the plan will need $14,400 in 20 years. If it invests in bonds with an interest rate of 4 percent, the amount for which the plan must provision – the *normal cost* – is calculated to be $14,400 × $(1 + 0.04)^{-20}$ or $6572. If the plan member has been working for 10 years, the plan's accrued liability for her service will equal 10 × $6572 or $65,720.

If the plan member has received a salary increase, then the estimates of normal cost made for earlier years have to be recalculated, because the current-unit method assumes that the cost for all years of service should be calculated using the latest salary. Assuming a salary increase of $3,000, the additional cost entailed by the raise would be equal to $3,000 × the accrual factor × years worked × annuity premium × the discount factor, or $3,286.

The *projected-unit* method uses a formula that is virtually identical to the current-unit method, with one crucial difference: Salary is projected forward to the period just before retirement. For example, it could be assumed that the plan member's salary would grow by 3 percent per annum between ages 45 and 65. That would bring it to $108,367 for her last year of work. The increment to her pension from the current year of service is now 2 percent of $108,367 or $2,167. To fund the increment in 20 year's time, the plan will require 12 times this amount, or $26,004. Discounted at 4 percent to the current year yields the normal cost determined by the projected-unit method, which is $26,004 × $(1 + 0.04)^{-20}$ or $11,870. Even if the plan actuary does not change the estimate of final salary, the normal costs that the projected-unit method calculates will grow from one year to the next, because the discount factor $(1 + 0.04)^{-t}$ will grow as t, the number of years to retirement, declines. The normal cost that the current-unit method calculates must rise above that which the projected-unit method calculates, as the service period lengthens to make up for the initial difference between them.

Source: Author's model and calculations.

Using the same ages and interest rates as the previous example, the present value of a stream of normal costs over a worker's career can be expressed as $PVNC = NC \sum_{i=35}^{65} 1/(1.04)^{i-34}$. This expression is set equal to *PVFB*, and solved for *NC*.

With the entry-age method, accrued liability is defined as the difference between PVFB and the present value of future costs (PVFC).[6] No liability has been incurred, by definition, if the normal costs that make up the funding all lie in the future, as is the case at the outset of service. Over time, PVFC does not grow as fast as PVFB, because the future value of benefits stays the same – meaning that its current value grows – while future costs are lowered by accumulated accrued normal costs.

Our example has calculated normal cost in currency terms – constant dollars, pounds, euros, or yen. Another way of calculating normal cost is as a constant percentage of salary. This has the advantage of keeping an important component of labor costs in line with the growth of wages and salaries. Both methods, in different ways, smooth the cost of plan service over the whole period of service of a plan member.

In a completely predictable world, the use of current rather than projected final salary to calculate accrued service cost would not be justifiable. In an uncertain world, the choice between these two methods of calculating the obligations of a pension plan is less clear-cut and arguments can be advanced for either. The choice depends to some extent on whether a plan is viewed as a going concern or an object of an explicit contract that can be terminated at any time. If it can be wound up at any moment, there would be little point in projecting salaries (Blake et al. 2008, 20). Even if the plan is a going concern, future wage increases are, at least partly, at the discretion of the sponsoring company, while the benefits measured at current salaries have already been earned and the sponsor is, therefore, committed to paying them (EFRAG 2008, 38). From this perspective it could be argued that using a final-salary estimate is mixing up a "hard" obligation with soft one (i.e., the part that depends on the future growth of salaries). On a related point, the unit-credit method does not rely, like the projected accrued-cost method, on an uncertain projection of wages and salaries many years into the future. In practice, the rates of salary increase are hard to predict even a few years hence, let alone 30 years hence.

Even if these predictions were always accurate, it has been argued that relying on a projection of salary in this way is inconsistent with the standard accounting approach that applies to wages and salaries: The cost of labor is never based on a projection, but on its current cost (Gold and Latter 2008). A related argument is that vested benefits are calculated on the basis

---

6   If PVFB is greater than PVFC, then the present value of future costs for which the plan provides is not enough to cover the cost of the benefits. The difference is the accrued liability, for which the plan is expected to provision. Provided it has made adequate provision, there will be no unfunded liability.

of the wage or salary earned by the plan member prior to separation, and not on the basis of projected wages.

Standard commercial accounting does rely on current and not projected wages, but the analogy between the accounting of wages and salaries and pension-plan accounting is flawed in one important respect. A commercial enterprise could, in principle, project its operating revenues and expenditures far out into the future, but as a practical matter it would not gain much from doing so. A company that is and intends to stay a going concern does not need to make long-range projections of wages to stay in business. Its main concern would be with its operating surplus, not the level of wages per se. Increases in wages and other current costs of production over time would usually be matched by increases in the price of its products.

When the wage level can be expected to increase over time, however, a funding rule based on a current measure of salaries always leaves the plan scrambling to keep up. A traditional pension plan makes a promise to pay a benefit that will depend on the long-term trend in salaries. If it is, for all practical purposes, certain that salaries will grow over time in nominal terms, the application of the current-unit method will invariably cause the pension liability to be understated. Viewed in this light, the issue is really *what* rate of increase should be assumed for salaries, and not should *any* rate of increase be assumed. Even a modest rate of increase is almost certain to be more accurate an assumption than one of no increase. If an assumption proves too pessimistic (too high) as time passes, a downward revision is preferable to an upward one.

Complications Posed by Early Separation

Plan members may quit before they become eligible for retirement, so that plan funding will also need to take account of the plan's vesting requirements. As an example, consider two plans A and B. Plan A has a vesting requirement of five years and plan B of seven years; they are identical in other respects. The funding requirements of plan B will be less than those of plan A if some workers work at least five years but quit before the end of their seventh year of service. Death on the job is a further complication, depending on how the death benefit is determined and whether it is included in the plan.

A traditional pension plan also needs to take account of the obligations entailed by workers who leave the sponsoring company after they have vested. The separation of vested workers affects the measure of pension-plan costs in different ways depending on how the cost of benefits is reckoned. The benefit that accrues to a vested worker is usually calculated by applying the accrual rate to a measure of final or career-average salary multiplied by the number of years of service in the company's plan. Typically, the benefit will not be paid until the worker reaches retirement age. In some countries it will be frozen in nominal terms until then. As Chapter 2 explained, this delay can cause a large decline in its real value.

Under the current-unit method, the accrued benefit of the separating worker will equal the accrued liability entailed by the worker's service calculated using his or her last salary, so that the early departure of the worker will have no effect on liabilities at the time of departure. If the plan has funded the pension correctly, the funded amount will exactly equal what is owed to the worker. However, if benefits are being calculated on a projected basis, then early departures, if unanticipated, will reduce the plan's obligations.

Under a final-salary plan, the early separation of one worker and his or her replacement by someone of the same age who is paid the same salary reduces the cost of the benefits the plan will pay, because part of the combined years of service of the two employees will be valued at the final salary of the second worker, and part at the final salary of the first. If the first worker had not quit, his final salary would have applied for the entire period. Under a career-average plan, however, the cost of the benefits paid out should not be affected.

Separation and death before employees reach retirement age mean that, as we have seen, a funding rule based on projected wages would overstate funding requirements. This said, separations can and are taken into account by estimating the probability that workers will separate early and shorten the length of their tenure. The issue is explored further in Appendix 2.

Choice of the Discount Rate

For both accounting and funding, the traditional pension requires a way of reducing the future stream of pension payments to a present value. There is no active market in any of the ten countries in the obligations of pension plans, making it hard to value them directly. Instead, the valuation of a plan's liabilities requires a discount rate, which is applied to the expected future stream of the plan's pension payments to determine their present value.

The choice of the appropriate discount rate raises difficult issues and has created considerable controversy. Financial economists and actuaries have in the past viewed the discount rate in quite different lights. Actuaries followed the practice of discounting the liabilities of a pension plan by a measure of the expected rate of return of the assets that fund them. The argument for basing the rate of return on the behavior of asset returns appears to be derived from studies of the long-run behavior of stocks, which show that typically stocks out-perform bonds, and that a reasonable assumption in projecting returns is to assume that they will continue to perform as they have in the past. Financial economists typically maintain that a risk-free rate of interest or perhaps a high-grade corporate bond rate should be used instead.[7] Because pension funds have normally allocated a large share of their assets to equities, which in the past have had an average rate of return substantially higher than high-quality bonds, the actuarial approach can substantially lower the calculated value of plan liabilities.

In recent years, the actuarial approach has lost ground to the approach of financial economists. International and national accounting standard-setters have been recommending adoption of a discount rate based on a high-quality corporate debt rate, or a risk-free rate, which in practice means the rate paid by national governments on their debt.[8] When a rate of return based on the expected return to a plan's assets is used, it can entail an unacceptably high risk of defaulting on a plan's obligations. This is easily shown in a simple example that assumes a plan's obligations are completely predictable, and that these obligations are inviolable (or with a very low probability of default). These assumptions make the obligations of a pension plan akin to government bonds.

Suppose that the rate of return on government bonds is 3 percent, and assume that a plan has been funding its liabilities with a portfolio composed two-thirds of equities with an expected return of 9 percent, and one-third of government bonds, resulting in an expected rate of return for the portfolio as a whole of 7 percent. There is an obvious advantage to the mixed funding. The plan can be funded by assets with a value equal to the present value of the future stream of plan obligations discounted at 7 percent rather than 3 percent.[9]

---

[7]   The issue of the divergent views of (some) actuaries and financial economists is addressed in AAA/SOA (2006).

[8]   EFRAG (2008) argues for the use of a risk-free discount rate. FRS 17 recommends that a discount rate be derived from the rate of return on a high-quality corporate bond (AA or its equivalent). The justification for a discount rate above a risk-free rate is that a plan sponsor has some discretion over the value of the benefits the plan pays [see EFRAG (2008, 148) where part of FRS 17 is excerpted].

[9]   As an example, suppose that a constant stream of pension payments begins ten years from now and lasts for 30 years. The ratio of the funding needed with the mixed strategy to that needed with the risk-free bond strategy is $\dfrac{\sum_{t=10}^{40} 1/(1.07)^t}{\sum_{t=10}^{40} 1/(1.03)^t}$, which equals 0.45.

Choosing the higher discount rate in this case cuts the funding requirement by more than 50 percent.

The problem with this strategy, assuming that the plan maintains no additional reserves, is the risk of shortfalls that it will entail. Even if the plan's assets achieve an average rate of return of 7 percent – and even if they achieve that every year – the plan can do no better than just cover its obligations. It stands a good chance of falling short, however. The fact that a pension plan's liabilities are of long duration does not affect this conclusion. As Bodie has often stressed (Bodie and Clowes 2003), the risk of a shortfall of *any* size will decline as the duration of the liabilities increases. However, the maximum possible shortfall will grow.

One basic test of whether a funding rule like this would be adequate is to consider what a buyer would require in compensation to take on the obligations of the pension plan. In the United Kingdom, a few insurance companies have been engaged in plan buyouts. The essence of such an operation is that an insurance company acquires financial obligations with a long duration, just as it would when issuing its own debt. In determining the cost of the obligations it was taking on with a pension-plan buyout, it would want to use its own borrowing rate or even a risk-free rate as a discount rate. It would not use a rate based on the average rate of return of the plan's assets.[10]

The financial economist's position is essentially that the discount rate applied to determine a plan's funding should be derived from the rate on securities with a similar probability of default. If the plan's obligations are viewed as certain to be fully honored, the appropriate rate is a risk-free rate. If the pension plan's obligations are not completely risk free, the discount rate used to derive the plan's liabilities should reflect that. The choice of a risk-free or high-quality corporate bond rate as discount rate does not require the plan to adopt a conservative investment strategy. It merely recognizes that the choice of discount rate should be based on the nature of the liabilities of a pension plan, and not on the average historical or expected rates of return on a plan's assets.

When a plan's liabilities are truly bond-like and must be honored, the argument for a risk-free discount rate seems watertight. Complications arise, however, when the stream of a plan's liabilities are not predictable. Typically, near-term liabilities will be more predictable than more distant ones. The stream of pension payments to be made to a 64-year-old employee

---

[10] In effect, the insurance company is "borrowing" money when it assumes the liabilities of a pension plan. If it were to use a discount rate higher than the rate at which it would borrow, it is short-changing itself. It obtains a smaller amount of funds for investment than it would if it simply borrowed an amount equivalent to the liabilities it was assuming and invested the borrowed funds.

who will retire shortly is more predictable than the payments that will begin (if they do begin) in 15 years' time to a plan member who is now 50 years old. Longevity risk and salary (cost) risk, which are especially important, have implications for the choice of discount rate. The implications of default by the sponsoring company also need to be considered.

Starting with longevity risk, let us suppose that a plan has enough members to reduce select or individual longevity risk to an acceptable level, but must contend with aggregate longevity risk. Let us suppose further that the probability distribution of the life expectancy of any cohort of men and women is known. Then the future stream of pension payments can be treated as a series of random variables.

Does this kind of risk call for a different discount rate? With a certain stream of payments, the use of the risk-free rate as the discount rate implies that the stream of obligations will definitely be honored. If the pension obligations are not certain, the risk-free rate is not the right choice.[11] In order to treat the obligations as default proof, either the discount rate will have to be lowered, the plan will need to provision for greater-than-projected experience losses, or an asset, like a longevity bond that is very highly correlated with the pension obligations will have to be found. If longevity bonds themselves are not free of default risk, then the plan will have to provision against that possible loss as well. Alternatively, the assumption that pension obligations should be treated as inviolable might have to be reconsidered.

Unpredictable trends in salaries may pose an even more serious problem for pension funding and the choice of the discount rate than aggregate longevity risk does. This unpredictability can be analyzed by splitting nominal-wage increases into two components: the part that maintains the real wage constant, and the rest of the increase, which can reflect the supply and demand for particular skills as well as economy-wide developments. If the rate of increase of this second component were constant and predictable, pension plans could conceivably invest in index-linked bonds [such as Treasury Inflation-Protected Securities (TIPS) in the United States]. These would serve as a hedge, because their value would perfectly correlate with the unpredictable part of wages and salaries. In these circumstances, a pension fund could hedge its exposure to wage inflation perfectly, and the use of a risk-free or low-risk discount rate would remain appropriate (see Box 3.2 for a demonstration).

---

[11] If the expected value of the payments is discounted by the risk-free rate to calculate the assets required to fund them, there will be a shortfall if actual payments exceed their expected values.

Box 3.2.   Funding with indexed debt when real-wage growth is perfectly predictable

The impact of inflation on funding depends on how predictable the real wage is. To demonstrate this, it is useful to decompose the growth of the nominal wage (W) into both real and inflationary parts. Specifically, equation (3.2) expresses nominal wages in period $T-1$ (W_{T-1}) in terms of the growth of real wages and the rate of inflation since the first year of work, period 1. [The rate of inflation in a given year t is p_t, and the (constant) rate of growth of the real wage is a.]:

$$W_{T-1} = W_1(1+a)^{T-2} \prod_{t=2}^{T-1}(1+p_t) \qquad (3.2)$$

Assuming that inflation in year T is projected to be p_T, and that the pension will be payable in year R, funding (F_{T-1}) as of year $T-1$ will be given by equation (3.3):

$$F_{T-1} = (T-1)\alpha \cdot W_{T-1}(1+a)(1+p_T)\frac{\ddot{a}_R}{(1+r)^{R-(T-1)}} \qquad (3.3)$$

The annuity factor $\ddot{a}_R$ is the cost of a dollar of lifetime income beginning in year R, the first year of retirement. Assume that funding consists entirely of inflation-indexed bonds. In year T, inflation proves to be higher than predicted by p_Δ. To be fully funded at the higher price level, funding for benefit accruals through $T-1$ should increase in period T to ($F_{T-1}{}^*$), as shown in equation (3.4).

$$F_{T-1}{}^* = (T-1)\alpha \cdot W_{T-1}(1+a)(1+p_T+p_\Delta)\frac{\ddot{a}_R}{(1+r)^{R-T}} \qquad (3.4)$$

Because the fund is invested entirely in indexed debt, the nominal value of the bonds automatically increases to $F_{T-1}{}^*$. The additional funding needed in year T will equal $\alpha \cdot W_{T-1}(1+a)(1+p_T+p_\Delta)\frac{\ddot{a}_R}{(1+r)^{R-T}}$. (The fund earns interest at the rate of r, which is why the exponent changes between equation (3.3) and equation (3.4)). The additional funding covers the increase in the value of the pension resulting from the last year of service. Its real value is not affected by unexpected inflation, and there is no need to increase funding to compensate for the impact of unexpected inflation on the cost of earlier years.

Source: Author's model and calculations.

Inflation-indexed bonds would be a perfect hedge for a pension fund if wages behaved in the way assumed here. However, the behavior of real-wage growth (i.e., nominal-wage growth minus consumer price inflation) is sufficiently erratic that indexed debt cannot serve this function. Wage-indexed bonds could do so in principle, provided either that an aggregate index tracked wages in particular sectors or occupations well, or that industry-specific wage indexes could be developed. However, wages can vary substantially across industries, and adequate industry-specific indexes have yet to be developed. Some pension economists have argued that equities are sufficiently well correlated with wages that, quite apart from their rate of return, including them in a pension portfolio will reduce the risk of funding to the plan sponsor, and would justify the use of a discount rate higher than the risk-free rate. The evidence on correlation between stocks and wages is, in fact, mixed. The correlation of short-run movements is not high at all.[12] Purely for the sake of illustrating a point, however, let us suppose that equity values and wages were perfectly correlated, that is, the expected rates of growth of an aggregate wage index and stock index were the same and had the same variance. Then the appropriate discount rate would be the growth rate of wages or that of equities, and the plan assets could be entirely composed of equities.[13]

The choice of a risk-free rate as the discount rate is tantamount to a claim that the debt of the company sponsoring the plan is as safe as government debt. However, even the most soundly run companies doing business in the most soundly managed economies are unable to borrow at the risk-free rate. Financial markets must be assuming some risk of default (and in the current global financial environment that perception would be contested by no one).

---

[12] FRS 17 notes that: "... research conducted by the Faculty and Institute of Actuaries demonstrated from past data that the correlation has not been close and that the best match for final salary liabilities was probably index-linked bonds" (EFRAG 2008,147).

[13] The growth rates of equities and wages do not have to be the same for this to hold. Set the fund's holdings of equities in period $t-1$ (E_{t-1}) equal to wages in $t-1$ (W_{t-1}) divided by one plus the growth differential (Δ) between equities and wages. The value of equities in period t will be given by the first equation, where g_E is the average growth rate for equities and (ε_E) is an error term.

$$E_t = \left(\frac{W_{t-1}}{(1+\Delta)} \right)(1+g_E)(1+\varepsilon_E)$$

Wages in period t are given by the second equation, where g_W is the average growth rate for wages and ε_W is an error term.

$$W_t = (W_{t-1})(1+g_W)(1+\varepsilon_W)$$

If we assume that the two error terms equal one another, then equities in period t will always equal wages (the base of pensions) in period t. Finally, because $\left(\frac{W_{t-1}}{(1+\Delta)} \right) = E_{t-1}$, it follows that $W_t = E_{t-1}(1+g_W)(1+\epsilon_W)(1+\Delta)$. In other words, the effective discount rate is the growth rate of equities.

Default risk being a fact of life, the question arises as to why the implicit claims on companies of the obligations of their pension funds should be valued at lower discount rates than their explicit debt. Informed opinion has not settled this question once and for all, although, as noted earlier, most key national and international bodies recommend the use of a high-quality bond rate rather than the risk-free rate as discount rate.[14]

The issue may be viewed from another angle; namely, the expectations that plan members, past and present, could be reasonably held to have about the security of their pension benefits. When pensions are viewed as deferred salaries, an active plan member with accrued benefits and a retired member both have a claim on the plan's assets and on the sponsor's assets if plan assets cannot cover liabilities. It can be argued that if bond holders understand that the price to be paid for the higher rate of return on a corporate debt is the possibility of default, then plan members should recognize that their claims on the plan are also risky. Assuming that both employer and employee contributions to a plan effectively come out of the pocket of the employee, then all contributions to a plan can be viewed as either a loan or an investment by the plan members. However, even if plan members do fully factor in their future benefits in their total compensation, it is a stretch to argue that they are also aware of the risk they are taking as participants in the plan.

The basic issue revolves around what the status of pension claims should be. Proponents of the risk-free view can argue, as Whittington (2006, 529) put it that "[pension] accounts are statements of stewardship," and that, in effect, the possibility of default should not be recognized. Interpreting the obligations of a plan as iron-clad might result in a plan sponsor's adopting not just a low discount rate, but consistently conservative assumptions regarding the management and matching of assets and liabilities, which would minimize the chances that they would default on the accrued benefits of their members. It could not ensure against the sponsor's bankruptcy. The choice of a high discount rate, however, would only increase the risk of plan insolvency or plan closure.

---

[14] The accounting standards board (ASB) of the United Kingdom raises doubts about using a rate above the risk-free rate in a recent statement, but appears to sit on the fence (Blake et al. 2008, 34). The United Kingdom's current reliance on a AA corporate bond yield was strongly criticized by the head of the Pension Protection Fund in the fall of 2008 for understating the real value of pension plans' defined-benefit liabilities (*Financial Times*, October 29, 2008). The massive disruption of financial markets resulted in a large increase in the spread between high, quality corporate and gilt (Treasury) rates, so that the discount rates that pension plans used increased markedly. In the event, the resulting reduction in measured liabilities was more than offset by the impact of crashing equity markets on plan assets.

Given the social function that private employer-provided pensions play, there is surely a strong case for a discount rate that minimizes the risk of insolvency. The discussion in this chapter points to the conclusion that the discount rate should not have an appreciable margin over the risk-free rate because of default risk. However, the appropriate value will depend on the availability of securities like longevity bonds and wage-indexed bonds and other hedges against the risks that pension plans confront.

Valuation of Assets and Its Implications for Funding

Current practice in most industrial countries is to apply fair-value accounting to the valuation of assets. This means that assets that are actively traded (which, for the typical pension plan, would account for the lion's share) would be marked to market. Assets that are not actively traded but that can be valued by reference to actively traded securities are marked to model – that is, their values are determined formulaically with respect to the prices of similar assets that are traded.

For both funding and financial-reporting purposes, however, assets and the net surplus or deficit of the plan may be valued quite differently. A common practice in determining the value of assets used to calculate a funding requirement is to smooth them. The gross assets figure does not typically appear in a corporate balance sheet, nor does gross liabilities; instead, the surplus or deficit is reported. In the United States, the net loss or gain for a particular period will appear in the income statement, but only the cost of current and past service will be included in the statement of operating profits and losses.

Since the eruption of the financial crisis, the practice of fair-value accounting has come under withering fire for its alleged shortcomings as a general financial accounting principle. Its application to pension plans has also been criticized. One argument against fair-value accounting that has been made in the past (not just with respect to pension fund accounting but also to insurance company accounting) is that in a financial crisis or a liquidity panic, the prices of financial assets can become distorted and behave in unusual ways. The same can be said of prices in a boom. These disequilibria could result from various factors: Some securities are thinly traded, and market psychology, be it irrational exuberance or excess of melancholy, can push the prices of some assets far from their equilibrium value. More recently, the panicky search for credit will cause the prices of less liquid but not necessarily risky assets to crash (*Financial Times,* July 28, 2008). An additional argument is the allegedly destabilizing impact of mark to market valuation on the accounts and stock market valuation of the sponsoring company.

The arguments against fair-value accounting that are based on there being a meaningful distinction between market prices and true underlying values have no application when it comes to financial institutions or traders that are funded on a short-term basis: It does not matter whether your asset is undervalued – what matters is the price that it will fetch if you have to liquidate a debt. In the case of insurance companies and pension funds, however, it has been argued that the long average duration of their liabilities means that what are possibly only short-lived declines in the market value of assets are not of great moment. One version of the argument might go something like this: Although a strong-enough dip in asset prices could wipe out a plan's reserve and make it technically insolvent, the typical plan will be able to pay its obligations for many years into the future before – assuming that asset prices do not recover – it runs out of money. In all likelihood, however, stocks will recover, because (so it is argued) they exhibit mean reversion (prices tend to revert to their average). Fair-value accounting might, therefore, create undue concern about the plan's financial situation.

If a market downturn causes a plan to be underfunded, opponents of the fair-value accounting argument might also argue that little or nothing need be done to increase funding. However, while stocks remain below their equilibrium values – assuming there are equilibrium values – and the sponsor's contributions do not increase, plan assets will fall short of their projected values. In the meantime, the plan's sponsor will have to hope that asset values do eventually recover, and recover sufficiently to make up for the losses realized in earlier years. To assume that this will necessarily happen is simply imprudent, however.

An alternative approach that an opponent of fair-value accounting might take is to rely on some concept of equilibrium-asset value in plan reporting, but use market valuations to determine the amount of extra contributions required of the sponsor. This approach would jeopardize plan funding less than the first would, but it would not win high marks for transparency.

The crash in plan assets has inspired acts of regulatory forbearance. In the United States, the shorter adjustment period introduced by the Pension Protection Act of 2006 was relaxed, so that pension plans have more time to make up what for many are very large shortfalls.[15] However, the practice of marking to market continues to apply. Similar acts of forbearance took place in other countries without the suspension or elimination of marking to market. The appropriateness of regulatory forbearance of this kind in an

---

[15] The law that included this measure was HR 7327.

exceptional situation, like the one in which defined-benefit pension plans found themselves in 2008–09 is taken up in Chapter 4.

The difficulty with the arguments against marking to market is that alternative valuation or pricing techniques are themselves artificial. There is no agreed upon way to measure the equilibrium or underlying value of a security. Market prices can, in a sense, be misleading, but they are an objective standard. A uniform alternative approach might be impossible to derive, and would definitely be impossible to interpret. It would reduce the amount of information contained in financial reporting (Escaffre et al. 2008). In the circumstances prevailing in 2009, fair-value accounting might arguably undervalue pension-plan assets, but it is at least a universal standard.[16]

Fair-value accounting does have important operational implications for a pension plan, however. If plan liabilities do not move in the same direction and by the same amount as assets – as would be the case if maturities of assets and liabilities were perfectly matched – then declining asset prices will require additional funding from the sponsor if the plan is to maintain the ratio of assets to liabilities it was previously maintaining. A key issue is how quickly any gap between assets and liabilities should be closed.

When Liabilities Exceed Assets

The nature of a pension plan's operations means the typical plan can sustain an imbalance between assets and liabilities for some time. This is particularly true of a plan that does not yet have a high ratio of retired to active members, unless the imbalance is very large in relation to its balance sheet. This basic feature of pension finance has long been recognized by plan regulators, who have normally allowed plans in deficit a long period to eliminate it. In choosing its investment strategy, a pension plan wants to avoid choosing a mix of assets that will entail an unacceptably large risk of a shortfall from which recovery could be difficult.

As the previous discussion of the advantages of high correlation of stocks with wages hinted at, the riskiness of a plan's assets cannot be judged independently of its liabilities. The ideal risk-minimizing strategy would be one where assets and liabilities were very highly correlated. In practice, this would require perfect matching. The simple model developed earlier in the chapter that used index-linked bonds is a model of perfect matching. The more assets were matched with liabilities in this fashion, the less

---

[16] Perhaps a variant of Churchill's well-known dictum about democracy should apply here: Fair-value accounting may be a terrible way to value assets, but it is less bad than all the rest.

would be the chances of a pension deficit exceeding any given target. The second section of the chapter will address these and other investment issues in more detail.

There can be no hard-and-fast rule for the pace at which a deficit should be eliminated, although very mature plans have less time to close or reduce a gap than growing plans. In principle, whether a pension plan should eliminate a deficit over 5, 10, or 15 years should depend on a reasoned assessment of the consequences of using each of these periods. Too slow a pace means that the plan could be seriously affected by a spate of experience losses, which would oblige the plan sponsor to take on a heavy contributory burden. Too rapid a pace could put an unnecessary strain on the finances of the sponsoring company. Careful modeling techniques could shed light on how quickly a plan should move, and of course the plan's regulators could and typically would set their own rule. The lack of hard-and-fast rules can both justify regulatory forbearance (relaxation) and possibly make regulators too susceptible to the pleas of sponsors of underfunded plans. The regulatory implications of these equilibrating adjustments are discussed in Chapter 4.

Issues in Investing for Traditional Plans

Preliminary Considerations

Discussions of pension-plan investing effectively treat the pension plan as a legal entity that is distinct from the sponsoring company. The sponsor has an obligation to ensure that the plan's solvency is never threatened, but the plan's finances remain separate from those of the sponsor. Many financial economists have taken a contrary position: The finances of the pension plan cannot be addressed independently of those of the sponsoring company. Before turning to the main subject of this section, we first consider the implications of this argument.

The premise of this "integrated finances" point of view is that the pension is effectively a division or department of the sponsoring company. The argument goes beyond the undeniable fact that despite a plan's legal status, the sponsoring company is expected to make good any shortfalls in the plan's funding. The extreme version of the argument would claim that no meaningful line can be drawn between the balance sheet of the plan and that of the company. This implies that, in principle, regulations regarding asset allocation and asset-liability matching aside, a company could shift assets at will between it and the pension plan. In addition, it could appropriate for itself any surplus the plan develops.

In practice, the sponsoring company cannot shift funds out of a pension plan at will to bolster its own balance sheet in any of the countries surveyed, either because such reverse transfers are forbidden, as they typically are in Europe, or because reversions are subject to punitive tax rates, as is the case in the United States. Nonetheless, if a plan develops a surplus, the sponsoring company can, depending on the regulatory framework, reduce its standard contribution, or even take a contribution "holiday."

If the extreme view of the financial integration of plan and sponsor is correct, then the question that arises is whether a plan's investment strategy matters, or whether the investment strategy may be dominated or strongly influenced by other considerations. In particular, the tax treatment of bond versus equity financing in most countries creates a definite incentive for the pension plan to tilt toward bonds, quite independently of its suitability as an asset-allocation strategy.[17]

It is clear that it is not possible to assess accurately the financial soundness of a plan without also assessing the soundness of the finances of the sponsor. Consider two different cases to illustrate this point. In the first case, the plan's finances are considered sound, but those of the sponsoring company, which is expected to make regular contributions to the plan to finance the additional benefits that plan members accrue, is insolvent. In the second, the plan's finances, viewed in isolation, are parlous, but those of the sponsor are in excellent shape. In case one, the plan will not be able to finance the additional benefits that should accrue to the company's employees. In the second, the sponsoring company can make good any excess of liabilities over assets that the plan experiences if the plan is not too large.

Despite the intimate financial links between a plan and its sponsoring company, the extreme view seems strained for various reasons. A plan still needs an investment strategy, and taking into account the regular contributions that the sponsor may make, that strategy can be appraised apart from the financial condition of the sponsor. The basic rationale for a separate investment strategy is to reassure plan members and their representatives that the sponsoring company has taken seriously its commitment to fund the plan adequately. Presenting a joint balance sheet – including the plan's liabilities with the company's and commingling the plan's assets with the

---

[17] For a discussion of this point with an example, see AAA/SOA (2006, 14–21). The basic idea is that the pension plan's bond income is taxed at a lower rate (if it is taxed at all) than the rate of the personal income tax applying to bonds. Shareholders (the owners of the company) are therefore better off reducing their direct holdings of bonds and holding more bonds indirectly through the pension fund. The opposite applies with equities.

company's assets – would imply, even if it did not contravene regulatory norms, that the sponsor did not take its fiduciary duties seriously. It would also make it impossible in practice for plan members, trustees, and regulatory authorities to gauge the soundness of plan finances. A further reason for segregating the finances of plan and sponsor is that, in most countries, the accrued pension rights of current plan participants and retirees are to be secured by a specific set of assets.

In light of these considerations, the rest of this section assumes that the assets the sponsoring company has earmarked to fund the current liabilities of the pension plan are held by the pension plan, so that the distribution of assets between the plan and the sponsoring company is not arbitrary, and is not influenced by fiscal arbitrage.

The Traditional Model of Financial Investment

The basic mean-variance model of financial investment (the Markowitz model) makes the investment decision one of maximizing the expected return of an investment for a given degree of risk. The basic version of the model assumes that a given sum of capital is invested among a number of risky assets (there is no explicit opportunity cost of capital), each with an expected return and variance. Given the covariances of the different assets, it is possible to calculate a set of efficient portfolios. Each portfolio is a combination of assets, the expected return of which cannot be increased without increasing the portfolio's variance. By assuming a certain degree of risk aversion, an optimum investment portfolio can be derived (for a description of the model, see Panjer et al. 1998, 378–83).

The Markowitz model's approach can, in principle, be applied to the investment decisions of a pension fund. However, a pension fund's investment decision is more complicated than either the single- or the multiperiod version of the model. To begin with, the nature or form of the optimization problem is quite different. Essentially, the sponsoring company could be represented as aiming to minimize the expected cost to it of the pension plan subject to a zero or minimal probability of default on its obligations to active and retired plan members. Taking the case of a noncontributory pension plan, this means that the sponsor would want to minimize its exceptional contributions subject to the no-default constraint.[18] Put another way, the sponsor's goal is to minimize its exceptional contributions without

---

[18] The value of the sponsor's regular contributions to the plan is determined by its wage and employment policy, the rate of separation of plan members from the company, and other influences. Its exceptional contributions are made to make up for shortfalls in the increase in net assets.

threatening the plan's solvency. This goal is qualitatively equivalent to the goal of the mean-variance model of investment of maximizing the expected rate of return subject to a constraint on risk.

Putting a plan's investment objective in this way raises the question of how to gauge solvency. Unlike a one-period model, a pension plan's assets may fail to cover its liabilities without precipitating a default. A plan's long horizon means that a state of underfunding can persist for some time. The share of liabilities that have to be liquidated in a given year can be small in relation to total assets, even if the plan is underfunded.[19] In practice, the amount and pattern of exceptional contributions will be determined by the applicable regulatory regime.

Given a set of simplifying assumptions, it is possible to show that a pension plan could eliminate risk by investing 100 percent of its assets in bonds. The necessary assumptions are that interest-rate risk, investment risk, and individual-longevity risk were the only uncertainties confronting the plan, and that the maturity of the plan's liabilities could be matched perfectly on the asset side. Because there would be no aggregate longevity risk, the aggregate nominal value of pension payments would be highly predictable. By matching each period's liabilities on the asset side, liabilities would always be covered 100 percent by assets. The asset portfolio is not risk-free, but the value of assets fluctuates with the value of liabilities as interest rates vary over time.

This strategy is a simple example of asset-liability matching.[20] The practicability of such a strategy depends on the existence of hedges for the risks that the simple model has excluded. If aggregate longevity risk were introduced and were the only risk, the same result could be achieved if a thriving market for longevity bonds were to develop. The additional introduction of unpredictable wage behavior, to name just one uncertainty, would make immunization impracticable, unless a market for wage-indexed longevity

---

[19] In the case of a typical firm supplying goods or services, if its net worth were negative, the firm's financial structure would not allow it the luxury of selling off assets to satisfy its creditors (assuming that it had not already filed for bankruptcy). In contrast, a plan's long horizon and the concentration of its assets in normally liquid financial instruments allow it to respond to an imbalance in this way.

[20] The easiest way to immunize a plan's liabilities would be through zero-coupon bonds, if they are available over a range of maturities that matches those of the plan's liabilities. The value of the zero-coupon bonds maturing on a given date is set to equal the value of the pension payments (which are assumed to be predictable) on that date. With exact matching, the duration of the plan's liabilities exactly equals the duration of its assets. However, regular coupon bonds could also be used provided their longest maturity matched that of the plan's liabilities. See Mackenzie (2006, 210–14) and Blake (2006b, 259–67). *Strips* are another possibility.

bonds or other instruments that could hedge these risks efficiently developed. In practice, however, an asset portfolio composed entirely of risk-free sovereign debt cannot eliminate risk, which opens the door to equities and other investments.

Asset-Liability Management

Asset-liability management (ALM) has been practiced by financial institutions for some time, but its application to pension finance did not become common until fairly recently. It remains more common in Europe than elsewhere. The basic idea behind ALM is not new, but was lost sight of during the bull market of the 1990s. That idea is that assets should not be managed independently of liabilities. For example, it does not make sense to set a goal of maximizing the expected value of assets subject to a constraint on risk without considering what the likelihood is that the policy could entail a significant deterioration in net assets.

When pension plans discounted their liabilities at a constant and unchanging rate, it might not have been necessary to worry about the behavior of net, as opposed to gross, assets. Measured liabilities would not have changed much from one year to the next, and would not have been affected by changes in the financial environment. This means that changes in gross assets would be a good approximation for changes in net assets. Ironically, pension plans in industrial countries were moving to market-oriented accounting at the time when both interest rates and equity markets were dropping. As Chapter 6 discusses, these developments entailed a large decline in asset-liability ratios.

Given the availability of the right kind of assets, as this chapter has discussed, a plan sponsor could prevent fluctuations in interest rates and wages from affecting the asset-liability ratio of a pension plan. In practice, assets with the necessary properties do not exist. Even if they did, their average return could be substantially lower than average returns to equities and other assets. In these circumstances, a plan sponsor prepared to make exceptional contributions when markets were down to maintain the plan's funding at the level required by the regulatory framework might do better with a more diversified and riskier portfolio.

ALM began with scenario analyses or stress tests, which were intended to show the impact on net assets of specific scenarios, like a drop in the value of the equity portfolio of 20 percent combined with a downward shift of the yield curve of 75 basis points. ALM has become more sophisticated over the years. Currently, ALM is usually conducted with a model using Monte Carlo simulations. ALM is most prevalent in the Netherlands, because the funding regulations give plans a strong incentive to adopt it. Because of its technical complications, most ALM work is contracted out.

ALM has two building blocks: a model of asset prices and a formalized trade-off between risk and return. To go beyond simple stress tests, it is necessary to have a model of the prices of the assets that affect the value of a plan's balance sheet. One fairly standard technique is to model asset prices with a vector autoregressive model (VAR), which makes asset prices a function of their past levels [see Bauer et al. (2006) for a relatively nontechnical discussion] and an error term. An assumption is made about the distribution of the model's error terms, usually that they are multivariate normal with zero mean. This statistical model is used to simulate the range of possible impacts of random fluctuations in asset prices on the funding ratio for a given asset allocation and duration of liabilities. Because simulations are conducted over a long period of time, an ALM exercise also needs to model retirements and separations, and make assumptions about the longevity of pension recipients.

Practices in modeling asset prices have not yet been codified. Ziemba (2003) stresses the importance of the phenomenon of mean reversion of asset prices. This is an important issue for a pension plan given its long horizon. The same author suggests that the probability distribution of asset returns be shifted to the left to allow for lower and more volatile returns.

A basic component of any ALM exercise is the specification of the optimization function, or the trade-off between risk and return. As already noted, a relatively aggressive investing strategy might reduce the sponsor's average contributions, but make them more variable. If wage-indexed bonds like those described earlier in the chapter existed, a very risk-averse sponsor might choose to invest a high percentage of plan assets in these instruments. A sponsor less averse to risk would invest more in assets with a high expected rate of return that was less well correlated with the return on liabilities.

The decision about how to trade off risk and return must also respect the regulatory environment in which the plan operates. If the actual funding ratio were allowed to adjust gradually to the ratio stipulated by regulation, a sponsor that wished to avoid abrupt changes in its contributions to the plan would have more leeway than it would if the regulations required rapid adjustment, as is the case in the Netherlands. With mark to market valuation of plan assets and liabilities, an accounting requirement that the plan sponsor must incorporate the plan in its own balance sheet could make the sponsor reluctant to pursue a strategy that risked substantial fluctuations in the funding ratio, even if gradual adjustment of the actual ratio to the ratio stipulated by the regulatory framework were condoned. More generally, the optimization function in an ALM model needs to reflect the special circumstances of the sponsor, including the regulatory environment in which it functions.

Some ALM exercises are conducted using a hybrid/simulation optimization model (Boender et al. 1998). A full-fledged optimization model should, in principle, cover all the possible scenarios (or, in the case of a continuous probability distribution, a very large number of scenarios) and simulate the effect of all possible asset mixes to determine the optimal policy. The hybrid approach is more tractable and less costly, which may appeal to smaller pension plans.[21] It might simulate the impact of 500 randomly generated asset mixes (60 percent stocks, 35 percent bonds, 5 percent cash, etc.) to see how each performs. The next step is to narrow down the set of policy mixes, and possibly simulate other policies that combined elements of the first set. The final step is to compare the policies according to the average contribution they require and, say, the instability of the funding ratio.

ALM can sidestep optimization altogether and take the less ambitious approach of finding an asset mix that gives merely satisfactory results, rather than striving for the optimal mix. For example, a plan might begin with its current asset mix, and conduct experiments with mixes that differed from it, but not radically. Based on these tests, the plan might then choose to make incremental changes to its asset mix. At the other extreme, a full-fledged optimization exercise could also include a feedback step. As an example, if the asset-to-liability ratio increases beyond expectations in one period, the model could include an automatic increase in the share of equities.

The complexity of ALM has prompted the criticism that it is a black box. ALM does not admit of simple rules of thumb, like "60 percent equities, 40 percent bonds." Both the properties of individual assets, if these include complex derivatives, and the overall results of simulation exercises may be hard to understand. British pension experts have expressed concern that the sophistication of ALM means that many trustees are unable to carry out due diligence in appraising the soundness of an investment strategy based on the ALM approach. The whole approach will simply be beyond them. This criticism may be overstated, because it should be possible to draw some fairly intuitive conclusions from an ALM exercise about the impact

---

[21] The most sophisticated form of ALM is not cheap. Together with the long-run outlook of pension plans, this explains why many plans conduct ALM exercises once every three years [Watson Wyatt (2009)].

of different strategies on risk-return outcomes. The notion of a quantifiable trade-off between some measure of risk and return may not be one that some trustees understand, but they can be shown the simulation output of an ALM exercise and judge whether the range of potential outcomes is one with which they are comfortable.

ALM has also been criticized for what amounts to an empirical bias; namely, making the eligibility of an asset for pension portfolios dependent on the existence of an adequate historical record from which to derive estimates of expected returns and variances. This approach allegedly discourages plans from investing in asset classes that might reduce risk (OECD 2004). This limitation is not inevitable, provided these assets can be incorporated in the ALM model without all the usual informational prerequisites.

An ALM exercise should help a pension-plan sponsor grasp the riskiness of a particular investment strategy, but cannot tell the sponsor how much risk it should be willing to take on. That will depend on a number of features of the sponsor's own operations and the characteristics of the plan. In principle, highly leveraged companies might wish to reduce the risk they were assuming in sponsoring a plan, because their balance sheet might already be exposing them to significant risk. A sponsor in this position might opt for a share of equities in the plan's portfolio that was lower than the share of the typical plan.[22] A sponsor's appetite for risk might also vary inversely with the size of the plan. A substantial degree of underfunding of a very large plan could entail a real strain on a company's financial position.

In addition, and as noted above, the volatility of a plan's asset-liability balance could also have more influence on a plan sponsor's attitude to risk if the applicable corporate accounting regime requires that the plan's financial position has to be fully reflected in the accounts of the sponsor. This influence would be heightened by the emphasis stock markets place on the short-term outlook. Finally, the attitude of both active and retired plan members could also have an influence: They might be more comfortable with an investment strategy that minimized the chances for and the likely size of exceptional contributions from the sponsor.

Some commentators have argued that plan sponsors and trustees should adopt a more aggressive stance when plans are immature, that is, when they are still accumulating reserves and pension payouts are only a fraction of contributions, if they have even started. The long duration of pension liabilities could tempt an investment committee to adopt a more aggressive

---

[22] If the pension plan increases its holdings of debt then the net combined indebtedness of the plan and sponsoring company declines.

strategy in the accumulation phase of the plan's life cycle, because a plan would have some years to recover from a downturn in financial markets. If stock prices are not mean-reverting, however, it can be shown that the mix of risky and safe securities in a pension plan's asset portfolio should not be changed over time just because its liabilities are of long duration (Jagannathan and Kocherlakota 1996).

Risk Budgeting and Liability-Driven Investment

Risk budgeting is a variant of ALM that derives ultimately from the mean-variance analysis of the Markowitz model. It has been defined as "a framework for analyzing both risk and return over the short and long term, where the units of risk and return are varied to be measures of relevance for each client's [plan's] situation" (Watson Wyatt 2009).[23]

In the case of a pension plan, risk can be measured in a number of ways. The risk-budgeting approach usually relies on the standard deviation of the plan's net assets relative to its liabilities. The first step in risk budgeting is for a pension plan's trustees and investment committee to determine how much total portfolio risk they are willing to take. Assuming that the plan's liabilities are valued at $10 billion, their acceptable level of risk might be an asset allocation that entailed a standard deviation of assets minus liabilities over one year of $300 million.

This risk is then allocated (budgeted) among the various asset classes the plan holds. Assuming that the plan's consultants can calculate the overall risk to the portfolio entailed by a given asset allocation, an optimal allocation will be achieved when, for all asset classes with positive holdings, the ratios of the expected return of each asset in the portfolio to the overall portfolio risk it entails are equal. If these ratios are not equal, then the overall return can be increased by reducing the allocation of assets with low ratios in favor of those with higher ratios.

Enunciating the basic principle of risk budgeting is easier than putting it into practice. The basic principle is an optimization principle, essentially the same as the principle of maximizing return subject to a given constraint on risk. To put the technique in practice, it is necessary to estimate the expected returns and covariances of the assets in which the plan will invest.

Risk budgeting has two advantages over a high-powered ALM exercise. It can be carried out more often – like once per year – and the rationale for the asset allocations it derives is probably more intuitive to those members

---

[23]   Studies of risk budgeting include Sharpe (2001), Urwin et al. (2001), and Mina (2005).

of investment committees without a strong technical background. It is less of a black box.

Liability-driven investment (LDI) is a variant of ALM that seeks to minimize risk by investing in a broader mix of assets. ALM, as it originally evolved, confined the choice of investments mainly to stocks and bonds. Because of the importance of managing asset-liability (surplus) risk, ALM simulation exercises suggested that bonds were underrepresented in pension-plan portfolios. Recently, however, a number of writers have pointed out that increasing the share of bonds in a portfolio could still leave the plan exposed to various risks. The most basic of these is interest-rate risk. With increasing longevity, the duration of pension-plan liabilities is substantially greater than the average duration of bonds, even government bonds (gilts in the United Kingdom). A related criticism specific to the United Kingdom is that the bond market does not have the capacity to provide a hedge for all the country's pension plans (Association of British Insurers 2005).

The problems of insufficient capacity and duration could be mitigated by the issue of sufficient quantities of very-long-term debt, and in recent years the governments of Germany, the United Kingdom, and the United States have increased the maximum maturity of their sovereign debt. The United States began re-issuing 30-year Treasury bonds in 2006 and the United Kingdom began issuing 50-year gilts both fixed interest and inflation-linked, in 2005.

Lengthening the maturity and increasing the supply of long-term fixed debt will not, however, address the problem posed by aggregate longevity risk, and the duration mismatch will not be eliminated overnight, even if it is possible to eliminate it entirely one day.

LDI can be seen as a concerted effort to hedge every possible risk (wage-uncertainty, interest-rate, investment, and longevity risks) by using derivatives. For example, if insufficient duration is a particular problem, a plan may borrow short term and swap the interest it receives on its floating-rate asset for a fixed rate of return, with the contract having a maturity that is longer than the available long-term debt. Similarly, the risk of unexpected wage inflation can be mitigated through a swap of the interest on a fixed-rate instrument for one that is linked to the consumer price index (retail price index in the United Kingdom). The best publicized adoption of LDI in the United Kingdom is that of W. H. Smith. In 2005, the company's trustees sold its entire portfolio of equities and fixed-income securities, and invested the proceeds in short-term paper, nearly all of which it swapped for a 50-year income stream that was intended to protect it against inflation and interest-rate risk (Sahai 2006).

Defined-Contribution Plans

Defined-contribution plans do not present the same challenges for plan sponsors as defined-benefit plans do, especially when they have no guarantees embedded in them. The defined-contribution plans found in Denmark and Switzerland, which do have guarantees, do raise the same kinds of investment issues as defined-benefit plans (see Appendix 1, Denmark and Switzerland), although they do not expose their sponsors to the same degree of risk.

In countries like Australia and the United States, guarantees typically do not apply to defined-contribution plans. In both countries, investments in defined-contribution plans are typically self-directed. Even self-directed plans raise fiduciary issues, which are considered in Chapter 4.

Defined-contribution plans entail substantial risks for their participants. The simulation model presented in Chapter 2 highlighted the risks confronting a retiree managing a nest egg consisting of risky assets. A working person confronts a similar problem, except that normally he or she is aiming to amass a nest egg, not run it down.

To zero-in on the investment risk faced by a plan member of a defined-contribution plan where investments are self-directed, let us imagine that the member can choose his or her contribution rate and predict the sum total of the contributions he will make during what remains of his working life, and that he aims to retire having accumulated a specified sum of money that is more than can be accumulated by investing solely in risk-free assets. To stand a good chance of achieving this goal, the plan member will have to act as a conservative defined-benefit plan sponsor would and aim high – that is, set a contribution rate (or average rate) high enough to make a shortfall unlikely. It is easy to show that this approach will result in a surplus most of the time, and one that may be sizeable.

A recent innovation in defined-contribution plan investing is the *target-date fund*. These funds assume that as an investor ages, the share of his investments in equities should decline, and the share of fixed-interest investments should rise. As already noted, it is possible to show that age should have no impact on asset allocation, but the proof of this assertion assumes that the investor has only financial assets and no human capital. That might be true of many older people, because they have few or no years of labor force participation ahead of them. It is not true of younger people, for whom a loss of financial capital is less catastrophic than it is for older people.

That said, the target-date approach has its own drawbacks. Consider, for example, someone of middle age who has invested hitherto heavily in equities, but had the bad luck to have suffered through a down market. The target-date strategy implies that as retirement comes closer, his asset allocation should become more conservative. Shifting out of equities into lower-yielding bonds will, however, effectively lock in the losses he suffered earlier. Target-date funds are, unfortunately, not a panacea.

Concluding Thoughts

Two financial downturns in the first decade of the twenty-first century, the second of which has come close to bringing the world's financial system to its knees, have created an intractable dilemma for the investment managers of traditional pension funds. A strategy of concentrating on the assets side of the plan's balance sheet has been soundly discredited, and most pension plans now practice ALM, often with the aim of minimizing (perhaps keeping at an acceptable level) the variance of the plan balance for a given amount of contributions from the plan sponsor.

As this chapter has pointed out, it is hard to derive rules of thumb regarding asset allocation from the ALM approach and to judge the soundness of the investment strategy that emerges from a modeling exercise. LDI is a version of ALM that concentrates above all on minimizing the variance of the plan balance by a strategy of asset-liability matching. LDI implies reducing the share of investments with high returns and acquiring bonds with a lower return if that will lower the variance of the plan balance significantly. One advantage of a strategy that matches the duration of assets and liabilities is that, in principle, it should be easier for regulators and plan board members to verify that assets and liabilities are balanced than it would be to evaluate the soundness of a strategy based on ALM. However, the full range of financial instruments needed for the comprehensive implementation of LDI is lacking.

4

Current Regulatory Issues

The Rationale for Regulation

The answer to the question "Why regulate employer-provided pensions?" may seem obvious. Nonetheless, a review of the rationale for regulating employer-provided pensions sheds light on why regulatory frameworks can differ from one country to another, and can also lead to a benchmark for evaluating certain features of a country's regulatory apparatus.

The most basic reason for regulating an employer-provided pension, especially a traditional pension, is that it is so complex a social and economic institution that *laissez-faire*, or self-regulation, will not be feasible. Too much can go wrong. A traditional pension plan channels a large share of the saving of working men and women into investments in order to pay a pension to the workers when they retire, which may represent a significant proportion of their income in retirement. The malfunctioning of a pension plan can jeopardize the welfare of many workers, and its complexity increases the chances of malfunction. Defined-contribution plans are less complex for the sponsor than defined-benefit plans, but they face their own risks. The possibility that defined-contribution plans will not perform as they should to provide a secure retirement is just as great as it is with traditional plans, perhaps even greater. A traditional pension plan's complexity derives from its long planning horizon and the sophisticated investment strategy that such a horizon demands, but also owes something to the rules the plan applies to determine eligibility for and the value of the benefits it pays.[1] These basic features in turn, as Chapter 3 has made clear, can bedevil pension accounting. The opacity that can characterize a pension plan's

---

[1] Pension plans can be a going concern for many years. The period from the date of a worker's first contribution to the plan to the time of his death (when he stops receiving a pension annuity) can stretch to as long as 80 years.

accounts is also a potential breeding ground for malfeasance, as the scandal of the Maxwell pension plans in the United Kingdom made clear.[2]

The long horizon of pension plans exposes them to risks that financial institutions, with the exception of insurance companies, do not normally face. Traditional pension plans must make projections many years into the future, which certainly must increase the risk of forecast error – errors in the projections of wage inflation, aggregate longevity risk, and the other determinants of a plan's liabilities. Another risk stems from the fact that the horizons of plan sponsors are probably much shorter than those of the plan. This mismatch of perspectives could result in the plan sponsors' making decisions that jeopardize a plan's finances. A plan sponsor, for example, can be tempted to reduce its contribution to the plan because of its own financial difficulties. Alternatively, the sponsor of a plan established as a trust might put pressure on the plan trustees to adopt a more aggressive investment strategy that, if successful, would allow the sponsor to lower its contributions but increase the risk of substantial underfunding.

This clash of interests is supposed to be mitigated by the oversight of trustees, but they will not be effective in this role unless they are honest, free of undue influence, and competent. The more sophisticated a plan's investment strategy, the greater the demands on the financial expertise of plan trustees. A very large plan may have less difficulty in recruiting trustees with the necessary acumen than a small plan, but the tendency to pick trustees from the executive ranks of the sponsoring company can entail a conflict of interest.[3]

Any society should be concerned whether a system of employer-provided pensions lives up to its promises: that the classes of employees that the plan's constituting document says are eligible should indeed be eligible; that the rules for eligibility should be transparent; that a plan's assets be invested to achieve the maximum return consistent with an acceptable risk of a shortfall of assets from liabilities; and that plan members receive the pensions to which their service entitles them.

A well-functioning legal system – with effective sanctions against misappropriation of funds and effective civil remedies for unjust or arbitrary interpretations of the rules – could go a long way toward ensuring that

---

[2] Robert Maxwell, a British media tycoon, was found after his death in 1991 to have looted more than £400 million (about $560 million) from the pensions sponsored by his companies (BBC News 2001).

[3] On a related point, small pension plans may be at another disadvantage compared to large plans, in that certain types of assets, including certain derivatives, may not be economical on a small scale.

these objectives are met. In fact, in certain respects, members of employer-provided pension plans should be better served by the legal system than individual savers with plans at financial institutions. The costs of legal action against unfair or arbitrary treatment can be spread over more people if more than a handful of pension members are directly concerned. Similarly, labor unions, especially if they have been involved in the negotiation of a plan's terms, will likely be prepared to represent the interests of a group of members seeking redress from a decision by the sponsor that they consider unjust. The collective nature of pension plans and the protective role of trustees may also lessen the need for consumer protection laws. One area where the legal system may need reinforcement is plan investment strategy, depending on how strong the incentives are for prudent, but not too cautious, investing.

A government can, however, be concerned with more than ensuring that the rules of the pension game are respected; it may wish to change the rules of the game. A private pension system may be well-functioning in the sense that it is properly funded and its rules are observed, but may be viewed as unfair because of its limited coverage, or some undesirable if heretofore legal discrimination in its treatment of different classes of worker. Employer-provided pensions began, as Chapter 1 discussed, with only particular groups of workers, usually long-serving clerical or professional workers, and decades elapsed before coverage was extended more broadly. A government concerned with making the second pillar of retirement security available to as many workers as possible will want to convert a private-sector welfare system into one that serves more of a social purpose. As an example, a government may be concerned not simply that vesting rules are observed, but that the rules do not deprive short-tenured workers of their accrued benefits. Similarly, they will be concerned not simply that covered workers receive the pension due them, but that all or most workers are covered.

There is a basic distinction between the two types of regulation. With the first, the regulatory framework is intended to make a system that would probably have come into existence anyway respect the relevant laws. It may be enough to rely mainly on the legal system to ensure that employer-provided pensions function as they should. The investment and funding functions might not be effectively regulated in this way, however. The very different time horizons of the plan and its sponsor, and the risk that trustees might favor the sponsor could mean that reliance on the prudent-person model and legal sanctions against excessively risky investment strategies would not be effective safeguards against imprudent investment.

With the second type of regulation, which is broader and more socially activist, the government is asking more of employers than that they should simply play by the rules; it is asking them to provide pensions to those employees that their plan might not otherwise cover on terms they might not otherwise offer. A government may simply require an employer to offer a pension to all of its full-time employees, for example, even if the employer would not do so if given the choice. Alternatively, it could adopt the U.S. approach and use the leverage of tax preferences by denying noncomplying plans those tax advantages they would enjoy if they complied.

A final reason for regulating pension plans is their sheer collective size as capital-market participants. Employer-provided plans account for a huge share of the financial assets of most of the countries surveyed. The decisions their investment committees make can have a significant effect for good or ill on the governance of companies in which the plans have a stake, and their asset-allocation strategies can substantially influence stock market outcomes. Even a single plan, if large enough, could wield considerable influence on the governance of some of the corporations in which it held shares.

These considerations suggest a regulatory hierarchy. The most basic task of regulation is to prevent or at least minimize the risks of malfeasance and misappropriation of funds. The Maxwell episode already mentioned illustrates that this risk should not be overlooked, even in a country boosting a venerable common-law tradition and ranking among the world's most highly developed financial centers.[4] The second task would be to ensure that pension plans were fairly and efficiently administered. This job, of protecting workers' pension rights, might be the responsibility mainly of the legal system, although regulation would also play a role. The third task would be encouraging prudent investments. The fourth, which corresponds to our second type of regulation, would be extending the coverage of the employer-provided pension system on terms that would make the system an effective second pillar of retirement security.

Pension-plan regulation is a huge subject. Apart from these stage-setting observations, this chapter will confine itself to addressing four regulatory issues of particular importance for the major themes of the book: (1) the role and implications of activist regulation, (2) risk-based supervision, (3) the scope of regulatory forbearance, and (4) the role of trustees and the risk of conflict of interest.

---

[4] The Madoff scandal is a painful reminder that even if pension-plan governance is beyond reproach, pension-plan finances are affected by regulatory lapses elsewhere in the financial system.

Activist Regulation

The purpose of activist regulation is to correct for perceived inefficiencies or inequities that the private employer-provided pension system, left to its own devices without corrective public policy, would manifest. The problems that governments would normally want to resolve besides overly narrow coverage are inadequate protection of survivors or divorced spouses, onerous vesting requirements, limited portability, unequal treatment of the sexes, and even inadequate pensions, as reflected in too low a replacement rate or less than full indexation. Governments typically require that employer-provided pensions offer a unisex annuity (as opposed to allowing sponsors to provide their female employees with a pension that, although it may be actuarially fair, is less than the pension received by a man with the same earnings history).

Some of these regulations could impose a substantial cost to employers. For example, a very broad coverage requirement could impose a burden on small and even mid-sized firms. Neither the unisex annuity nor a survivor's pension need impose an extra cost on the *average* plan sponsor, because they simply entail a redistribution of the pension between the sexes or within a family. A unisex annuity will raise costs for employers in industries that employ women in disproportionate numbers. Establishing a survivor's pension could entail some contentiousness between members of a couple, because they might have differing views on how large the survivor's pension should be, and the priorities set by the government might not be the same as those of either the employee or the employee's spouse. These differences could be minimized by allowing some flexibility in the terms of the pension.

Coverage

Inadequate coverage may be the most basic problem, because it ensures that many workers will be left with little or no occupational pension to supplement their public (first-pillar) pensions. As Chapter 1 discussed, the rates of coverage of any kind of employer-provided pension vary enormously among the countries surveyed. The United States applies *nondiscrimination rules* to ensure that coverage of less well-paid workers and their pensions are not excessively low in relation to highly compensated workers. However, employers are not required to offer a pension to any of their workers if they choose not to. Unless broader coverage is required by the government, it will remain restricted.

The most likely reasons for this are that pensions, especially traditional ones, are an expensive form of compensation, particularly for the low-paid worker, and a benefit that they may not appreciate as much as a more highly compensated worker would. As Chapter 1 discussed, the traditional pension was as much a device for ensuring loyalty and hard work among career employees as it was a means of facilitating their saving for retirement. The payoff to the employer of extending coverage might simply be insufficient to justify it. Countries like the Netherlands and Denmark do not, strictly speaking, require employers to offer a pension to their entire workforce, but the key role that collective bargaining plays in their economies means that broad, even near-universal coverage has effectively been a condition of agreement on the overall package of labor-management issues. In Canada, the United Kingdom, and the United States, countries with a more individualistic tradition, coverage has effectively been left to the employer.

Some governments, as Chapter 1 makes clear, have successfully required nearly universal coverage from employers. Implementing such a policy requires a decision about exceptions – both exceptions to the rule that all employers offer a plan, and the rule that every employee be included in it. A considered decision about universal coverage should be based on a view of the impact of the policy on employers' labor costs, and on how they could be expected to react to any cost increase.

Whether or not labor costs would increase will depend on a number of things, and not just the administrative cost of the pension. Take the case first of a noncontributory pension, where the employer's contribution is set to equal the cost of the pension rights a worker accrues. If the worker values the compensation in the form of the pension as highly as he does his pay – meaning that the worker is relatively longsighted – he will be prepared to take a cut in take-home pay equal to the contribution to the plan made on his behalf.[5]

The cost to the employer in this case would be reduced to the cost of administering the pension plan. The resulting increase in the cost of labor could conceivably reduce the employer's demand for labor. Whatever the significance of this effect, it would be greater in proportionate terms for low-income workers than it would be for high-income workers if the fixed-cost element of administrative expense was significant. In the case of a longsighted worker, it makes no difference whether the contributions to the plan are paid by the worker or by the employer.

If workers did not value the pension as highly as take-home pay, they would perceive the requirement to participate in a plan as tantamount to a

---

[5] With favorable tax treatment, a worker in this position would be willing to accept a reduction in gross salary that exceeded his or her employer's contribution to the pension plan.

cut in pay. They would balk at accepting the cut in take-home pay that would keep their employer's labor costs unchanged. Standard economic theory suggests that with a shortsighted workforce, some decline in employment would be the price to pay for a higher rate of coverage of the employed. Australia's experience, however, suggests that this need not be the case (see Appendix 1, Australia).

No employer-provided pension system enjoys 100 percent coverage, and even in a system that aspires to universality there may be categories of workers for whom coverage is not feasible. One such category may be part-time workers, especially casual workers, who tend to be less well-paid than full-time workers. In light of the fixed-cost element in plan administration, requiring the inclusion of part-time workers in an employer-provided plan may entail a heavy burden in costs for the employer. For similar reasons, requiring small employers to offer a pension to their workforce without assistance from the government may not be feasible.

Exceptions invite gaming. In particular, the exemption of part-time workers creates a strong incentive, if the laws permit, for employers to replace full-time workers with part-time workers. The technology of the workplace, the demands of a job, and workers' preferences will all influence how widespread recourse to this stratagem is. In the United States, workers logging less than 1,000 hours per year need not be covered by a plan, and there are some industries where part-time work is common (AARP 2009, 4–18). One way to defeat this ploy would be to do as Australia has done, and define part-time worker so that it includes only those employees who work no more than a few hours a week. The lower the cutoff point, the harder it would be to substitute multiple part-time workers for one full-time worker.

A variant of a policy of universal coverage has gained considerable attention in the United States, and is the mainstay of the U.K. reform to be introduced in 2012. It could be described as a policy of soft universal coverage because, although employers with more than a stipulated number of employees are required to offer their employees a pension, their employees are not required to participate. In the United States, the vehicle proposed for this policy is the automatic or auto IRA. The auto IRA is intended for small employers for whom a conventional defined-contribution plan like the 401(k) is too costly. The auto IRA is a much simplified defined-contribution plan benefiting from the same favorable tax treatment that established plans enjoy. Its key feature is its default setting, which entails participation unless workers explicitly opt out. Chapter 7 discusses this type of policy innovation further, but here it can be noted that the goal of universal coverage, soft or hard, is facilitated by encouraging less costly plans.

Vesting and Portability

Vesting requirements are a key feature of an employer-provided pension, especially a traditional pension but also a defined-contribution plan. Nearly all traditional plans require that a worker achieve some minimum period of service before obtaining the right to the benefits he or she has accrued to date. This feature was consonant with the original motivation for these plans, because it rewarded long service and penalized early separation from the sponsoring company's employ. However, as Chapter 2 discussed, a long vesting period could leave many workers with little or no pension rights, particularly given a trend to shorter tenure. In effect, workers with comparatively short tenures were subsidizing the pension paid to workers with long tenure.

Other things being equal, shortening the vesting requirement of a transitional pension plan is justifiable on the grounds of equity, as well as the more pragmatic grounds that more workers would be able to draw a pension.[6] The policy should, in principle, reduce the chances that a worker with several employers and a cumulatively long period of membership in several plans ends up with no pension. However, the policy also increases the cost to the employer of providing the pension, because the employer will now be paying pensions to workers who had previously not vested. To keep the employer's costs unchanged, the terms of the pension would have to be made less generous by such changes as lowering the accrual rate, increasing the number of years used to calculate the pensionable base, or moving from a final salary to a career-average plan.

Changing the terms of a pension plan can be both expensive and a source of friction with the workforce. However, assuming it can be done, predicting the workforce's reaction to changes in the structure of the pension is very difficult. The probability that a plan member receives a pension increases given no change in tenure patterns, but the value of the individual pension actually received would decline. The total value of the pensions paid out should not change, but payouts would be redistributed in favor of short-tenured workers. That one group of workers would benefit from the change in policy while another would be hurt raises the question of whether it would be popular with the workforce as a whole. These considerations illustrate how a social policy may have side effects – in this case, a decline

---

[6]   A defender of an unreformed system could argue that workers willingly choose to enter a lottery in which they win the prize if their tenure at the company is long enough for them to vest. However, the choice of staying in a job until the employee is fully vested is not always his or hers to make. Consequently, the contributions made on behalf of an employee during the vesting period are tantamount to a risky investment.

in the average pension of workers with long tenure – that need to be taken into account, because they may be unpopular with most of the workforce, who do not benefit from the change.

The portability of benefits under a traditional pension is another facet of employer-provided pensions that governments could regulate. As Chapter 1 explained, there is some difference across the ten countries with respect to the portability of the benefits of traditional plans. In the United Kingdom and the United States, pension rights acquired under one traditional pension plan cannot generally be transferred to another. Instead, the benefits will be paid to the former plan member at retirement age. There are two problematic aspects to this procedure. First, plan sponsors may go out of business, plan records can be lost, and a former plan member can lose touch with the plan sponsor. Problems arising from this sort of communication failure would not affect every former vested employee, but could certainly affect some.

The second problem is occasioned by separation that takes place after benefits are vested but well before the normal retirement age, and was discussed in Chapters 1 and 2. The benefits a separated plan member will ultimately receive are typically fixed in nominal terms. They are neither indexed nor do they earn interest. Indexing or applying a market-related rate of interest to acquired benefits poses no technical challenges to a plan actuary. However, requiring indexation or the application of interest increases the cost of the plan to the sponsor and, as was the case with shortening the vesting period, will require that the plan be made less generous to long-serving employees.

Provision of Information

The growing popularity of defined-contribution plans has given critical importance to one particular regulatory issue – the provision of adequate and comprehensible information on the choices plan members must make. It is addressed here, in the section on activist regulation, although it could equally well be considered as one of the topics of the conservative legal approach to regulation with which this chapter began.

Members of any employer-provided plan need to make elections among the plan's options in the course of their service. However, the type of decision and the frequency with which decisions need to be reviewed are typically much greater for the defined-contribution plan than they are for the defined-benefit plan. In the case of the traditional plan, members need make only a small number of benefit-related decisions, and these usually do not require frequent or continuous review. One decision that is normally made early is the choice of designated beneficiary (if the pension has a death benefit). In the period leading up to or at retirement, a worker will choose the method of distribution of benefits – if there is a choice – and the survivorship features of an annuity, if he has elected an annuity.

Members of defined-contribution plans, especially if investments are self-directed, must make many decisions during the accumulation phase of the plan. In addition to decisions about the asset allocation of their plan balances, they may need to decide how much to contribute. At the distribution phase, the typical defined-contribution plan offers its members substantially more choice than the traditional plan does. For example, with a traditional plan the distribution may take the form of an annuity payment, which cannot be changed. With some defined-contribution plans, the amount to be withdrawn at any point during the distribution phase may be entirely at the member's discretion.

In order to make informed decisions about asset allocation, members of defined-contribution plans should at a minimum receive reliable and timely information on the total value and asset composition of their plan's investments, and the fees they pay for the investment and administration of their account. This information is necessary even for members of plans where the sponsor determines asset allocation, because the overall performance and riskiness of a plan has an obvious bearing on the member's decisions regarding his or her personal pension plan, if he or she has one, and is especially important for self-directed plans. Plan sponsors will not necessarily provide all the information that a plan member might reasonably expect to have; as well, they may not have all the information themselves. This is a real problem with 401(k) plans in the United States (see Appendix 1, United States).

Financial Education

Financial acumen or financial literacy is especially important for defined-contribution plans where investments and distributions are self-directed, and remains important even for plans, like the traditional pension, where the participant's role is largely passive. All of the governments of the ten sample countries have demonstrated concern over the ignorance that most of their citizens display about financial matters in general.

There are three dimensions to financial literacy. The first is basic knowledge of relevant institutions and facts. In the case of older Americans, these would include the basic information needed to make a sensible decision about the right age at which to claim Social Security or the coverage that Medicare provides. The second would be a basic understanding of financial relationships – not just facts, but why, for example, bond prices fall when interest rates rise, or why investing in your company's stock to any extent is a bad idea. The third is what could be called practical knowledge – the ability to follow good financial advice. This is the faculty that allows us to stick to a saving plan and not spend impulsively.

Depending on exactly how much scope for choice a defined-contribution plan provides, all three aspects of financial literacy come into play. For our purposes, the key issue is whether or how the provision of financial education can be regulated. Economists often point out that education is a public good and is at risk of being undersupplied, because its benefits do not accrue solely to the student. This point is more relevant at lower levels than higher levels of education, and might not seem to apply to financial education beyond basic arithmetic and knowledge of basic banking and the like. However, to the extent that bad decisions by an individual affect the rest of the community, for example, by making it more likely that he or she will need social assistance, then financial education may be seen as a public good. The basis for a more financially literate population is probably an educational reform that would insert the subject more firmly in traditional subjects such as arithmetic and mathematics, as well as in specialized courses. This said, there is probably a limit to what even thoroughgoing reform could achieve.

As far as regulation is concerned, there is obvious scope in some countries for at least greater clarity and completeness in the presentation of information on investment performance. Similarly, regulation may reduce the prevalence of seriously misleading claims by the financial industry about its products.

Risk-Based Regulation of Pension Plan Balance Sheets

The Traditional Standard

In most countries, the investment decisions of pension funds have been subject to the prudent-person rule, with some additional quantitative restrictions on asset holdings intended to limit the plan's holdings of the stock of a particular company, or to impose limits on broad asset classes (e.g., equities, fixed-interest securities, and real estate).[7] The prudent-person rule arises from Anglo-Saxon trust law. It does not lay down hard-and-fast rules for asset allocation or day-to-day investment management. Instead, it

---

[7] For a summary of these quantitative limits that covers seven of the ten survey countries, see Davis (2001).

enjoins trustees to act prudently, which is to say, to act as a prudent person would act were he or she in the same position. As Clark et al. (2003) have observed, the prudent-person standard concerns the way in which trustees should conduct themselves in carrying out their duties, and is not a guarantee of a particular outcome. The emphasis is on process, not result.

Until quite recently, the application of the prudent-person rule to investing in general is thought to have encouraged overly conservative investing, because the rule was interpreted as forbidding the inclusion of any risky assets in a portfolio, even if their inclusion might increase expected returns without increasing overall risk.[8] In the United States, the prudent-person rule has given way to the prudent-investor rule, which explicitly accepts the importance of diversification. ERISA, §404(a) enjoins a fiduciary to diversify "the investments of the plan so as to minimize the risk of large losses, unless under the circumstances it is clearly prudent not to do so. ..." Even this version of the rule fails to recognize explicitly the need to take the duration of liabilities into account when deciding on asset allocation.

The prudent-person/investor rule lays down no hard-and-fast rules for investing, let alone asset-liability management. For the rule to work well, some basic preconditions must be satisfied. First, there has to be some generally accepted idea of what prudent investing entails; it cannot be either too risky or too conservative. The rule could not provide reasonable guidance without such a standard. Second, there must be strong incentives for pension plans to seek advice from competent and honest investment advisors. This, in turn, will require that the relevant professions maintain high standards, and that the legal system must function well enough to provide effective redress against both fraudulent and incompetent investing and bad investing advice.

Whether the absence of hard-and-fast rules is a serious weakness of the prudent-investor rule is uncertain. Clearly, much will depend on what a country's financial community thinks is prudent and whether it works. One advantage of the lack of specific rules may be that notions of what is prudent may evolve in a more flexible way than they would if they were set out in regulations.

Pension-plan investments could, in principle, be regulated by imposing quantitative restrictions on their asset allocation. Quantitative restrictions are the regulatory instrument of choice for some classes of financial institutions in emerging market countries. In some industrial countries, they

---

[8]   Mackenzie (2006, 87–93) and the references therein discuss some of the implications of the prudent-person rule, especially as it applies to life insurance companies.

are used to reinforce the prudent-person rule. The basic problem with sole reliance on these restrictions is that they tend to be either too loose or too tight. They can either impede efficient, risk-reducing diversification, or fail to check an overly speculative investment stance.[9] In addition, they ignore completely the liabilities side of the balance sheet.

Risk-Based Supervision

Whatever the merits of the prudent-person/investor rule, the combination of falling share prices and declining interest rates in the early years of the current century made pension-plan managers acutely aware of the need for investing strategies that matched assets with liabilities. This experience has contributed to the development of models of asset-liability management that pension plans can use in deciding on their asset allocation. The models make possible and indeed require a very sophisticated form of supervision of plan investment strategy known as risk-based supervision (RBS). To date, among the ten countries, the Netherlands, Germany and Australia are most advanced in its application, and a framework for RBS is in place in Denmark.

The Dutch System of Risk-Based Supervision

The general approach that the Netherlands has adopted is similar to that of Solvency II, the euro-area directive on RBS in insurance companies. Perhaps the most novel and innovative aspect of the approach is that it essentially treats pension plans as if they were large, systemically important financial institutions. The version of RBS that the Netherlands has adopted is complex. Explaining it in detail would take many pages. Instead of doing that, we highlight its most basic features.[10] The supervision of risk management in Dutch pension funds is based on two different exercises. The first of these is essentially an appraisal of the risk-management practices of a pension fund. The second consists of two different solvency tests based on a model of the plan's balance sheet.

The appraisal of risk management by pension plans, which has the acronym FIRM (for financial institutions risk analysis method), begins by creating a comprehensive description of the pension plan. This profile is used as a basis for identifying potential weak spots in risk management and the significance of the inherent risks – which are grouped in nine different categories – to which the fund is subject. The risks include not only those that

---

[9]   See Davis (2001) for a thorough treatment of the drawbacks of quantitative restrictions.
[10] This section draws heavily from Hinz and van Dam (2008).

are specific to the activity of a pension plan, like the risk that demographic projections prove to be inaccurate, but risks that arise from the conduct of business.[11]

Having evaluated the significance of each of these inherent risks, FIRM then evaluates the effectiveness of what are termed risk-specific controls, as well as more general controls (like the quality of management). The same type of risk may show up in more than one of a fund's areas of operation. FIRM quantifies the severity of each manifestation of that risk on a scale from 1 to 4, and also quantifies the effectiveness of controls. A particular risk may get a high score but be neutralized by an effective control, so that the "combined" score is reduced to an acceptable level. These estimates are aggregated, and the result, multiplied by three, is added to a similar figure for the assessment of management and organization to yield an overall score.

The Nederlandsche Bank (usually known by its Dutch acronym DNB) is well aware of the arbitrary character of the assumptions underlying this exercise and sometimes may choose to override the result; there is no doubt that much is left to the judgment of the responsible supervisor from the DNB. Nonetheless, the exercise in quantification is believed to give the overall exercise a rigor and consistency that it might otherwise lack.

The measurement of assets and liabilities on which these tests are based reflects recent developments in pension accounting. Assets are marked to market, and the discount rate for plan liabilities, which was previously set at 4 percent regardless of the maturity of liabilities, is now based on the term structure of zero-coupon euro-area bonds. Future salary increases are not taken into account in the calculation of liabilities. The longevity assumptions are to be based on a current mortality table, but should reflect the plan's judgment about the longevity of plan members as well as the possibility of additional improvements in life expectancy. All plans are expected to maintain an asset cushion of 5 percent of the value of technical provisions. Should a plan fail to do so, it must submit a recovery plan to the DNB with a recovery period of no more than three years, which the DNB can choose to shorten to just one year.

The framework for solvency tests, known by its Dutch acronym FTK, applies two tests to gauge a pension plan's solvency. The first assesses the

---

[11] The nine types of risks are: external (e.g., financial contagion), operational (including staffing and information management adequacy), IT-related, legal (noncompliance or violations of laws), moral (fraud, tax evasion), actuarial (unfavorable experience), maturity mismatch, market risks (declining stock prices), and credit (failure of issuer of a financial instrument to comply with terms).

sensitivity of the plan's surplus to a variety of shocks to financial and non-financial variables over a single year. For the purposes of the test, interest rates are assumed to change according to a schedule that relates the size of the percentage-point shock to the duration of the instrument. Assets are divided into a number of classes, with a specific value assigned to the shock: for example, 25 percent for mature market equities and 35 percent for emerging market equities. The test also includes a shock for currency risk (a uniform depreciation of 20 percent of all other currencies against the euro, the home currency), a commodities shock (a drop in the benchmark index for commodity prices of 30 percent), credit risk and insurance risk (e.g., the risk that assumptions regarding longevity are conservative). The values of the shocks have been picked on the assumption that the combined worst outcome will only occur with a probability of 2.5 percent.

The solvency test relies on a formula to derive an aggregate risk index. It is given by the square root of the sum of the square of the impact of each shock, plus a factor assuming some correlation between interest and equity risk. The formula is reproduced as equation (4.1), where S_1 stands for the interest-rate shock, S_2 for the equity shock, and S_3 through S_6 for the shocks attributable to currency risk, commodities risk, credit risk, and insurance risk, respectively. The equity shock S_2 is derived from a separate subformula aggregating the shocks attributable to the holdings of each class of equity. The formulation assumes that the equity and interest-rate shocks (S_1 and S_2) are partially correlated, while the other shocks are not correlated to each other or to the equity and interest-rate shocks. The measure of the interest-rate shock takes account of its impact on both assets and liabilities, and by so doing captures the vulnerability of a plan to maturity mismatches.

$$\text{Total risk} = \sqrt{S_1^2 + S_2^2 + 2 \times 0.5 \times S_1 \times S_2 + S_3^2 + S_4^2 + S_5^2 + S_6^2} \quad (4.1)$$

As an example of how the formula would work: If a plan had an equity exposure of 40 percent, all in mature markets, then S_2 would be 10 percent (40 percent of 25 percent). If interest-rate risk amounted to 10 percent and there were no other risks, total risk would be calculated as 17.3 percent, which is the amount of extra capital the plan would have to provide to satisfy the solvency rule.[12]

How a pension plan fares under this test clearly depends, among other things, on the extent to which the duration of its assets and liabilities are

---

[12] Pension plans may develop their own model for solvency tests. The model must be vetted by the DNB, and must pass the same solvency test when subject to the set of shocks that the DNB uses.

well matched, and the share of fixed-interest securities in the portfolio. The test will discourage international diversification to some degree, if investing in securities outside the euro-area will expose a plan to currency risk, but not further diversify the portfolio. The 15-year recovery plan that a pension plan must submit to the DNB if it fails the test need not necessarily include a suspension of full indexation, although conditional indexation (see Chapter 1 and Appendix 1, Netherlands) may be necessary given a plan's particular situation.

In addition to the solvency analysis, funds are expected to carry out a continuity analysis. Its aim is to gauge the plan's vulnerability over a long period (15 years) to both foreseeable trends and random events. In making its projections, the fund is expected to maintain minimum values for real wage growth, consumer-price inflation, real short-term interest rates, and other variables. The discount rate is to be derived from the forward swap curve. The assumptions should be subject to sensitivity analysis, and deviations of experience from assumptions should be analyzed. Stress testing is also to be employed, and the model employed must have a stochastic element to it. A continuity analysis should be performed every three years or more often if changed circumstances warrant it.

The Dutch regulatory system confronts a pension plan with a trade-off. It may increase its average expected rate of return by maintaining a high share of its assets in equities, in which case it will have to maintain a high level of funding, but still be vulnerable to market corrections. Alternatively, it may try to structure its portfolio to reduce its vulnerability to such shocks, and emphasize matching of maturities. In this case, however, it will have to increase its average contributions to the plan.

Observations on the Dutch System

Two features of the Dutch system stand out immediately: It is highly complex and costly. Its complexity is reflected in the considerable sophistication that it requires of the risk-management techniques of pension plans. In particular, pension plans must be able to assess rigorously all the sources of risk that impinge on the plan and the effectiveness of the controls adopted to minimize them. The stress testing and simulation exercises are similarly demanding. Some of these tasks may be contracted out, but part of the test would be the ability of in-house personnel to deal with risk and make portfolio allocation decisions that did not expose the plan unduly to the risk of losses.

No figures are available on the cost of regulation to the regulator, but there must be a limit to the number of plans that DNB regulatory staff can be expected to handle, especially given the high degree of technical sophistication they would have to command. Let us take a very rough guess and assume that one staff-member year of the regulatory agency's time can handle 24 plans, or about one plan every two weeks. With 768 plans in the Netherlands, almost all of which are defined-benefit plans, some 32 officials would be needed. A comparison with the United States is instructive. That country had about 29,000 defined-benefit plans alone in 2007, so assuming the same rate of surveillance some 1,200 officials would be needed. Even if this estimate is scaled to take account of the difference in size of the two economies by dividing it by 20, the U.S. figure is about twice the Dutch figure. The difference reflects the fact that most Dutch plans are industry-wide. Bearing in mind that in 2005 there were no less than 631,000 defined-contribution plans in the United States, and assuming that the investment strategies of defined-contribution plans were to be regulated in a similar way, the implications for the size of the regulatory function are staggering.[13] It may be that pension plans have to achieve some minimum average size to reduce the cost of RBS to what is feasible.

Such a resource-intensive regulatory process must put a premium on realizing economies of scale with pension plans. Tripling the size of a pension plan will not triple the cost of regulating it or complying with the regulations. In fact, there should be no increase in cost unless large size means a more complex investment strategy.

One way of reducing the cost of RBS as practiced in the Netherlands would be to eschew a comprehensive approach, and instead rely on a more selective approach, like the audit programs that tax departments conduct. This approach could make do with a smaller regulatory staff, but it suffers from some significant drawbacks. Taxpayers do not need to be audited every year because the penalties for fraud and evasion are severe enough that even a moderate chance of a thorough audit can deter illegality. However, RBS is concerned with current practices. The element of discretion in official supervision and the need in the case of smaller pension plans for guidance argue against infrequent contact.

RBS may be simply too costly for some countries. If it is, then a country that does not want to rely on quantitative restrictions will need to fall back on the prudent-investor rule. Its effective use would require that it be modified (or interpreted) to ensure that the rule does not simply apply to the assets side of the pension balance sheet.

---

[13] The sources for the U.S. numbers are: for defined benefit, Pension Benefit Guarantee Corporation (2007), and for defined contribution, Employee Benefits Research Institute (2008a). The Dutch figure comes from Brunner et al. (2008).

Risk-Based Supervision and Defined-Contribution Plans

The Dutch system of RBS is intended for defined-benefit plans almost by definition, because defined-contribution plans cannot ordinarily become insolvent as they have no explicit or contractual liabilities to plan members. This said, the need for risk management, and therefore RBS, is as acute for defined-contribution plans as it is for defined-benefit plans, and a quantitative approach is as feasible for defined-contribution as it is for defined-benefit plans, particularly in the case of plans where a participant's choice of investment strategies is limited.

The approach of the Australian Prudential Regulatory Authority (APRA) is quite similar to that of the DNB (see Appendix 1, Australia). Defined-contribution funds have an obligation of prudence to their members, which is taken to mean that the overall level of investment risk of funds should not be excessive, and that safeguards against other risk (counterparty, fraud, etc.) should be in place.

One way of implementing the equivalent of a solvency test in the case of defined-contribution plans would be to assume that plan members have a target replacement ratio they wish to achieve in retirement. Specifically, they might wish to accumulate a balance in their accounts by the day they retire that is sufficient to purchase an annuity that would either generate an income that equals or exceeds some specified percentage of their final salary or some specified value.[14] By assuming a premium per-dollar figure for the annuity they would buy or have bought for them, a targeted final balance follows directly. By making assumptions, presumably conservative, about wage and salary growth, it would be possible to calculate the average rate of return necessary to pay for the annuity. This, in turn, could be the basis of Monte Carlo simulations, which would produce an estimate of the risk that different investment strategies would fall short of the desired goal.

In the case of self-directed plans with many investment options, simulating the range of outcomes for each account holder may not be feasible. A less useful but more feasible approach would be to require stress tests to determine how sensitive the asset allocation of accounts with varying shares of equities would be to the kinds of shocks already described. The results of such a test could be included in an annual statement sent to plan members, along with a simple explanation of stress testing and its limitations.

---

[14] Blake (2006c) uses a procedure like this to conduct simulation exercises to show how risky some investment strategies can be with defined-contribution plans.

RBS is of obvious importance for defined-benefit plans, because the plan sponsor has an obligation to pay pensions, the value of which is not dependent on financial-market performance. In none of the countries surveyed, apart from Denmark, Germany, and Switzerland, do sponsors of defined-contribution plans routinely offer a guarantee or a minimum rate of return. Nonetheless, the mere obligation to undergo stress testing or testing of the risk that a targeted replacement ratio will not be achieved would make sponsors of defined-contribution plans and their members more aware of the risks their investment strategies entail.

Regulatory Forbearance When Plans Are Underfunded

One key regulatory issue, touched upon in Chapter 3, is whether or when it is appropriate to relax the rule that determines how quickly a shortfall of assets from liabilities should be eliminated. A standard argument against such regulatory forbearance is that it encourages moral hazard: If seriously underfunded plans are let off the hook, then a signal is sent to both them and to better-managed plans that a significant degree of underfunding is acceptable. The standard argument against holding the line (and not allowing a slower pace of adjustment) is that plan sponsors may suffer undue hardship, or may even be forced out of business. Both arguments have been advanced recently in North America.[15]

If a policy of forbearance is implemented, one key question is how uniform its application should be. Should plans that have remained reasonably well funded be excluded? It could be argued that this type of policy simply increases the risk of moral hazard, making it more likely that sponsors of both well-funded as well as underfunded plans will relax their own funding standards in the future. Including the better-funded plans in the policy's ambit runs a similar risk, however. This suggests that a policy targeted to benefit plans in some financial difficulty is the better course.

The best rule to follow might be to recognize that in certain extreme situations, the rule for closing a funding gap was too onerous to honor, and that a more relaxed schedule was acceptable as a temporary expedient. The relevant authorities would, however, have to communicate the exceptional nature of their action convincingly.

---

[15] In late 2008 to early 2009, Canadian union representatives criticized the forbearance extended to plans in Ontario, arguing that it could fundamentally weaken the financial positions of the affected plans. In the United States, plan sponsors argued that without forbearance, plans would be frozen. Congress heeded their request.

Conflict of Interest Issues in the Appointment of Trustees[16]

The Anglo-Saxon trust does not normally impose restrictions on the choice of pension-plan trustees, with the possible exception that they be deemed to be persons of good character and well qualified. It is standard practice to appoint officers of the sponsoring company, but member representatives may also be appointed, and in some countries joint representation is required.

An employer-sponsored pension plan is normally (or at least was normally) an important part of the employer's personnel policy. To the extent that it is seen as a means of increasing motivation and enhancing productivity, the employer has a strong interest in the plan's being adequately funded and efficiently managed. Nonetheless, conflicts of interest could arise if the sponsoring company came to believe that the plan had outlived its usefulness, or if the company's finances had deteriorated to the point that its solvency was threatened.

Addressing this kind of conflict is not easy, as recent experience in the United Kingdom attests. As summarized by Byrne et al. (2006, 10) [The Pensions Act of 2004] in the United Kingdom requires that "… trustees must maintain a written statement of their policy for securing that the SFO [statutory funding objective] is met. If the SFO is not met, the trustees must prepare a recovery plan setting out the steps to be taken to meet the SFO and the period within which that is to be achieved." This seemingly innocuous provision aroused many British pension experts.

An unidentified pension lawyer was particularly outspoken: "The 1995 Act also recognizes this conflict and trust law has done so for hundreds of years. Conflict is good – it gets different views out on the table and stimulates discussion. The issue has always been to spot when a conflict becomes unmanageable. What has changed is that the new Act appears to positively encourage conflict rather than conciliation. The Regulator is encouraging trustees to take an aggressive and confrontational approach in negotiations with the company" (Byrne et al. 2006).

The possibility of serious conflict of interest depends upon the amount of discretion trustees have in administering the plan and determining its investment policy. No pension plan can run on automatic pilot, although the scope for discretion will vary from one jurisdiction to another. In the United States, once a plan becomes underfunded (or when assets fall short of liabilities by a specified percentage), the plan sponsor must make

---

[16]   This section is of special relevance to the Anglo-Saxon countries.

additional contributions to the plan that fill a certain fraction of the gap.[17] In the United Kingdom, the trustees of a pension plan are expected to come up with and endorse a program that will eliminate the gap under reasonable assumptions within a specified period of time. This second rule gives trustees more leeway than the first if they can choose, within limits, the assumptions regarding rates of return, tenure, and longevity that underlie their plan. In part because of this greater involvement of trustees in the financial aspects of plans, recent U.K. legislation has required that trustees receive appropriate instruction in pension finance.

Apart from measures to curtail trustees' discretion, the basic protection pensioners have against an abuse of fiduciary obligation is the lawsuit. Another protection might be a law requiring some minimum degree of representation of both active and retired plan members. Yet another might be the appointment of third-party trustees.

These remedies raise the question of how much influence over plan management a sponsoring company needs to go on funding it. Some further remedies are available that would not necessarily entail a dilution in the sponsor's control. A more specific standard of fitness for trustees, if one is not now applied, could increase the competence of trustee decisions. Greater transparency regarding investment strategy and its underlying assumptions would lessen the chances that key parameters and assumptions are massaged to minimize the need for exceptional contributions from the sponsor. All this said, the appearance if not the reality of conflicts of interest may be the price to be paid for a pension trust.

---

[17] The Pension Protection Act (2006) stipulates a minimum funding obligation equal to the target normal cost of the benefits for the year in question plus one seventh of the shortfall of assets from the value of benefit obligations.

Public-Sector Employer-Provided Pensions and Recent Innovations in the First Tier

This chapter has two parts which address two different issues. The first part is concerned with public-sector employer-provided pension plans, and with a number of specific issues that these plans raise. The second part appraises some recent innovations in the design of public-pension (first-tier) plans. Both employer-provided public-sector plans and first-tier plans are financed by the taxpayer, and both are affected by population aging. Because most second-tier public-sector plans are funded, demographic change affects them differently than it does first-tier plans.

Public-Sector Pensions – Introduction

The pensions that public-sector employers – national and subnational governments, public utilities, and public enterprises – provide their employees deserve a prominent place in a study of the decline of the traditional pension. In most industrial countries, coverage of civil servants and other public-sector employees is near universal. In seven of the ten survey countries, public-sector pensions are either overwhelmingly or exclusively defined benefit.

The combination of the sizeable share of civil servants in the labor force and the predominant role of the traditional pension plan in the public sector means that enrollment in public-sector plans accounts for much of the coverage of the traditional plan in the Anglo-Saxon countries. This is particularly true of the United Kingdom, where public-sector employees account for more than 80 percent of the membership of open plans. Even in the United States, where general government is smaller in relation to gross domestic product (GDP) than it is in the other industrial economies, active members of state and local government pension plans represent about 10 percent of the labor force, which means that more than one in two traditional pension plan members are in the public sector.

Public-sector pension plans tend to be much bigger on average than their private-sector counterparts. The California Public Employees Retirement System (CalPERS) had, as of the end of June 2008, over 838,000 active members and 409,000 annuitants, and held assets of over $238 billion, and is large by any standard, although the plans of New York and Florida rival it in size.[1] The sheer size of a plan like CalPERS gives it a major role in some important corporate decisions and allows it to engage in social activism on a large scale. Public-sector pension benefits tend to be generous, and the deferred compensation that they represent accounts for a larger share of total compensation than private-sector benefits.

Public-sector pensions are of special interest to this study, because the traditional form of the pension plan has continued to flourish in that area. It is possible that the same erosive forces at work in the private sector are also working, albeit with a lag, in the public sector. If so, they are working very slowly. By studying why the defined-contribution plan has, to date, made little inroad into the public sector, we may have a better idea of why the traditional pension has declined so markedly in the private sector.

To set the stage for this analysis, the first part of the chapter continues with an account of the basic features of public-sector plans. It surveys the main features of public-sector plans in all ten countries, but then turns to concentrate on the United States and Canada, where the relevant data and related studies are more readily accessible than they are for the other eight countries. Next the chapter addresses the reasons for the continued dominance of defined-benefit plans, while noting the implications of the stock market crash for funding. Finally, part one addresses a number of issues that have arisen recently with public-sector plans: whether their special characteristics mean that they should be allowed to employ a rate of discount derived from the rate of return on the assets in which they invest; the appropriate target for the ratio of assets to liabilities; and the appropriateness of their engaging in social investing.

Basic Features of Public-Sector Plans

Public-sector plans cover 90–100 percent of the public-sector labor force in each of the ten countries of the study. Typically, participation in a pension plan is a requirement for a regular position, although part-time

---

[1] The estimates for CalPERS come from the Public Fund Survey, available at www.publicfundsurvey.org. This project contains basic data on 125 state and local plans, and has near universal coverage of U.S. state and local pensions.

employees may be excluded. It is common for central government civil servants to be covered by an unfunded plan, but uncommon at lower levels of government.

The basic forms that public-sector pensions take, as well as the legal and regulatory framework in which they must operate, vary a good deal across the ten countries. The traditional pension predominates in the public sectors of the Anglo-Saxon countries and the Netherlands, as well as in Germany and Japan. In Sweden, there is a mix of defined-benefit and defined-contribution plans. In Australia, most public-sector defined-benefit plans have been closed or wound up; in Denmark and Switzerland, civil servants belong to hybrid plans.

Chapter 3 explained why it would be unwise for a private company to try to operate an unfunded plan. Unfunded plans are more feasible in the public sector, because a plan's dependency ratio would not be as affected by the same swings as a private plan's dependency ratio would be. Pension outlays are, in consequence, treated as another current expenditure item in the accounts of many governments. Among the six countries where the traditional plan predominates, the prevalence of funding varies considerably. In Germany, the only public-sector plans that are funded are those of two Länder (i.e., regional governments) (Maurer et al. 2008). In the Netherlands, all public-sector plans are funded, and in Canada and the United States, most plans are funded. In the United Kingdom, local authority plans are funded, but the plan that covers the National Health Scheme is not. In Denmark and Japan, the plans that cover the civil service are not funded.

Even if a public-sector plan is funded, it may or may not be subject to the regulatory framework that applies to the private sector. In Australia, the Netherlands, and Switzerland, public- and private-sector plans are subject to the same regulations. In the Anglo-Saxon countries, public-sector plans have their own rules, which can vary across jurisdictions. In the United States, for example, state and local plans have much more latitude with respect to funding strategies, and their benefits are not insured by the Pension Benefit Guarantee Corporation. In the United Kingdom, funded public-sector plans are not subject to IFS17, the accounting standard that applies to the private sector. When plans are unfunded, they are *ipso facto* outside the regulatory framework.

United States
The traditional pension retains its dominant position in state and local government in the United States. Only Alaska, Missouri, and the District of

Columbia have closed their defined-benefit plans to new entrants. Seven other states offer their employees a choice between a defined-benefit and a defined-contribution plan, and three states offer hybrid plans. Twenty states offer defined-contribution plans to specific occupations, but these tend not to have long tenures (Mattoon 2007).

A survey of 125 state and local plans in the United States provides valuable information on plan coverage and financing.[2] As of the end of June 2007, these plans were estimated to have 13.3 million active members, or about 90 percent of all full-time state and local employees, and 6.5 million annuitants.[3] Actuarially estimated assets amounted to $2.5 trillion and liabilities to $2.9 trillion, implying an unfunded liability of $0.4 trillion (about 3 percent of GDP in 2007), and a funding ratio of 86.4 percent.[4] The median value of the discount rates the plans used to calculate these estimates was 8 percent, which was well above the rate for long-term Treasuries, the usual proxy for the risk-free rate, at the date of valuation, but also above the AA (i.e. high quality) corporate bond rate that the Pension Protection Act of 2006 is phasing in.

The individual plan-funding ratios varied from 45 percent to 116 percent, with most falling in the 70–100 percent range. Twenty of the plans had funding ratios equal to or exceeding 100. However, the 13 largest plans (measured by assets), which account for almost 50 percent of the survey membership's assets, had a collective funding ratio of 95 percent. The smaller plans tend to be the outliers.

There is substantial variation in funding ratios within states (most states have more than one plan in the sample), as well as across states (Mattoon 2007). Munnell et al. (2008) find that some of the variation in fundedness may be explained by the choice of cost-accounting method: the current unit method discussed in Chapter 3, which some but not all plans use, entails increases in cost as the workforce ages.[5] The Munnell study also finds that teachers' plans are relatively underfunded, but that large

---

[2]   See footnote 1.

[3]   Pension plans cover most if not all state employees in all 50 states. Much of the expansion in coverage took place between 1930 and 1950, and 45 states had plans by 1961. The Social Security Act, which was passed in 1935, excluded state employees from coverage because of a legal issue regarding the federal government's right to tax states' payrolls. The expansion in coverage was in part a response to the exclusion of state employees and intended to provide them with some coverage of their own (Clark et al. 2008).

[4]   The median valuation date was end-June 2007. Valuation dates varied from plan to plan.

[5]   The current unit method, as Chapter 3 explains, uses the current and not the projected salary level to estimate the current service cost of a plan. The older and more experienced the workforce, the higher its average current salary will be. A measure of cost based on projected salaries would not be affected by the aging of the workforce in the same way.

plans and plans with separate investment committees are more likely to be well funded.

Unlike their private-sector counterparts, most state and local government plans index the retirement benefit partly or wholly. Some plans are indexed subject to a cap, so that full indexation applies until the rate of inflation exceeds some specified ceiling; others fully index an initial tranche of the pension, but not the rest. Some plans fix an annual adjustment in advance, such as 3 percent. Others make ad hoc adjustments (Mattoon 2007, 24). These rules are effectively stop-loss provisions to avoid a situation in which the pension plan is exposed to an unlimited liability, and they may be overridden when the plan's financial situation is comfortable.

In addition to some degree of indexation or adjustment for inflation, many states give favorable tax treatment to plan benefits. Many states exempt benefits entirely from the state income tax (which most states levy), while others partly exempt them. Only a few states tax the entire benefit (Mattoon 2007, 24).

Clark et al. (2008) find that most states have substantially increased the generosity of their pension plans over the past three decades. Specifically, the study compares the findings of three other studies undertaken between 1979 and 2007, and concludes that a worker retiring in 2007 with 30 years of service would have had a replacement ratio 10 percentage points higher than that of a worker with the same earnings history retiring in 1977. The same study concludes that replacement ratios tend to vary with a state's population growth – a proxy for economic growth, because states with dynamic economies attract new residents from other states – and inversely with its funding ratio.

The stock market crash has hit state and local pension plans hard, especially considering the fact that many plans were underfunded to begin with. About 54 percent of the aggregate portfolio of state and local plans was invested in equities, which is similar to the share of equities in private-sector plan portfolios.[6] The crash must have caused a huge increase in unfunded liabilities, possibly of the order of $600–$650 billion, which would bring them to over $1 trillion and reduce the aggregate funding ratio to about 60 percent.[7] Many plans would now be gravely underfunded. If the rate used to

---

[6]   The Pension Fund Survey estimated that the average holding of equities for the 98 systems for which data was available was 54 percent.

[7]   As of end-2008, the S&P 500 index was about 45 percent below the level of June 30, 2007. A simple estimate of the impact of the crash on plan asset values can be made by multiplying the percentage decline in the market by the estimated share of plan assets allocated to equities as of June 2007. A decline of 45 percent in 54 percent of the total assets of the plans entails a drop in assets of about $610 billion.

discount plan liabilities were based on the AA corporate bond rate that the private sector is obliged to use, the picture would be even worse.

Even if state and local plans were given many years to reverse the increase in the funding gap caused by the market's crash, relying on contribution increases alone would require a substantial increase. The annual wage and salary bill of state and local government full-time employees is estimated to be about $800 billion. A 3 percentage point increase in contribution rates would yield initially $25 billion per annum. On the basis of some simple illustrative calculations, the increase in the contribution rate might reduce the funding gap by about $480 billion.[8] If there were strong resistance to an adjustment based entirely on the revenue side and borne by the current generation of workers, then cuts in benefits will be necessary, especially if the continued existence of traditional pensions in the public sector encounters strong political opposition. In the case of some plans, the gap must have become so large that they will be unable to honor the pension obligations coming due in the next few years.

The plight of the state and local plans, like the plight of many private plans in industrialized countries, is in a way ironic. Inasmuch as the aggregate information available permits a judgment, state and local plans have been allocating their assets in much the same way as private-sector plans. Their investment strategy has been "prudent," because it has been in line with what has been, until now, the received wisdom of pension investing; namely, that equities warranted a high share. What the U.S. state and local plans did not do was to practice asset-liability management, and their investment strategy could not be described as liability driven.

Canada

The structure and coverage of public-sector pension plans in Canada and the United States are similar. Total membership as of the beginning of 2006 was 86 percent of public-sector employment and 18 percent of the total labor force. About 60 percent of plan membership is at the provincial level. Membership in defined-benefit plans accounts for over 90 percent of total public-sector plan membership.

The typical plan bases its benefit on an average of the 4–5 best years of an employee's career, making it effectively a final-salary plan, and the typical accrual rate is 2 percentage points. Membership in plans with partial or full

---

[8] This figure is calculated by starting with the estimated state and local wage and salary bill in 2009 of about $800 billion assuming annual growth in real terms of 1 percent, and a discount rate of 3 percent for a period of 25 years.

indexation to the consumer price index (CPI) accounts for three quarters of public-sector plan members (Pozzebon 2008).[9] Average plan membership is smaller than it is in the United States, because no Canadian public-sector plan, with the possible exception of those of Ontario and Quebec, including the civil servants' and teachers' plans, can rival the largest U.S. state plans. Nonetheless, as of the beginning of 2007, 73 percent of plan members were in plans with 30,000 members or more. Only 21 percent of private-sector plan members were in plans of this size.

Information on the funding ratios of Canadian public-sector plans is not readily available in the aggregate, although many plans post plan assets and liabilities for a recent valuation date on their websites. The marked contrast with the United States in this regard might have something to do with the fact that for many years, plans were simply a part of the government and financed on a pay-as-you-go basis. The move toward a separate fund did not gain real momentum until 1990. Pozzebon (2008) notes that the Ontario Teachers' Pension Plan Board was a forerunner in adopting a separate fund.

Some information is available on asset composition, which breaks total assets down into four categories: equities, bonds, pooled mutual and investment funds, and other assets. Equities and pooled funds each accounted for slightly over 30 percent as of the end of 2006. Assuming that one-half of the pooled-funds category is equity, total equity holdings would be close to 50 percent. The lack of aggregate data means that it is not possible to estimate the impact of the stock market crash on funding ratios. It is likely that the impact on assets was less than but about the same order of magnitude as the impact on U.S. state and local plans.

The Survival of the Traditional Pension in the Public Sector

Pension coverage depends on the interaction of demand for pensions by plan participants, and supply by plan sponsors (employers). Certain differences in public- and private-sector labor markets, the organization of work, and the accounting rules that apply to pensions in each sector could explain both why public-sector coverage has always been higher, and why it has not changed appreciably while coverage in the private sector has declined so much in some countries.

The special factors working to keep coverage high in the public sector could be: (1) plan size; (2) plan accounting rules that lower the cost of

---

[9]   Most of the data on Canadian plans in Chapter 5 come from Pozzebon (2008).

funding and give sponsors considerable flexibility in addressing a funding shortfall; (3) less onerous supervision, which reduces compliance costs, (4) lack of profit-and-loss accounting in the public sector; (5) longer tenures in the public sector than in the private sector and a more farsighted workforce; (6) a desire by public-sector employees (and perhaps their employers) to increase the share of compensation that is deferred; (7) the greater role played by unions; and (8) greater trust by civil servants in the durability of their employer and in the reliability of the employer's pension promise. The first four of these influences reduce the perceived cost of offering a pension plan in the public sector as compared with the private sector, and the last four increase the demand of public-sector employees to participate in a plan.

Plan size. Average plan sizes are considerably larger in the public sector than they are in the private sector. Because administrative costs per plan member fall considerably as the number of members increases, the average costs of public-sector plans should be lower than those of private-sector plans. To the extent that public-sector plan managers are sensitive to administrative costs, the same proportional increase in administrative costs in the public sector would not have the same impact on the relative attractiveness to employers of this particular form of compensation. This said, the numerous examples in both the United States and the United Kingdom of large private-sector plans being closed to new members, or even closed to further contributions from old members (subject to a soft or a hard freeze in American parlance) suggest that plan size by itself does not hold the key to a plan's survival.

Plan accounting rules. Many public-sector plans are not funded, but financed, as already noted, on a pay-as-you-go basis. The government will make regular projections of future pension payments as it does for the public-pension system, but the concept of fundedness does not have the same meaning as it does for a plan with funded benefits.

The plans at the state (or provincial) and municipal levels in North America are funded, however, and are required to carry out periodic evaluations of their fundedness ratio. State and local government plans have two notable advantages over private plans in calculating their asset-liability ratio and responding to an imbalance: They can use a higher discount rate, and they are not required to adhere to the rules, recently revised for U.S. plans by the Pension Protection Act, for closing the gap between assets and liabilities. This makes it easier for public-sector plans, if they are underfunded, to adopt a strategy of awaiting the next stock market boom.

The lack of profit-and-loss accounting. Public-sector accounting differs in important ways from private-sector commercial accounting. With regard to pensions, the public sector is not generally subject to the same scrutiny as the private sector, and public-sector accounts do not typically include the investment losses of their pension plans. In contrast, U.S. corporations are required to include investment losses of their pension plans as a charge on income, without any smoothing of losses allowed.

Longer tenure and greater foresight. The more likely a plan member is to become either vested or eligible for an early- if not a full-retirement pension, the greater the attractiveness of the plan. Civil servants have traditionally had comparatively long tenures. Their employers may find the traditional plan a more efficient means of promoting good performance than a defined-contribution plan if the build up of human capital specific to the job is more important in the civil service than in the private sector. The nature of the work may also attract cautious people who are more content than the average person with a steady job that typically has no spectacular promotion prospects but much less risk of loss. Such people might be particularly attracted by the promise of a lifetime income postretirement.

Pensions as a less prominent form of compensation. Civil-service pensions are often an easy target for the conservative press. Increasing the share of deferred compensation in the form of a traditional pension might reduce the incidence of complaints that their public servants are overpaid. This would require that an annuity paid by a traditional pension be less visible than the deferred compensation from a growing balance in a defined-contribution plan, which could be the case if the plan's accounts have a more tangible presence than a claim on a future income stream.[10]

Unions. Chapter 6 will explore this topic at greater length because the argument is equally relevant for private- as for public-sector unions. Ghilarducci (2008) and other economists have argued that there is a direct link between the share of the labor force that is unionized and the importance of traditional plans. Despite the general decay in the role and influence of the union in the private sector, public-sector unions have remained quite strong in many of the ten countries, notably in Canada and the European countries. In some countries, union or labor representatives serve as trustees in the public sector, just as employee representatives serve in the private

---

[10] An argument against the view that a traditional plan somehow hides part of a plan member's compensation is that, if the employer makes no contributions to a defined-contribution plan, then the plan member appears to be paying for 100 percent of his or her retirement. With a defined-benefit plan, the employer usually makes regular contributions, making it appear that the pension is being subsidized.

sector. For the reasons that Chapter 6 sets out, a strong union presence would help preserve the role of the traditional pension in the public sector. Contributing to the influence of unions in some U.S. states is the obligation stipulated in the state constitution to pay civil-service pensions. Finally, civil servants as a group may weld considerable political power, because they can bring the machinery of government to a halt.

The pension promise. Private-sector employers in some of the industrial countries have been unable at times to keep their pension promises, and their insolvency typically means that the government has to intervene to compensate for the employer's failure. In industrial countries, whether the private-sector pensioner gets 100 cents on the dollar or 100 pence on the pound depends upon the terms of the government agency offering the guarantee, if there is one. All this being said, however, default or even partial default is rare.

In contrast with private enterprises, which come and go, governments are immortal – or so someone has said. They have a monopoly on the power to levy taxes and their income sources are typically more stable than those of private concerns. There are no cases on record of public-sector pension plans in industrial countries being unable to fulfill their pension obligations. (This is not true of emerging market countries, however.) Nonetheless, even among the industrialized countries, the power to levy taxes does not mean that a government cannot become insolvent. It is simply that a governmental budget constraint is usually softer than that of a private enterprise. It is quite possible that economic and political forces will lead to a scaling back of second-tier pensions in the public sectors of more than one industrial country.

In sum, the greater staying power of the traditional pension in the public sector is a reflection of the durability of the public sector, less rigorous accounting rules, the lack of a role for a plan's financial performance as a closely monitored indicator of financial performance such as net profit, long tenures and less restless employees, and unions and the political power of civil servants.

Three Current Issues for Public-Sector Plans

Is a Risk-Free Discount Rate Wrong for Public-Sector Pension Plans?
In the American setting – although the issue has obvious relevance for other countries – some pension experts have argued that public-sector plans can and should be allowed to operate under assumptions that differ from those that apply to their private-sector counterparts. In particular, they argue that

the current practice in the United States of allowing public-sector plans to use a discount rate derived from average historical or expected rates of return of their assets is fully justified. Chapter 3 set out the reasons why the choice of such a rate – a rate much higher than the risk-free rate – would result in misleading valuations and excessively risky funding decisions in the private sector.

Two related arguments, ones we have just encountered, have been advanced supporting special rules for public-sector plans: the alleged immortality of governments and their ability to levy taxes. Specifically, the immortality of government (the institution, not a particular administration) and government's power to tax make it almost certain that public-sector pensions will be honored. The fact that government is less likely to default on its obligations is said to justify the use of the higher discount rate.

The fact that government may be for all purposes permanent, and (in most countries) highly unlikely to default, may give it more leeway in funding its pension obligations. More specifically, it does not have to consider the possibility that the plan will be terminated. The valuation of the liabilities of a private pension plan upon its termination can be higher than the valuation made when the company is a going concern because of the costly benefits that can be paid to active participants when a plan is terminated. In addition, if a private plan sponsor pays an insurance company to assume its liabilities, the insurance company's bid will be based on actuarial assumptions that are more conservative than those used by the plan sponsor to value its liabilities.

The second source of leeway is the additional amount of time that a public-sector plan is thought to enjoy in making up any shortfall in assets from liabilities. As Chapter 3 discussed, the use of a discount rate based on the expected or average past rate of return on assets in place of the risk-free rate increases the chances that a plan will incur a funding shortfall for a given asset-allocation strategy. However, if a private-sector company and plan sponsor becomes insolvent, it will normally be unable to close the funding gap, so that plan members will not receive the benefits that they have earned unless the country in which they reside has a public agency that insures pension benefits fully. In other words, the consequence of using an asset-return-based rate of return are more serious for private-sector plan members than for public-sector ones.

A third argument is that the use of a risk-free discount rate by public-sector plans would unnecessarily burden the current generation at the expense of future generations. The lower the discount rate, the higher taxes have to be. If, as some economists have argued, future generations can confidently be expected to enjoy a higher standard of living than the present generation, there is a case for shifting forward part of the risk of funding a public-sector pension plan. Future generations are burdened if plans become underfunded, but they benefit when investment returns are above average. The same argument must apply to private-sector plans, however. The difference that advocates of the higher discount rate point to is the public sector's superior ability to shift burdens across generations. This difference justifies the special rate of discount.

The third argument ignores one important issue that arises with fringe benefits: Who is really paying for them? A standard assumption used in tax-incidence studies is that labor supply is inelastic, so that payroll taxes are always ultimately paid by the employee however the law distributes them between employer and employee. If we apply the same argument to compensation, and argue that a buck is a buck, then contributions to a pension plan – be they from employer or employee – are simply a part of total compensation. If this is true, then there is no shifting forward of burdens.

Moreover, it might be presuming too much to assume that future generations would foot the bill. In the United States, the burdens of future tax-payers are almost certain to increase, and the same is true of most other industrial countries. In the United States, it is the growing burden of the publicly funded health care programs; in other countries, it is public pensions. The fact that a plan is in the public sector cannot rule out the possibility of a taxpayer revolt or an inability by the public sector to pay. As Waring (2008, 7) puts it: "Ultimately the plan might earn the full expected return, but it might not, and one could question whether hoping to 'get lucky' is the proper role of the fiduciary."

The claim that a public-sector pension, especially one that is funded directly by a government that can levy taxes such as a state or province, has more leeway to deal with a funding shortfall is plausible. The pertinent question, however, is whether it is good public policy to have recourse to a higher discount rate, not whether it is feasible.

Sometimes parables can shed light on thorny issues. Consider two persons, Prudence and Felicity, who are saving for retirement. They are the same age and have the same earnings history and assets (at the beginning of the story). Prudence uses a risk-free discount rate to determine how much she has to save; Felicity, on the advice of her financial planner, uses a rate that is derived from average historical rates of return for the stocks and bond funds in which she invests. We assume that both are aiming to accumulate the same lump sum by age 65. Prudence must plan to save more than Felicity, because she assumes that her savings will accumulate at a lower rate, although she does invest in risky assets. In addition, Prudence, unlike Felicity, does not have a rich uncle.

So what happens? Let's say that the performance of financial markets during the two women's working lives is disappointing but not disastrous. Prudence has been saving more than Felicity and achieves her retirement savings goal. Felicity, who has been saving less, falls short of hers. However, her rich uncle's grandchildren come to the rescue and bail her out. Her choice of discount rate has made a shortfall probable.

The deeper meaning of this little fable for public policy should not be an ineffable mystery. The rich uncle and his descendents are meant to represent the government, and the lesser (or nonexistent) threat of bankruptcy of sponsors of public-sector plans. The rich uncle's progeny are the next generation, who could refuse to help Felicity. Nonetheless, there is a basic parallel between this story and the situation of public- and private-sector employees. Why would a public-sector pension plan want to adopt a strategy with such a high risk of a funding shortfall? The answer might be that the plan is not presented with the bill to be paid.

Finally, the position of a public-sector traditional pension plan can be compared to the position of a universal defined-contribution plan (like a compulsory second tier) for the private sector, because the issue of the discount rate arises with both of them. Who would consider it good public policy to recommend that account holders assume a rate of return based on the historical average return of an index of risky assets? That would be tantamount to recommending that every private account holder behave like Felicity. Who, having decided that the use of such a discount rate for the individual accounts was a bad idea, would consider it a good idea for a traditional public-sector plan?

Shortfalls and Speed of Adjustment

As Chapter 3 discussed, the long duration of a pension plan's liabilities means that the consequences of a shortfall of assets from liabilities is not as serious as it would be if a plan's liabilities had a very short duration. As a result, regulatory authorities normally allow a private-sector plan some time to close a funding gap, so that a plan's funding ratio may slip below 100 percent for a time, provided it does not slip too far. The corridor approach that some regulatory authorities apply is an example of this tolerance.[11]

---

[11] With the corridor approach, no adjustment is required until the asset-liability ratio falls below some floor, like 90 percent. Once this is breeched, a reduction in the gap between the actual ratio and 100 percent equal to some specified fraction per year may be targeted.

A policy that countenances the gradual elimination of a shortfall and a funding ratio that falls somewhat short of 100 percent for a time can presumably apply to public-sector plans as well as private ones. However, the question arises whether the speed of adjustment could be even more gradual, and the targeted funding ratio could be even less ambitious for public-sector plans than private-sector plans. We assume that the same discount rate is used for both types of plans.

Suppose that a public-sector plan and a private-sector plan are substantially similar – the salary history of their active members is similar, the ratio of active to retired members is similar, and the same discount rate is used. Are there grounds for thinking that the public-sector plan should be permitted to adopt a less-ambitious funding target, and adjust more gradually to shocks? The same considerations arise as those arising when considering allowing public-sector plans a higher discount rate. The issue now is not that a shortfall is more likely with the public-sector plan. Instead, a public-sector plan will typically be less well-funded than a private plan. The farther from being fully funded a plan is, the greater the likelihood that a bad investment experience will make it seriously underfunded. The argument for special treatment of public-sector plans is further weakened by the fact that bankruptcy is a less likely prospect for governments than it is for the sponsors of private plans. In sum, public-sector plans are not entitled to special dispensation when they need to adjust to a shortfall.

Investor Activism and Social Investing

The largest public-pension plans can wield considerable clout at the boardroom table. Their portfolios are so large that they can hold a significant share of the equity of even large companies. CalPERS, the California state pension plan, is known for using its position as a large shareholder for instigating the replacement of management teams thought to be depressing share values below their potential. It has also lobbied for changes to voting rules and other measures that strengthened shareholders' rights.

Barber (2008) estimates that the giant fund's activism on behalf of investors may have increased share values of the firms it has targeted by $1.9 billion. CalPERS' own "shareholders" – its members – would have benefited from these interventions as a result of the appreciation in the value of the CalPERS plan's holdings of these stocks. Barber notes that CalPERS' action creates positive externalities for other investors, both institutional and individual. Its huge size allows it to absorb these costs without difficulty, although the presence of externalities would mean that the amount of activism undertaken would be less than optimal.

In contrast with shareholder activism, social activism – including social goals in the investment decision – may not be in the interest of plan members. For example, a decision not to invest in pharmaceutical or tobacco companies might conceivably reduce the return earned by the plan's portfolio at a given level of risk. This is a direct conclusion from the standard model of the investment decision: Any additional constraint imposed on the asset-allocation decision can at best only leave the risk-return frontier unchanged.

Private-sector plans do not normally engage in social investment unless the law obliges them to do so. If they did, the plan's trustees could be held accountable if investment performance was unsatisfactory. Public-sector plans, depending on the jurisdiction, are not subject to the same restrictions, and as a result may be used as a tool of public policy with objectives that have nothing to do with their primary purpose. The plans are effectively saddled with an unfunded mandate.

Setting aside the question of whether social investing is an efficient way of furthering particular social or political objectives, another question arises as to its implications for plan funding. The great difficulty involved in appraising social investing is that the costs it entails to the pension plan are not easily measured. A mandate to make social investments is not the same as a mandate to make charitable contributions. In the latter case, the plan incurs an obvious and measurable cost.

Measuring the impact of a ban on investing in shares of a particular industry is more difficult. One way of doing it could be to make a measurement after the fact: to compare what a plan's assets might be if it has retained its holdings of the shares of some notorious source of negative externalities instead of making alternative investments. Barber (2008) follows this approach when he analyzes the divestiture of $365 million of tobacco company stock from CalPERS' portfolio in October of 2000. He estimates that the divestiture had a cost of $1 billion by assuming that the alternative investment's return was that of the S&P 500, given that the value of tobacco stocks subsequently increased by almost fourfold. A problem with this approach is that it is after the fact, but it is better than nothing.

If a plan is obliged by the government that employs its members (or a higher level of government) to undertake social investing, transparency in public accounting would arguably require that the plan receive a compensatory transfer from the government. But precisely because of the difficulties of establishing a unique measure of the cost of social investing, the rationale for this practice may seem less compelling. That said, adding additional objectives to the investment function of a public-sector plan is not in the best interest of its members.

Innovations in Public-Pension Systems

Preliminary Considerations

The finances of traditional pension plans are manifestly affected by population aging: At an unchanged retirement age, increasing longevity increases the cost of providing a pension of a given amount. However, pay-as-you-go first-tier plans are transparently vulnerable to demographic changes.[12] This dependency is easy to demonstrate with a basic PAYG model, which assumes that the system's expenditures must always be equal to revenue. Equation (5.1) illustrates the relationship between the system's basic parameters – payroll tax and average pension – that this equality implies. The system's revenues are decomposed into the product of the average payroll tax (τ), the average wage (w), and the number of contributing workers (L), and its expenditures into the product of the average pension (P) and the number of retired workers (R).

$$\tau \cdot w \cdot L = P \cdot R \tag{5.1}$$

By re-expressing average pensions as the product of the replacement ratio (ρ), which equals P/w, and the average wage, and slightly rearranging equation (5.1), the relationship between a system's financial parameters and the dependency ratio is made clear:

$$R/L = \tau / \rho \tag{5.2}$$

Equation (5.2) illustrates how demography impinges on the finances of tier-one plans.[13] Provided the dependency ratio does not change over time, a given average replacement ratio can be sustained without requiring a change in the payroll tax rate, and the system's financial balance is maintained. If the dependency ratio increases, however, then maintaining financial equilibrium will require some combination of an increase in the payroll tax rate or a decline in the replacement ratio.

---

[12] The impact of demography on a first-tier defined-contribution plan is less obvious, but equally unavoidable. A given increase in the number of pensioners relative to workers poses the same burden under either type of system. To sustain a given standard of living among the elderly at an unchanged level of output per worker, the level of consumption per worker must decline. Similarly, sustaining the working generation's consumption requires a sacrifice by the older generation. See Barr (2001, 96–100) for further discussion.

[13] Note that in any real-world system, the parameters τ and ρ are determined by the specific definitions of the taxable base and accrued pension rights that characterize the system.

The huge literature on public-pension plans provides many examples of the difficulty countries have experienced in maintaining equality between a system's revenues and expenditures. Quite apart from the impact of demography, a political system that awards short-term gains in welfare excessively creates incentives for designing a system that will not be financially sustainable.[14] Even with a system that is sustainable at a given dependency ratio and not subject to maturation effects – as when the average pension is growing because of increases in the average contributory period – population aging may require that major adjustments be made to keep it so. Some industrial countries have been affected by increasing longevity more than others, but all have had to deal with the financial imbalances this phenomenon has caused.

Notional Defined-Contribution Systems

The basic idea behind a notional defined-contribution (NDC) system is that it should adjust the parameters of the tier-one pension system *automatically* to forestall the emergence of these financial imbalances. Ideally, the adjustments are taken out of the political arena altogether. Unlike a conventional defined-benefit plan, the benefit is determined by the contributions a worker makes over his or her working lifetime, accumulated at an artificial or notional interest rate that the system sets, and by an annuity factor, which the system sets as well, that determines the rate at which the accumulated balance is converted to an annuity upon a worker's retirement.

Unlike a true financial defined-contribution plan, each contributor's account balance is purely notional. It is not invested in the financial markets. An NDC system, despite its superficial resemblance to a defined-contribution system, remains a PAYG system and its parameters are set and reset, so that contributions remain equal to benefits (although not necessarily continuously). The system's rate of return reflects a promise by government of a future benefit, and is neither a market rate of return nor a guaranteed rate of return based on past financial market performance.

The relationship between a conventional public-pension system and an NDC can be illustrated by assuming that the conventional (defined-benefit) system is in a steady state. This system has its own internal rate of return (i.e., the rate of return that equalizes the discounted contributions and expenditure of each age cohort), which is given by the rate of growth of

---

[14] For example, if a system requires a certain minimum contributory period as a condition for a benefit, it can run a cash-flow surplus during the first few years of its operation even if the payroll tax rate will ultimately have to be increased to maintain financial balance.

contributions.[15] Suppose an NDC system is introduced that collects exactly the same amount of revenue as the previous system did and promises the same average benefit.[16] From a macroeconomic perspective, there has been no change. However, the internal rate of return of the conventional system becomes the rate of return that the NDC system explicitly offers; the benefit is now determined in a different way, and can change if contributions change or if the system's notional rate of return is altered.

This conversion of a conventional PAYG system to an NDC system replaces a system that relies on a payroll tax and a set of formulae that determines replacement rates, by one that relies on a contribution rate, a notional rate of return to contributions, and an annuity conversion factor. The two sets of parameters behave differently in response to changes in the economic and demographic environment. The impact of changes in their values on the system's financial position also differs.

Consider the impact of declining growth in the wage bill due to declining rates of growth in the working-age population. With an NDC system, where the implicit rate of return is set equal to the rate of growth of the wage bill, future pension payments are automatically reduced even if the contribution rate does not change. An increase in the contribution rate could compensate for the effect of declining growth of the wage bill on pensions. This is not the case with a conventional system, although revenues would, of course, increase. A change in the annuity conversion factor due to increased longevity automatically changes expenditures. No such mechanism exists with a conventional plan.

The advocates of NDC systems claim many virtues for them.[17] First, they are transparent, in the sense that the relationship between contributions and ultimate benefit is more straightforward: Workers get their contributions and the interest that has accrued on them at retirement, although the balance in the account will be automatically converted to an annuity. In addition, the rationale for changes to the system's parameters may be more easily explained. Second, needed changes to the parameters are likely to encounter less political resistance because they are more technically determined. For example, changing an annuity conversion factor because

---

[15] With a simple two-period life-cycle model, the generation that works in period one and retires in period two receives as pension income the contributions of the generation that follows it and that works in period two. Because contributions grow at a rate equal to the sum of the rate of growth of the labor force (l percent) and the real wage (w percent), the rate of return to the first generation's contributions will be ($l + w$) percent.

[16] The revenue that is collected between the start of the new system and the payment of the first pensions under it finances the obligations of the old system.

[17] For a comprehensive list, see Börsch-Supan (2006).

of increasing longevity is more palatable than simply announcing a reduction in accrual factors – or some other change to the system that reduces replacement rates – and giving the same reason. Third, changes to the system's parameters can, in principle, be made automatically – this is most apparent with annuity conversion factors. Fourth (and a related virtue), changes can be made more regularly and thus forestall the emergence of large financial imbalances. Fifth, NDC systems are said to be less distortive of labor market decisions – both the decision to supply labor when young and the retirement decision – because they create and maintain an explicit link between contributions and benefits. As a result, contributions may be perceived more as involuntary saving than as a tax.

What NDC systems do not and cannot do by themselves is to resolve the intergenerational conflicts that lurk beneath unbalanced public-pension systems. For example, determining the rate of interest by the rate of growth of the wage bill undoubtedly reduces the financial imbalance that slowing labor force growth will cause. However, it also puts all the adjustment on the back of the existing generation of workers, which may not be acceptable politically or perceived as fair.

Similarly, adjusting the annuity conversion factor to reflect the increasing longevity of successive cohorts implies a steady decline in the real income of successive cohorts. Although the accumulated balance in the account at retirement may not change from cohort to cohort, it is conceivable that the welfare of pensioners will decline, if the effect on welfare of the decline in income outweighs the effect of increasing longevity. This is most obvious when pensions are near subsistence level. Pushing down annual incomes to pay for increases in the life expectancy of a cohort may not seem fair. A concern with equity requires that an NDC system includes a minimum benefit, as Sweden does. This benefit is means-tested and financed by general tax revenues so that it does not affect the finances of the system.

A more general issue with any such system is that it is difficult to design it so that its signals cannot be overridden.[18] Students of the Swedish reform, discussed next, have noted the importance of a careful, gradual, and inclusive reform process, which was undoubtedly facilitated by Sweden's open parliamentary democracy.

---

[18] A similar issue has arisen in the United States with the Social Security "lock-box." Specifically, fiscal conservatives have expressed concern that there is no mechanism (lock-box) to prevent a surplus in the OASDI trust funds from being used to finance additional expenditure by the federal government, which would nullify the fiscal impact of Social Security reform.

The Swedish System[19]

As the introduction noted, the current Swedish system, which took full effect in 1999, includes both an NDC component and a financial defined-contribution component.[20] A brief account of the Swedish NDC system may shed light on how an actual NDC system works. The contribution rate is set at 16 percent, with a limit on the salary base of about 1.5 times the average salary. The system allows Swedes to earn noncontributory pension rights during periods of sickness, unemployment, participation in other social insurance programs, military service, and time spent raising children as well as periods of education.

Rather than use a measure of the wage bill to derive the system's rate of return, Sweden chose to use a measure of the average economy-wide wage. A lagged value of the measure is used, which is not necessarily equal to its value in the period in which the adjustment is made. The choice of the average wage reflected concerns about pension adequacy, given Sweden's slow- growing or even declining labor force. The choice has implications for the system's financial stability.

The minimum retirement age in Sweden is 61. There is no maximum retirement age. The balance in the account buys a unisex annuity, which is priced on the basis of periodic estimates of life expectancy at 65 and an assumed rate of return of 1.6 percent. This feature means that the system's annuities are not actuarially fair after the age of 65, and would presumably dampen the enthusiasm for retiring at a later age. In practice, most workers leave the labor market before the age of 67, and the average retirement age is 62 (Könberg et al. 2006, 462)

Two aspects of the system's design are potentially important sources of financial imbalance. First, the choice of the average wage means that account balances – and hence future pensions, all else remaining unchanged – will grow faster than the wage bill (and contributions) when employment is falling. This effect could be aggravated in a period of declining wage increases because of the lagged adjustment of the wage index, or by a discrepancy between the calculated average wage increase and the actual average wage increase of plan members. Second, the calculation of life expectancy at age 65 does not take account of any further improvements in longevity that might occur during the remaining life of a particular cohort of retirees. To prevent these design features from causing serious financial imbalance, the

---

[19] The main sources for this section are Könberg et al. (2006) and Turner (2009).
[20] Sweden is one of a small group of countries, which includes Italy, Latvia, and Poland, that has implemented an NDC-type reform, and is probably the best known.

Swedish system includes an automatic adjustment mechanism that requires a suspension of indexation of pension benefits when a measure of plan assets falls below plan liabilities.

Automatic Adjustment Mechanisms

Adopting an NDC is not the only way to insinuate an automatic adjustment mechanism (AAM) into the first tier. A slightly broader group of countries has included an AAM of some kind in their public-pension systems without adopting the NDC model. Using Turner's (2009) classification scheme, these mechanisms fall in one of the following groups: those that index the pension benefit to changes in life expectancy; those that index either the early or normal retirement age to changes in life expectancy; and those that include an automatic solvency mechanism.

The most common way of adjusting pensions for changed life expectancy is to calculate the impact of the change in longevity on the present value of the stream of pensions, and make an appropriate change in the average pension. For example, if the increase in life expectancy would increase the present value of pensions received by a particular cohort by 2 percent, pensions would be reduced by approximately 2 percent to keep the present value of pensions constant.

The practical application of this adjustment requires that the measure of life expectancy be specifically defined. For example, life expectancy at the relevant age might be taken from the period tables prepared by a country's statistical agency, and the size of the adjustment derived from a comparison of the calculated value of life expectancy at age 65 between the current set of tables and the previous set. If period life tables were prepared at a frequency of less than one year – say every three years – annual adjustments, if thought desirable, could be derived by interpolation.

The retirement age – both the minimum and the normal age – can be indexed to life expectancy as well. One way of doing this would be to maintain life expectancy at retirement constant. With increasing life expectancy, this would increase average working lifetimes and reduce the dependency ratio. If pensions were not increased to compensate for the increased age at which retirement began, the system's financial position would improve.

The U.K. Pensions Commission proposed a more sophisticated adjustment target, which was maintenance of the ratio of life expectancy at retirement to average working lifetime. In the event (Turner 2009), the United Kingdom adopted a rule that would increase the retirement age slowly over several decades and by predetermined amounts. To give the workforce adequate time to adjust to these changes, the changes applied only to those cohorts 15 or more years away from the new retirement ages.

Solvency mechanisms

Several industrial countries have maintained the basic structure of their public-pension system but have adopted an adjustment mechanism to restore financial balance automatically when demographic or economic change threatens to create an imbalance. The Swedish NDC includes this type of mechanism, but it is not necessary to adopt an NDC system to put it in place.

Germany's AAM was introduced in 2004 and took effect in 2005. When the system's dependency ratio rises, the AAM requires a reduction in the benefit for a given wage and employment history. The faster the increase in the dependency ratio, the greater will be the reduction in the benefit. The system has been designed so that the financial adjustment to a higher dependency ratio is not borne entirely or even mainly by benefits; payroll tax rates must increase as well. A circuit breaker of sorts applies to the adjustment process: Pensions in nominal terms are not allowed to decline.

In Japan, a 2004 reform introduced a "reduction factor," or modified indexation, to be in place until 2023. Pensions are to be reduced by the sum of the percentage decline in the number of contributors and the rate of increase in life expectancy at age 65. A circuit breaker like that of Germany applies, as well as a floor on the replacement ratio.

The Canadian adjustment mechanism provides yet another example. The basis for the adjustment is a triennial actuarial review of the sustainability of the system. Should the chief actuary conclude that the system is not sustainable (roughly speaking, that the present value of revenue falls significantly short of that of expenditure), indexation of benefits will be suspended for three years unless the ten provincial finance ministers, who act as trustees for the system, agree upon an alternative corrective measure (Turner 2009). The Canadian system thus blends automatic adjustment with political discretion and achieves a flexibility that systems relying purely on a mechanistic adjustment will not enjoy.

PART TWO

6

The Causes of Decline

Introduction

Over the past two decades, seven of the ten survey countries have either witnessed a substantial decline in the prominence of defined-benefit plans in their employer-provided pension systems (the United Kingdom, the United States, and, to a lesser extent, Canada, Sweden, and Switzerland), or have enacted legislation that paves the way for such a development (Germany and Japan). In the Netherlands, the traditional pension has continued to dominate, but some flexibility in plan parameters has been built in. In two of the ten countries (Australia and Denmark), defined-contribution pensions remained dominant (but with a guarantee feature in Denmark's case that gives Danish pensions a hybrid character). Chapter 6 aims to explain why the share of defined-benefit plans in employer-provided pension coverage behaved as it did in the group of seven countries where role of the traditional pension has slipped.

Some Issues of Method

A satisfactory account of the changing role of defined-benefit plans in the ten countries must explain why its role has diminished in the three Anglo-Saxon countries – especially in the United States and the United Kingdom – and in Switzerland and Sweden. However, it also must explain, or at least shed light on, the slower pace of change in Germany and Japan, and the evolution of the Dutch employer-provided pension system.

The global character of the trends in occupational pensions suggests that the forces or influences behind the changes must themselves be global. One obvious global influence is financial instability, given the way national financial markets are interlinked. As Chapter 4 has discussed, another influence is the convergence in accounting rules. Although the repercussions of the decline in global equities and interest rates in 2000–03 may seem tame in comparison with subsequent financial chaos, it was not perceived in that way at the time. In any case, the crash of 2008 is too recent to have a bearing on what has happened to the role of the traditional pension since then.

The hypothesis that financial instability was a major cause of the declining importance of the traditional pension in the Anglo-Saxon countries requires an explanation of why global financial developments did not have more of an impact in other countries. Specifically, to be valid, the hypothesis that the marked decline over the past five to seven years in the role of traditional pension plans in the United States and the United Kingdom was caused by the bursting of the dot.com bubble in late 2000, has to explain why similar declines in coverage did not take place in other countries. To rescue the hypothesis, it is necessary to show that there were countervailing forces or institutions in these other countries that prevented financial instability from having the expected effect on the role of defined-benefit plans.

Another issue arises when the legal and regulatory framework in which employer-provided pensions function discourages or effectively prohibits alternatives to defined-benefit pensions. This was the case until recently in Germany and Japan – defined-benefit plans were the only plans that the law allowed employers to offer their employees. Consequently, it appears as if there is nothing to explain, apart from developments in the eight or so years since the reforms were passed. The dominant role of the defined-benefit plan would not be affected by financial and even regulatory developments, at least not until after the enactment of the new laws.[1]

The absence of legally sanctioned alternatives to the defined-benefit form of pension plan may be a formally adequate explanation of their continued dominance of defined contribution plans. If employers may not offer their employees a defined-contribution plan, no switch from defined-benefit to defined-contribution plans will take place. Letting the matter rest there is not, however, fully satisfactory. The laws and regulations governing employer-based pension systems are not chiseled in granite, even if some inherent legal, political, and social inertia renders them hard to revise or revamp. A fully satisfactory answer would explain why the legal framework was not changed earlier to accommodate defined-contribution plans.

---

[1] Defined-contribution plans might not be allowed, but unless employers were required to offer traditional pensions, their coverage could be affected by the financial environment and other influences.

That said, there is an inherent difficulty in explaining a discrete change in the structure (in this case, the legal framework) of the economic and social environment. It is reasonable to posit some inertia in the reform process as it applies to pensions, especially in a country such as Germany where the role of the social partners is especially important. The same forces at work in countries where a swing to defined-contribution plans was unimpeded by law might well have been at work in Germany and Japan, but these countries would have needed time to create adequate momentum for structural change.

The fact that the basic legal framework had been fundamentally changed to allow defined-contribution plans could be interpreted as the culmination of a build-up in pressures to change the system. In that respect, it would be akin to the swing in plan coverage that took place in countries that had no legal impediments to defined-contribution plans to begin with. In other words, the legal reforms, although they did not immediately bring about a major increase in the role of defined-contribution plans, accomplished something similar by making it possible.

The Analytical Framework

General Considerations

Chapter 2 argued that the benefits of a pension plan can be assimilated to deferred compensation or a fringe benefit, although their contingent character implies that the terms of the trade-off between compensation today and a pension tomorrow may be neither simple nor transparent. The demand by workers, either directly or through their representatives, for a particular combination of fringe benefits can be affected by any number of factors, from the tax treatment of pensions to the perceived trade-off between pension benefits, other benefits, and regular pay. Similarly, the willingness of employers to offer a pension benefit of a given amount, and the type of pension plan they will sponsor, will depend on many factors.

This chapter assumes that the decline in the relative importance of the traditional defined-benefit plan has resulted from some combination of increases in the relative cost to employers of offering or maintaining such a plan, and a decline in its perceived attractiveness to employees. The influences at work on employer costs are supply-side influences, and on attractiveness to employees are demand-side. In light of the previous discussion of the legal limits on the variety of occupational pension-plan forms, the discussion recognizes that the impact of these demand-side and supply-side factors on the relative importance of defined-benefit plans may be inhibited by limits that employers face in choosing a plan for their employees.

The cost to the plan sponsor and the attractiveness of a plan to participants depend not only on predictable costs, but also on the type and degree of risk the plan requires them to bear. The sponsor of a traditional defined-benefit plan bears both investment and longevity risk. Assuming that plan sponsors are risk averse, this means that the cost to them of a traditional defined-benefit plan will depend not only on the values they project for the rate of interest and the life expectancy of pensioners in a base case or middle of the road scenario, but on financial volatility and aggregate longevity risk. An increase in financial volatility that is not accompanied by an increase in the expected return to financial investments or some other offsetting factor can be expected to raise the perceived costs to employers of a traditional plan. The reverse should be true of plan participants: the greater the uncertainty surrounding life expectancy and financial market volatility, the greater the risk of a defined-contribution plan, and the greater the appeal of a defined-benefit pension plan. This conclusion assumes that plan participants or their representatives can gauge these two risks reasonably accurately.

One important influence on the cost to employers of a defined-benefit plan is the flexibility of its terms and conditions – that is, the ease with which they can be altered if the plan's finances deteriorate. How flexible a plan's terms are depends, in turn, on its institutional framework. For example, in the Netherlands, where plan terms are agreed collectively by labor and management, a sense of social solidarity might countenance changes to the formula of defined-benefit plans that would share investment and aggregate longevity risks more broadly – not simply between active members and sponsors, but also among active members, sponsors, and retirees. With such institutions, defined-benefit plans could be more flexible than they would be in a more adversarial environment.

The Range of Supply-Side Influences

Pension experts have identified a long list of possible supply-side influences. In addition to increasing aggregate longevity risk and underperforming or volatile financial markets, the list includes historically low interest rates, an onerous regulatory burden that is subject to legislative or administrative caprice, and a publicly provided guarantee that may encourage a combination of overly risky investment of plan assets and inadequate provisioning by plan sponsors. Some commentators would add increasing longevity (i.e., longevity increases that are predictable as opposed to aggregate longevity risk, per se), and the environment of cutthroat competition that globalization is widely held to have fostered in many industries. In the United States, rising health costs (which are borne mainly by the private sector) are also thought to have shifted the composition of the compensation package in favor of health insurance and away from pensions. All of these possible influences could diminish an employer's willingness to sponsor a traditional defined-benefit plan, and the generosity of that plan.

The Range of Demand-Side Influences

On the demand side, the list would include declines in average employee tenure, declining confidence of plan participants in the security of future benefits that plans promise them, and increased shortsightedness of plan participants. Given a plan's vesting rules, increased labor-force turnover increases the chances that an employee will separate with inadequate pension rights. Consequently, a decline in average job tenure encourages both employees and their representatives to prefer a pension plan that is more portable than the typical final- or average-salary plan, and it increases the appeal of early vesting. Employees' assessed value of the benefit from a final-salary pension plan will also depend on their expectations regarding the salary they will draw in their final years of work.

Employees' confidence in their employer's role as trustee of their acquired pension rights may have declined in a number of the ten countries under study, both because of the perception that the continued existence of even large companies is far from assured, and because employees simply repose less trust than they used to do in the probity of their employer. Even if employees' accrued pension benefits were to be vested, they may prefer to participate in a defined-contribution plan that vests quickly and also allows them to transfer their balance to a similar plan with another employer or to a personal savings vehicle. The clearer separation that a defined-contribution plan maintains between the plan's finances and those of the sponsoring company makes it all the more attractive.

Some degree of skepticism by pension-plan participants in some countries about their plan's promises is healthy. Although an Anglo-Saxon, employer-sponsored pension plan is a trust, and a legal entity distinct from the company that sponsors it, its financial position will still depend on the company's finances. In particular, the various risks impinging on an average- or final-salary pension plan or even a cash-balance plan mean that the sponsor may be asked to make exceptional contributions, which its financial position makes it impossible to meet. The financial difficulties of the company may make it impossible to meet even its regular obligations.

Outright fraud or malfeasance on the part of pension-plan trustees or sponsors is also a concern, as Chapter 4 noted.

The uncertain finances of the plan sponsor can affect both active and retired plan members. If the plan is dissolved, active plan members can no longer count on the pension they had been expecting to receive at retirement, and may even not receive all of their accrued benefits. Retired members may have to take a cut in their pension.

Increasing shortsightedness of plan participants could also contribute to the declining popularity of traditional defined-benefit plans. If participants discount the future benefits payable under an average- or final-salary plan at a high rate, their present value will compare unfavorably with the value of the balance accumulated in a defined-contribution plan or cash-balance plan with the same combined contribution rate. Shortsightedness could make a defined-contribution plan appear more valuable to participants even if they had no control over the rate of contributions, as is normally true of defined-benefit plans. If participants can choose their contribution rate within limits, as is the case in the United States with the typical 401(k) plan, then any significant degree of shortsightedness could tip the scales decisively in favor of the defined-contribution plan.

Anyone who wrestles with so complex a socioeconomic phenomenon as the diminishing role of traditional pension plans in industrial countries must wish for the acute judgment of Inspector Jules Maigret, the intuitive genius of Georges Simenon's *romans policiers*. The canny inspector carefully takes the measure of each possible person of interest before he apprehends the true culprit. However, the decline of the traditional pension, even if it may be compared to a murder mystery, is in some respects more like Dame Agatha Christie's tale of *Murder on the Orient Express*, where the famous Belgian detective Hercule Poirot deduces that no less than a dozen assassins had a hand on the knife.

The account that follows will sift the evidence in the manner of Simenon's phlegmatic protagonist, but will conclude that this particular mystery, unlike most fictional mysteries but like most real-life ones, has more than one villain. Some suspects can be let off. Specifically, the case against financial instability is weak, and the impact of declining interest rates and increasing aggregate longevity risk has been overstated. The real culprits are declining job tenure, an unnecessarily complex and changeable regulatory environment, declining unionization, and the reduced trust of employees in their employers, reinforced by an increase in myopia among plan participants and some misunderstanding of the relative merits of defined-benefit and defined-contribution plans.

Analysis of the Supply-Side Influences

Aggregate Longevity Risk

Both life expectancy at birth and conditional life expectancy at advanced ages have been increasing for decades around the world. In some countries, the increase has been quite spectacular. Among the ten countries in the study, the OECD estimates that the life expectancy of women aged 65 in Japan has increased by 8.1 years since 1970, bringing it to 23.4 years as of 2006 (Table 6.1). Denmark is the laggard of the group, because the increase in the life expectancy of 65-year-old women in that country since 1970 was 2.5 years as of 2006, which raised it to 19.2 years. For seven of the ten countries, the increases since 1970 cluster within 2 percentage points of each other.

The life expectancy for men has also increased, and the pattern of increases across countries is similar to that for women – notably, the increase in life expectancy is the second greatest for Japanese men and the

Table 6.1. *Trends in life expectancies for 65-year-old men and women in ten industrial countries (in years)*

	Women				Men			
		Change since				Change since		
	Life expectancy (in 2006 except where noted)	1970	1980	1990	Life expectancy (in 2006 except where noted)	1970	1980	1990
Australia	21.5	5.9	3.6	2.5	18.3	6.4	4.6	3.1
Canada[a]	21.4	3.9	2.5	1.5	18.2	4.5	3.7	2.5
Denmark	19.2	2.5	1.6	1.3	16.2	2.5	2.6	2.2
Germany	20.5	5.6	4.2	2.8	17.2	5.3	4.4	3.2
Japan	23.4	8.1	5.7	3.4	18.5	6.0	3.9	2.3
Netherlands	20.1	4.0	2.1	1.2	16.7	3.4	3.0	2.3
Sweden	20.8	4.0	2.9	1.8	17.6	3.4	3.3	2.3
Switzerland	22.1	5.8	3.9	2.4	18.5	5.2	4.2	3.2
United Kingdom	20.1	4.1	3.5	2.2	17.4	5.4	4.8	3.4
United States[a]	20.3	3.3	2.0	1.4	17.4	4.3	3.3	2.3

[a] Changes are from 1961, 1971 and 1981.
Source: OECD Health Division.

least for Danish men. The gap between female and male life expectancies increased in some countries and widened in others, including Japan and Switzerland (Table 6.1).

Demographers and pension-plan actuaries predicted some of the increase in life expectancy at ages 65 and older that took place in the mid- to late twentieth century. Their failure to predict more of it might be put down to a combination of poor modeling techniques and bad luck. Private pension-plan actuaries have not always allowed for increases in longevity that in retrospect were predictable. However, forecasting errors could also have reflected an increase in aggregate longevity risk.

The distinction between the two types of error is important. The first type, in principle, can be corrected by the adoption of better forecasting techniques; even if no further improvement in techniques is possible, it is not likely to cause another large error. A type-one error should not increase the amount of risk currently borne by sponsors of defined-benefit plans, at least not those offering benefits in the form of a life annuity. Actuarial losses would increase and might be heavy, because retired employees were living longer than plans had assumed, and plan parameters would have to be changed or contributions by employers increased to maintain actuarial balance.[2] However, with improved forecasting techniques in place, the risk to which the plan was subject would not increase.

The second type of error is less tractable. An increase in aggregate longevity risk would increase the risk borne by the sponsor of the standard final-salary or average-salary plans, because the predictability of the stream of annuity payments to retired plan members had declined. As Chapter 7 will explain, plan sponsors might be able to hedge this increased risk, but only partially.

Aggregate longevity risk could vary from country to country, because increases in longevity might be more predictable in some countries than in others. In Denmark, for example, the increase in longevity for both men and women from one decade to the next has tended either to fall or to vary little over time (Table 6.1). In other countries, the pattern is hard to characterize.

The evidence on the significance of aggregate longevity risk in most of the countries surveyed is limited. Brown and Orszag (2006) argue, based on indirect evidence, that aggregate longevity risk has increased the cost of

---

[2]   There is one circumstance, however, in which a predictable increase in longevity would increase the risk borne by final-salary pension plans, and that would be when there was a shortage of long-dated bonds. In this case, there would be an additional element of risk in the price of the annuity that plans would buy from an insurance company, because of the mismatch between long-dated liabilities and assets.

a life annuity (and presumably a typical final-salary pension) by no more than 5 percent in the United States.[3] This study does not attempt to estimate any trend in aggregate longevity risk, nor does a recent study by Friedburg and Webb (2006). Antolin (2007) estimates a longevity function for each country of a selected group of OECD countries, and then uses the errors the simulation generates as the basis for a Monte Carlo study of the possible variation in longevity. He finds that for some countries, this variation can be substantial, but as with the previous studies cited, it is difficult to infer whether aggregate longevity risk has worsened over time.

Much uncertainty surrounds both the degree of aggregate longevity risk and its trend. There is yet no agreed model of the maximum life span, and until there is, there is likely to be disagreement over the pace of improvements in life expectancy. However, if the burden of proof lies on those experts who think aggregate longevity risk has increased, the available evidence does not make their case for them.

Financial Market Instability (Investment and Interest Rate Risk)
The global financial crash may well have momentous consequences for both defined-benefit and defined-contribution plans. Nonetheless, this section concentrates on developments in the decade leading up to the fall 2008 crash, because, as noted previously, the timing of the crisis does not allow us to draw specific conclusions about its impact on pensions.

That said, some general observations can be made about the consequences of the crisis for employer-provided pensions. There can be no doubt that the crash would have dampened the enthusiasm of sponsors of defined-benefit plans to maintain them. Because most plans allocate a large share of their assets to equities, the rate of return on their assets in the first ten months of 2008 ranged from a loss of 7.0 percent for Denmark, to a loss as high as 21.5 percent for the United States (OECD 2008c). In the United Kingdom, an increase in the spread between the risk-free and high-grade corporate bond rates temporarily offset the impact that this fall in asset values

---

[3]   This estimate is based on a calculation of the money's worth ratio, which measures the ratio of the actuarially fair value of the income stream of an annuity to its cost. In a theoretical world of costless financial intermediation and no aggregate longevity risk, the ratio should equal one. Brown and Orszag (2006) refer to a study by Brown, Mitchell, and Poterba (2001), which estimates a money's worth ratio of 0.95. The calculation uses mortality tables for U.S. annuitants and the yield curve for Treasury bonds to discount the annuity's stream of income. Brown and Orszag, using the estimated ratio of 0.95 as a benchmark, argue that the cost entailed by longevity risk cannot exceed 5 percent of the cost of an annuity, because if it did, the money's worth ratio would have to be lower simply to allow annuity suppliers to break even.

had on plans' funding ratios. In general, however, the defined-benefit plans of industrial countries have become seriously underfunded.

Defined-contribution plans have been as severely affected as defined-benefit plans, because in most countries with defined-contribution plans, participants have been heavily exposed to equities. The difference is that the losses have been borne by plan members and not their sponsors. Australians and Americans have both suffered huge losses in their retirement saving plans because of the fall in equity values. In the United States, the drop in the balances of 401(k) plan members and IRA holders between September 2007 and March 2009 amounted to no less than $2.7 trillion (Soto 2009). In Australia, average losses on superannuation accounts during 2008 were estimated at 19.7 percent (theage.com 2009). As a result, it is likely that many defined-contribution plan participants are wishing that they had been members of a traditional plan, especially participants in those plans without a guarantee. The financial crisis has increased the relative attractiveness of these plans to participants as it has shaken the willingness of employers to offer them.

The decade prior to the financial crisis was itself not free of instability. The bursting of the dot.com bubble and the ensuing decline in global stock markets in 2000–03 caused jarring falls in the asset values of defined-benefit plans in most of the countries under study, particularly in the United States, the Netherlands, and the United Kingdom, where the share of equities by value in pension-plan assets is upward of 40 percent (OECD 2006, 7). In most of the other countries, the share of equities ranges from 25 to 30 percent, still high enough for the dot.com crash to have inflicted substantial losses.

Among the major markets, the stock market decline was the greatest in Germany. From its peak in early 2000 to its trough in early 2003, the DAX (a broad stock market index) fell by over 70 percent. In the United States, the S&P 500 index fell by about 50 percent from its peak at end 1999 to its trough in early 2003. In the United Kingdom, the FTSE 100 declined by close to 50 percent between December 1999 and March 2003. Finally, in Japan, the Nikkei 225, which by late 1999 had fallen by over 50 percent from the peak reached in December 1989, had declined by a further 50 percent by early 2003, when it reached its low point (Figure 6.1).

The impact of the global decline in equity values on pension-plan assets would have been tempered by the impact on bond prices of the subsequent global decline in interest rates. In the United States, the mitigating effect of bond holdings in plan portfolios would have been small. At the end of 2005, holdings of credit market instruments (including treasuries and

Figure 6.1. Performance of broad stock-market indexes in major financial centers, May 1997 to May 2008 (May 1997 = 100). *Source*: Yahoo, Deutsche Bundesbank.

government-sponsored agency and corporate securities) are estimated to have amounted to about 20 percent of the total financial assets of private defined-benefit pension plans (Federal Reserve Board 2007). In the other countries, the share of bonds in 2005–06 ranged from about 30 percent in the United Kingdom (Mercer 2006) to 35–40 percent in Canada, the Netherlands, and Japan.[4] In Switzerland, where the guaranteed minimum rate of return and the fixed ratio applied to accumulated balances to determine annuity income give what is nominally a defined-contribution plan a defined-benefit character, the share of bonds was about 25 percent.

The impact lower interest rates would have had on pension-plan assets would have been more than offset by the impact of lower long-term rates on plan liabilities, especially given the likely mismatch in most countries between the average duration of plan liabilities and the duration of assets. The decline in interest rates would have entailed a concurrent and large increase in the present value of plan liabilities, because the discount rates used for both accounting (financial disclosure) and funding purposes are now market-related in nearly all countries (OECD 2005, 38).

---

[4] In Canada, data on the composition of assets are not available for defined-contribution and defined-benefit plans separately. However, because the share of defined-contribution plan membership remains below 30 percent, the share of bonds in total pension assets, which is similar to the share of bonds in the Netherlands and Japan, is likely a good estimate of the share of bonds in the assets of defined-benefit plans.

The Impact of the Financial Market's Decline on Plan Funding

The stock market's correction and the decline in long-term interest rates together caused a noticeable deterioration in the net-asset position of defined-benefit plans in all ten countries, one that was large enough to cause a significant gap to open up between the actual level of assets and the level required to fund plan liabilities. However, the post-2003 recovery in equity markets and increases in interest rates substantially reduced this gap in most countries.

Data on the degree of underfunding over the recent period are available for some of the ten countries. For the United States, the Pension Benefit Guaranty Corporation (PBGC, 2007) has estimated that total underfunding of single-employer plans rose dramatically from $164 billion in 2002 to $420 billion in 2003. Underfunding stayed at about that level for two years before declining in 2006 to $314 billion, and to $225 billion the following year. The decline undoubtedly reflected in part the gains enjoyed by the U.S. stock market, together with the increase in interest rates between 2003 and 2007. Nonetheless, underfunding remained at levels that were high by historical standards because of the problems of large pension plans in the airline and steel industries.

In Canada, a similar improvement in the finances of defined-benefit plans took place. The solvency ratio – the ratio of assets to liabilities calculated on the assumption that the plan would be dissolved on the date of valuation – is estimated to have increased from 93 percent as of end-2003 to 95 percent as of end-May 2006 (Armstrong 2006). It almost certainly increased further in the following year given further gains in the Toronto Stock Exchange and Wall Street, and the increase that took place in interest rates during that period.

In the United Kingdom as well a substantial degree of underfunding emerged in the wake of declining interest rates and stock prices. Mercer (2006) estimates that the net plan deficit as calculated by applying IAS 19 principles for the firms that comprise the FTSE 350 index (which would account for the vast majority of defined-benefit plan assets and membership) amounted to £74 billion (about $120 billion or 7 percent of the U.K. GDP) at the end of 2002. The estimated funding ratio was 79 percent. By end March 2007, the overall deficit is estimated to have declined to £36 billion, and the funding ratio to have risen to 93 percent (Mercer 2007a). In May of 2007, other pension consultancies were reported as saying that U.K. corporate pensions were mostly in the black. The decline in pension-plan deficits reflects both the recovery of the stock market and an increase in long-term interest rates.

A much more conservative method of valuation than that underlying these estimates is based on an estimate of what a company that is sponsoring a pension plan would have to pay an insurance company to relieve it of its obligations to current retirees and its accrued obligations to current employees. Mercer (2007b) estimates that this buy-out-based valuation of the FTSE 350 companies (which it derives by increasing conventionally measured liabilities by 40 percent) would have amounted to £230 billion at end of March 2007.[5]

Underfunding has also been evident among European pension plans. Mercer (2006) estimates that the pension deficit for the 50 largest companies in the Euro zone amounted to €117 billion at end 2006, partly reflecting a deliberate policy of underfunding in some countries The Dutch pension system has no book reserves, and its average funding ratio followed the pattern of other countries, declining from 150 percent in 1999 to 108 percent in 2002, before beginning its recovery (International Monetary Fund 2006). Finally, in Japan, where data on assets and liabilities are not readily available but figures on the number of employee pension funds that are over or under funded are, the number of plans in surplus declined from 30 percent of the total in 1998 and 82 percent in 1999, to 5 percent in 2002 before recovering to 34 percent in 2003 (Government of Japan, Ministry of Health, Labor and Welfare, n.d.). The ratio of surplus funds is likely to have recovered further in 2004–07, given the performance of Japanese equities.

In sum, the recovery in equity prices in all the major markets after 2002 had brought prices close to or above their previous nominal peaks by mid-2007, and had contributed to a substantial improvement in pension-plan funding.

Despite the recovery of major stock markets, institutional investors might have become less willing to hold risky assets than they previously were if returns to financial assets had become more volatile. For risk-averse plan sponsors, an increase in the volatility of stock and other financial markets is tantamount to an increase in the cost of funding the plan, and they will seek the shelter of a less risky investment portfolio. This is, in fact, what happened with European life insurers following the bursting of the

---

[5] The Canadian solvency valuation and the U.S. termination-based valuation differ from a valuation of an ongoing plan because they take account of termination benefits, which for younger workers could be higher than their accrued benefits. Similarly, they should reflect early retirement pensions, which may have a higher actuarial value than regular retirement pensions. A buy-out valuation makes more conservative assumptions about mortality (i.e., assumed life expectancies are greater), and uses a lower discount rate. The relevance of a buy-out-based valuation is not particularly great, however, if plans will not be wound up *en masse*.

equity bubble (IMF 2004b), although a change in regulatory norms also contributed.

Volatility can be quantified, and its measurement might shed some light on whether investors have rational grounds for unease. Volatility is normally measured in two ways. The first is based on a measure of the variance of an asset's price or return. This measure is after the fact and backward looking: It is a gauge of how variable asset prices *have been*, and not a prediction of how variable they *will be* in the future.

The second measure is based on the behavior of options prices. An option is a derivative instrument that gives its holder the right to sell the underlying asset at a predetermined price on or before a date specified in the contract. Options become more valuable the greater the expected variance of a stock. Consequently, a measure of implicit volatility may be derived from the behavior of options prices. This measure is forward looking, although the short maturities of the options prices from which it is derived mean that it gives an indication of the state of short-term, not long-term, expectations.

Both historical and forward-looking indexes imply that the volatility of all the major equity markets (London, Frankfurt, Tokyo, and New York) picked up in 2002 – not surprisingly, given the correction taking place – but then declined to the levels of the mid-1990s (International Monetary Fund 2002, 10–11; 2007a, 147). Similarly, both indicators imply that the volatility of global bond markets has been declining since 2000 (International Monetary Fund 2007a, 148). Most gauges of global financial volatility imply that it returned to relatively low levels after the dot.com bust.

The behavior of inflation is a more indirect indicator of financial volatility, but in some ways a more general one. A high (or rising) and variable rate of inflation is almost certainly a harbinger of more systematic financial volatility, much as a high fever will be a symptom of a whole-body illness. Rising inflation normally prompts a central bank to raise its policy rate or take other measures that give its policy a restrictive stance, leading to increases in interest rates at all maturities. Holders of long-term bonds demand an inflation or term premium on the rate their assets earn, which will be high and possibly unstable if inflation is high. If the discount rate that pension funds use to value their liabilities is market-related, high inflation can indirectly lead to a decline in pension fund liabilities, but can also prompt a large decline in equity values.

Something like this occurred in the U.S. financial markets in the late 1970s and early 1980s, when the Federal Reserve's resolute attack on inflation sent both nominal and real interest rates to unprecedentedly high levels, contributing to a severe recession and a slumping stock market. The international transmittal of high U.S. interest rates had similar effects abroad.

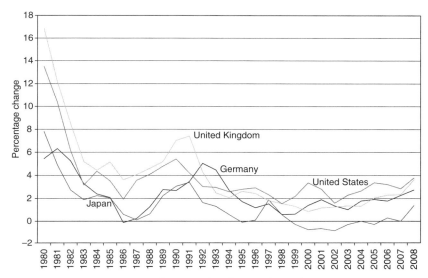

Figure 6.2. Consumer price inflation in four large industrial countries, 1980 to 2008. *Source*: International Monetary Fund, WEO Database.

By comparison with this difficult period, the financial markets of industrial countries were comparatively calm from the late 1980s until 2007, and inflation has been comparatively low and stable in the industrial world. In Japan, prices stopped falling for a time, but the rate of change of the price level has been very stable by historical standards (see Figure 6.2). The comparative calm of major financial markets in 2002–07 did not last. It is clear, however, that financial markets until 2007 were not particularly volatile by comparison with earlier periods, and that average rates of return on financial assets were not low.

No matter how carefully volatility indicators may be defined and measured, they are not necessarily reliable guides to investor psychology. The assessment by pension fund managers of investment risk might not have moved in lock step with the objective indicators, and there is always the question of how much weight managers will give to the recent past. Institutional investors might simply have been spooked by the dot.com bust.

The English poet Phillip Larkin famously wrote that sex was invented in 1963, not that volatile stock markets were conjured up at the turn of the twenty-first century. Stocks were, are, and always will be a risky investment. An influential commentator like Robert Shiller (2000) was arguing persuasively before the dot.com bust that the 1990s boom displayed all the classic features of a bubble, and it was undoubtedly prudent for pension fund managers (and, indeed, any investor) to assume that a correction was in

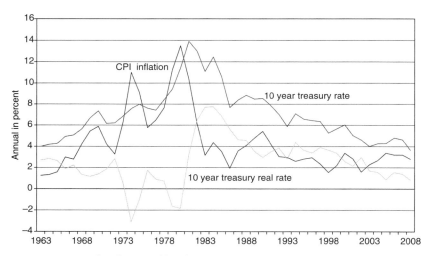

Figure 6.3. U.S. real and nominal bond rates, 1963 to 2008. *Source*: Federal Reserve Board.

store. With the 20/20 vision that hindsight can bestow on us, the decline in the market in 2001–02 was not a great puzzle, even if its extent and timing could not have been foreseen.

Turning back to the liabilities side of the pension balance sheet, the decline in nominal interest rates since the late 1990s in U.S. and other major financial markets will permanently increase the cost to sponsors of funding the benefits of new employees, or the additional service of existing employees, should it not be reversed. As noted, pension-plan actuaries in most of the ten countries use market-based rates in their funding calculations, although they may have some discretion in the choice of rate (OECD 2005, 38). The decline in rates has not, however, brought them to historically low levels. In the 1960s and 1970s, real interest rates were often lower than their contemporary levels (Figure 6.3). Viewed in an even longer-term perspective, real interest rates are not especially low (Catão and Mackenzie 2006), and long-term rates were starting to rise in mid-2007.

Because our concern is with the *relative* attractiveness of defined-contribution versus defined-benefit plans, it is important not to focus exclusively on the impact of a decline in interest rates on the cost to the sponsor of a defined-benefit plan. A permanent decline in interest rates and in the risk-free rate of return does increase the cost of a defined-benefit plan, but it does not increase the attractiveness of defined-contribution plans relative to that of defined-benefit plans. If we compare a defined-contribution plan in the same financial environment as a defined-benefit plan, and with contribution rates exactly equal to those of that plan, a decline in interest rates would require that the defined-contribution plan increase its contributions by as much as the defined-benefit plan if it wished to provide the same benefit. Alternatively, both plans could leave their contribution rates unchanged, in which case their benefits would have to decline. A farsighted and financially sophisticated plan participant would realize that the decline in the rate of return should not alter the *relative* attractiveness of the two plans. In practice, many participants in defined-contribution plans would overlook the fact that the stream of income their accumulated balances could finance will fall by exactly the same amount.

A similar point can be made about investment risk. An increase in investment risk increases the cost to the plan sponsor of maintaining the plan, but should increase the cost to participants in a defined-contribution plan of achieving a given goal of income in retirement. (In fact, if plan sponsors are less risk averse than participants, an increase in investment risk would increase the relative attractiveness of a defined-benefit plan.)

The analysis of the impact of interest and investment risk on the relative attractiveness of defined-benefit and defined-contribution plans raises an issue that crops up anytime a plan sponsor might want to change the parameters of a defined-benefit plan: Is changing the terms of a plan sufficiently difficult that an alternative like freezing the plan and offering employees a defined-contribution plan instead is the preferable course? This course of action is more likely if plan participants misunderstand the effective return to participation in the two types of plans. For example, heightened investment risk requires a change to the parameters of a defined-benefit plan, like a decrease in the accrual rate, if the risk the sponsor bears is not to increase, but with a defined-contribution plan, no change to the plan's contribution rate is necessary to shift the cost to participants: They bear all of the extra risk automatically. This point is taken up again in Chapter 7.

The Impact of Regulatory Reform and Tax Policy

As earlier chapters have discussed, the occupational pension systems of all ten of the countries this book considers have had to cope with periodic revisions to their regulatory frameworks. These revisions were particularly significant in the larger countries, and notably in the United States and the United Kingdom. In Japan and Germany, some significant modifications of the regulatory framework combined with fundamental reforms to the structure of employer-provided pension plans could well spell the end of the dominance of defined-benefit pensions.

The aim of this section is to judge whether the burden of regulatory complexity, especially the burden on defined-benefit plans has become heavier over the past decade or so, and whether plan sponsors or plan participants (or their representatives) have good reason to believe that the regulatory framework is now less stable than it formerly was.[6] A finding that the regulatory burden on defined-benefit plans has increased in comparison to the burden on defined-contribution plans in a particular country may shed light on the decline of defined-benefit plans in that country. Similarly, a finding that, quite apart from the burden it currently entails, the regulatory framework for defined-benefit plans is perceived as unpredictable would further tip the scales in favor of the alternative.

Some of the costs that a regulatory framework imposes can be estimated reasonably accurately, while the cost of others cannot. As an example of the first taken from the American experience, the direct cost to a plan sponsor of compliance with the extremely complex nondiscrimination rules that Employee Retirement Income Security Act of 1974 (ERISA) introduced could, given enough information, be quantified. The same is probably true of paperwork and reporting requirements.

In contrast, an estimate of the cost of rules that prescribe plan reserves would require some assumptions about a stochastic variable, in particular, the rate of return on alternative assets. As a third example, the perceived cost entailed by fiduciary responsibilities that expose the plan sponsor to the risk of liability claims and lawsuits could be very high but fail to be captured simply by the extra cost of in-house council or legal fees. [7]

These examples suggest that estimates of the administrative cost of pension plans, even if they are readily available, are not enough by themselves. They need to be supplemented by a qualitative appraisal of the impact of major changes to the regulatory framework. As is the case with a tax reform, some changes to the regulatory framework for pensions may ease the task of plan sponsors and reduce compliance costs; others may increase them. Unless the costs of these changes can be reckoned in dollars, euros, pounds, or yen, appraising their combined effect will not be an easy matter. It is less difficult when there is a general direction to reform.

---

[6]   A comparison of the state of the regulatory framework at two different periods could have four possible findings, because its cost in the later period may be higher or lower than its cost in the earlier period, while its perceived stability may be greater or lesser. Changes to the framework that make it more complex and costly and that heighten the sense of uncertainty about its stability would be the worst of the four possible outcomes.

[7]   An estimate of this cost could, in principle, be based on the cost of liability insurance, were it available.

Some data on administrative costs are available for the United States and the United Kingdom, and their implications are considered before the more general question of regulatory complexity for these and the other eight countries. For the United States, Hustead (1998) finds that for defined-benefit plans of companies with 10,000 employees, the administrative cost per active plan member almost tripled between 1981 and 1996, from about $23 to $68 in 1996 dollars, or from roughly $30 to $90 in current dollars. Some, but not all, of this increase may reflect the foreseeable increase in the ratio of retired to active members entailed by plan maturation.[8] The cost for defined-contribution plans of same-sized plans increased by less over 1981–96, although it did double, so that a gap of about $30 per member in current dollars opened up between the two types of plans. To the author's knowledge, no estimates of administrative costs are available for the United States for 1996–2009.

For small- and medium-sized firms, the estimated cost of plan administration is very high. The cost per plan member for a defined-benefit plan with 15 members is more than $800 in current-dollar terms. With costs this high, defined-benefit plans are not a feasible benefit for small employers to offer, unless they can realize substantial economies of scale through joining a multiemployer plan. (The administration of defined-contribution plans is also burdensome for small- and medium-sized employees, although less so than the administration of defined-benefit plans.) Much of the difference in per-capita cost between small and large firms probably reflects the burden that compliance with the nondiscrimination rules, intended to ensure that the coverage of and benefits paid to lower-paid workers are adequate, poses for small firms. In addition, small plan sponsors would not reap the benefits of economies of scale in various functions, including record keeping, legal and actuarial work, and investment policy and activity.

As for large firms, Hustead's figures imply that the administrative cost per annum of defined-benefit plans amounts to about 0.2 percent of the average economy-wide annual salary. The difference between the administrative cost of defined-benefit and defined-contribution plans for large firms is estimated to amount to less than 0.1 percent of the average annual salary. This difference does not look large enough to tip the balance against defined-benefit and toward defined-contribution schemes. In any case, this is not a comparison of like with like. The typical defined-benefit plan offers

[8] The cost estimates are expressed as a ratio of costs (measured in constant dollars) to active participants. As a pension plan matures, it normally experiences an increase in the ratio of retired participants to active participants. This trend would increase cost per active plan member even without a change in the administrative-cost function or in cost inflation.

the worker a substantially larger expected benefit than the typical defined-contribution plan, and quite apart from the size of the expected benefit, a final-salary plan normally comes with longevity insurance included.

In the United Kingdom, a survey by the Government Actuary (U.K. Government Actuary's Department 2006) found, unsurprisingly, that in the case of defined-benefit plans, costs per plan member tended to decline dramatically with increases in plan size, reflecting the same economies of scale that are evident with U.S. plans. For plans with 10,000 or more members, total costs, including the cost of the investment function, were about £86 ($130) per plan member. Administrative expenses alone were a mere £12. The responses from defined-contribution plan administrators were too patchy to permit the drawing of a similar inference for these plans, and data on earlier years are not readily available. The data available on defined-benefit plans in Britain imply that their administration is less expensive than that of their American counterparts.

Before turning to the task of characterizing the change in the overall burden and stability of the regulatory framework in each of the ten countries, there is one trend in reform that should be addressed first, because it has crossed national boundaries. This is the recent reform in pension accounting, as represented by the new standards mandated by the Financial Accounting Standards Board (FASB), Accounting Standards Board (ASB), and International Accounting Standards Board (IASB).

The aim of these revised standards was to bring the conventions of pension accounting into line with current financial accounting principles. Even if funding gaps are not to be filled immediately (usually they cannot), they should be measured in a way that is consistent with the principles of modern finance. Consequently, with mark-to-market valuation of assets, as Chapter 3 discussed, a decline in a pension plan's assets should be reflected immediately in the balance sheet. Without a compensating change in asset composition, this reform means that balance-sheet volatility will increase.

For these accounting reforms to have an effect on the perceived financial position of a pension fund or its sponsor, it must be the case either that the old accounting regimes effectively hid the true financial position of pension funds, or that shareholders and the financial market generally are influenced more by the way information is presented than by the facts it conveys. In the United States, the information necessary to measure the net assets or liabilities of a pension plan at market value formerly were included as a memorandum item in the supporting statements to the financial statements, and a well-trained financial analyst should not have had difficulty in consolidating it. If investors could pierce the financial veil and adjust for the way information on pension-plan funding was conveyed, the change in accounting regime would have no real effects. Casual empiricism and some studies argue for the importance of presentational effects, however. In particular, Coronado and Sharpe (2003) find that the U.S. stock market focuses on the estimates of the impact of those operations of a pension fund that are included in the net income statement. Clark and Monk (2006) cite other studies with similar conclusions.

Because they tend to increase balance-sheet volatility, the practices of marking to market – as now mandated by FASB, FRS 17, and IAS 19 – and the consolidation of the pension plan's financial position with that of the sponsoring company are said to have contributed to the decline of the defined-benefit plan. Given how recently they have been implemented, these accounting reforms cannot explain the longer-term trend to decline in the share of defined-benefit plans in the Anglo-Saxon countries. Nonetheless, the *prospect* of an increase in balance-sheet volatility could contribute to further decline, particularly in countries where the share of equity in plan assets is high. To the extent that balance-sheet volatility is perceived as undesirable and in need of dampening, an increase in the share of bonds in plan assets becomes desirable, because it could be expected to reduce volatility (and because it reduces duration mismatch).[9]

The evolution of pension-plan regulation in the ten countries has reflected both common influences, like accounting reform, as well as the special circumstances and institutions of each country. In the United States, a good understanding of recent changes to the regulatory framework requires some appreciation of the impact of ERISA. The start of the decline in the role of defined-benefit plans dates more or less to its enactment in 1974. As Salisbury (2006) has pointed out, it is possible that the secular trend to decline in the role of defined-benefit plans reflects the key elements in that legislation, rather than any subsequent laws. In particular, ERISA substantially liberalized vesting requirements to protect workers with short-average job tenures. This measure would have reduced the subsidization by these workers of co-workers with long tenure that Chapter 2 discussed and that had previously prevailed, and would have increased plan costs by increasing pension accruals. A plan's parameters can, in principle, be changed, however, and the issue of how feasible such revisions are, which cropped up in the discussion of the impact of low interest rates, arises again.

---

[9] If the rate of return used to project plan income is a weighted average of the historical rates of return of the asset classes a plan holds, increasing the share of bonds would reduce the rate of return, which would increase the measured imbalance between assets and liabilities, and oblige the sponsor to make additional contributions.

The three decades since the passage of ERISA in 1974 are best analyzed if they are divided into two periods. ERISA introduced substantial complexity into U.S. pension regulation, and during the first period, which ended in the early 1990s, a series of laws consolidated some of ERISA's most important provisions. The measures taken during this period were often motivated by concerns over the large tax expenditures that resulted from the preferential tax treatment of both defined-benefit and defined-contribution plans. For example, the Tax Reform Act of 1986 lowered the maximum defined-benefit pension and defined-contribution limits that ERISA had introduced to reduce tax expenditures.[10] Similarly, the Omnibus Budget Reconciliation Acts of 1987 and 1993 (OBRA 87 and 93) reduced defined-benefit plan funding limits.[11] The Tax Reform Act of 1986 also enhanced ERISA's vesting requirements, which might not have further increased a plan's administrative burden, but did increase the cost of a plan to its sponsor (Schieber 2005, 32).

Other changes to pension funding and accounting regulations had the effect of reducing pension tax expenditures by lowering permissible employer contributions. In the late 1980s, FASB required pension plans to adopt the projected unit-credit method, described in Chapter 3 for calculating accrued benefits (McGill et al. 2005, 702–3). Because the majority of plans were using the entry-age normal-cost method, this decision gave their sponsors some initial relief. However, by back-loading the contributions made over a plan member's career, its initial fiscal impact was to lower pension tax expenditures. Overall, changes to the regulatory framework during the first period increased the costs of sponsors of both defined-benefit and defined-contribution plans: It is difficult to say which plan was more affected.

During the second period, in response to growing unease about the declining coverage of defined-benefit plans, the failure of private employer-provided pension coverage as a whole to increase, and perhaps also some

---

[10] A tax exemption for employer contributions (and, for certain plans, employee contributions) to pension plans is a tax expenditure in a classical income-tax system, because it subsidizes contractual saving. However, in a consumption-tax system, which many economists consider superior to an income-tax system because it does not create a wedge between the before- and after-tax rates of return to saving, such exemptions would be the norm. Schieber (2005) and Groom and Shoven (2005) argue that the "tax-expenditure" view was driving pension policy in the 1980s and early 1990s.

[11] OBRA 1987 reduced the limit on aggregate funding from 100 percent of projected liability to the lesser of 100 percent of projected plan liability and 150 percent of accrued benefits, while OBRA 1993 reduced the level of individual employee compensation that could be taken into account in funding and contributing decisions (McGill et al. 2005, 704–6).

abatement of concern over pension-plan tax expenditures in light of an improved federal budgetary position in the late 1990s, measures were taken to reduce the administrative burden ERISA entailed, and reverse at least partially the measures taken to curb the tax cost of private pensions. As an example of the first type of measure, the nondiscrimination rules, as they applied to defined-contribution plans, were considerably simplified. As for the second, the Economic Growth and Tax Relief Reconciliation Act of 2001 (EGTRRA) provided for substantial temporary increases in the limits applying to the maximum benefits of defined-benefit plans and the maximum contribution for defined-contribution plans. The Pension Protection Act of 2006 made EGTRRA's temporary increases in these limits permanent (Deloitte 2006).

The Pension Protection Act of 2006 has substantially limited the extent to which smoothing can muffle fluctuations in asset values for funding purposes, and has reduced the amortization period that applies in the event of a funding shortfall.[12] This change would increase a plan sponsor's costs by shortening the period over which the sponsor would be required to make up the shortfall. However, the Act has also sanctioned a change in the discount rate from a weighted average of current and lagged Treasury bond yields to a discount rate derived from corporate AA yields. The change in discount rate is being phased in. In addition, the Act protects hybrid plans against future claims of age discrimination under various laws, subject to certain provisos.

The Pension Protection Act has also simplified the administration of 401(k) plans in various ways. The Act's most important changes affecting defined-contribution plans, however, are the protection and encouragement it gives to plans with automatic-enrollment provisions, and the legal protection (safe-harbor provision) it gives plan sponsors who offer investment advice to their employees (subject to certain safeguards for the employees).

On balance, defined-contribution plans have benefited more from the changes to the regulatory framework in the second period, even if the overall burden on defined-benefit plans did not increase. It is fair to say that the basic framework established by the landmark legislation of 1974 has not been fundamentally altered for either type of plan, apart from the passage of legislation to encourage plan sponsors to set appropriate defaults for

---

[12] Smoothing will be restricted to a period of two years, and the resulting value must be in a range of 90 to 110 percent of the current market value. Funding shortfalls now need to be made up over 7 years in level installments. Previously, the period of amortization could be as long as thirty years, depending upon the source of the shortfall.

the basic choices that defined-contribution plan participants must make. ERISA's major changes to the private pension system were arguably its participation (nondiscrimination) and vesting requirements. The vesting rules remain in place, while the measures to ease the administration of the nondiscrimination rules have mainly benefited defined-contribution plans.

In sum, the most recent regulatory changes in the United States have generally been in the right direction – from the point of view of the plan sponsor – but more so for defined-contribution than for defined-benefit plans.

Any answer to the second question – whether uncertainty regarding the future shape of the regulatory framework has increased or not – is inevitably conjectural. In the United States, there has been considerable uncertainty over the legality of conversions of final-salary plans to hybrid schemes. The Pension Protection Act addresses this issue prospectively, which should clear the way for new conversions, even if it does not deal with the ones that have been stalled. Consequently, frozen plans are more likely to become hybrid plans than to be terminated. Other recent changes can be seen as addressing ERISA's more problematic features, and in the particular case of accounting rules, bowing to the inevitable, and moving to a consistent mark-to-market valuation principle. Consequently, they might not be judged too critically by plan sponsors. The judgment that regulatory reform has overall favored defined-contribution plans should stand.

In the United Kingdom, the regulatory framework has been undergoing revision for some time. Over the past quarter century, various laws have been enacted to ease vesting requirements, ensure the equal treatment of men and women, and discourage the accumulation of excessive plan surpluses (see Appendix 1, United Kingdom). The tax regime applying to pension funds underwent a swingeing change in 1997 that entailed an increase in their tax liability of £5 billion ($8 billion). Nonetheless, the regulatory framework was and is less complex than the U.S. framework in one important respect: British plans do not have to cope with nondiscrimination rules.

The Pensions Act of 2004 has brought about a major change in the British regulatory framework. It revamped the regulations governing funding by replacing the minimum funding requirement of the 1995 Pensions Act with a requirement that is better tailored to the situation of particular plans, but which is perceived as more rigorous on the whole.[13] The Act also increases

---

[13] Under the new rules, trustees, in assessing the appropriate level of technical provisions, are expected to take into account such factors as the ability and willingness of the employer to provision for future events and the plan's maturity [i.e., the average duration of its accrued liabilities (The Pensions Regulator n.d.)].

the fiduciary responsibilities that trustees bear, and is thought by some observers to have increased the potential for conflict between plan trustees and corporate management (Blake 2006a; Byrne et al. 2006), and to have impaired the quality of pension finance decision making. Other measures have been aimed at improving funding and investment decisions. In addition, the responsibilities and powers of the new regulatory authority (the Pensions Regulator) are greater than those of its predecessor.

However necessary these reforms may have been, the regulatory burden imposed on British defined-benefit plans is now heavier than it used to be. Moreover, the increase in the burden on final-salary plans appears to be greater than that for defined-contribution plans, where funding issues are less relevant and fiduciary concerns less acute.

The pace of change in the regulatory framework may have contributed to the decline between 2000 and 2007 from 4.1 million to 1.3 million in the active membership of open private-sector defined-benefit plans (U.K. Office for National Statistics 2008). The new institutions and rules introduced by the Pensions Act of 2004 have not been in effect for long, and there appears to be considerable uncertainty about how they will function. The Pension Regulator has spent its initial period of operation in formulating and disseminating its position on basic features of the new approach, and notably in helping trustees of underfunded plans who are obliged to formulate recovery plans to understand the funding framework. A survey carried out for the Pension Regulator in November of 2006 found that 61 percent of defined-benefit/hybrid plan trustees polled had a good or very good understanding of the funding framework (The Pension Regulator 2007). This was an improvement over the previous survey, carried out about 18 months earlier, which reported a figure of 43 percent, but suggests that many trustees have yet to rise to the top of the learning curve. Similarly, there appears to be some uncertainty about the finances of the Pension Protection Fund, which had to raise the risk-based component of its levy very substantially for the 2007/2008 year. The still uncertain regulatory environment must combine with the increase in the regulatory burden to incline plan sponsors to freeze their final- or average-salary plans.

In Japan, significant changes in the structure of occupational pensions have taken place together with reforms of the regulatory framework that were intended to adapt pension funds to a more liberalized financial environment, and to bring certain practices into line with international best practice. These reforms have taken place against the backdrop of a very difficult financial environment (the "lost decade" of 1990–2000). The Employee Pension Funds (EPF) became more and more unfunded in 1990–2000 because of the deep decline in share prices and fall in interest rates. The ensuing losses prompted the government to intervene with measures that would allow the EPFs to "substitute" that part of their employees' pensions that the government had previously substituted out to them. The legislation enacted in 2001 created two varieties of defined-benefit plans and two types of defined-contribution plans – one for individuals, the other for employees of corporations (see Appendix 1, Japan). These new plans are subject to tighter regulatory oversight than their predecessors were.

Meanwhile, the rules applying to pension-plan accounting and investment were being revised, as they were in other countries, to bring them more into line with international best practice. In 1995, the prudent-person rule replaced the quantitative restrictions that had applied to asset composition. In the next few years, mark-to-market accounting was adopted, and pension fund balances were included in the balance sheets of their corporate sponsors. The projected benefit-obligation method (like the projected unit-credit method) of accounting for liabilities was also introduced, and pension plans may now hire or consult with investment advisory services.

These changes to pension fund accounting might have made the EPF and the defined-benefit corporate pension plans (DBCPP) somewhat less attractive relative to defined-contribution plans, but how much so is hard to say. However, some of the other changes (or decisions not to change) may have reduced the cost of maintaining defined-benefit plans. The adoption of the prudent-person rule could, in principle, have made it easier for pension fund asset managers to achieve a given rate of return at an acceptable degree of risk. By not liberalizing the very conservative vesting and portability rules that applied to the older plans, the reform may have prevented an increase in plan costs.[14]

The advent of defined-contribution plans has not yet dented the dominant position of defined-benefit plans. Part of the tepid popularity of defined-contribution plans may reflect the current low annual limit on tax-deductible contributions of ¥276,000, equivalent to about $2900 that applies when the employer offers another plan. This could make defined-contribution plans unattractive to better-paid employees and, as well, to employees at all income levels if the low limit caused managerial fees to be high, because that could make the net rate of return to contributors uneconomically low (Clark and Mitchell 2003).

---

[14] Given the typically long tenure of Japanese workers, a change in the law might have had little impact on the cost of sponsoring a plan, but lifetime employment is becoming less common than it used to be.

Some inertia is built into the system by the requirement that the replacement of an EPF by a corporate defined-contribution plan requires the consent of a union or person representing the majority of the plan sponsor's employees (Morito, n.d.). The poor performance of the stock market for most of the recent past may also discourage the spread of personal plans, or even corporate defined-contribution plans, although a corporate plan must offer a fund with a guaranteed rate of return along with at least two other funds. In sum, the spread of defined-contribution plans has probably been inhibited by their relatively unfavorable tax treatment, the innate conservatism of both Japanese investors and trade unions, and the continued high rate of long-term job tenure. The limits on contributions to both forms of the defined-contribution plan are expected to be raised, which should address, partly if not fully, at least one of these inhibiting factors.

In Germany, the changes in the structure of the occupational pension system are similar in some respects to the changes that have taken place in Japan, especially regarding the passage of legislation authorizing defined-contribution plans. (Like Japan, Germany also enacted legislation to create individual pension plans – hybrids that look like defined-contribution plans.) For our purposes, the key issue is the implications of German regulatory reform of employer-provided pensions for the relative attractiveness of defined-benefit plans. However, one issue to be kept in mind is the significance of any regulatory reform given the continuing importance in Germany of book-reserve plans, which are not directly supervised, and whose funding is not normally directly affected by financial market fluctuations.[15]

The major change to the regulatory framework was the move toward risk-based assessment of financial institutions, including pension plans, under the aegis of the Federal Financial Supervisory Authority (BaFin). Risk-based supervision meant a move away from reliance on quantitative restrictions, and could, in principle, give pension fund managers more flexibility in their asset allocation decisions. Its introduction does not have to entail any increase in the relative cost of sponsoring a defined-benefit plan.

That said, even if the only change to the occupational pension landscape in Germany had been the introduction of defined-contribution plans, a strong preference for these plans could normally be expected to increase their coverage of the labor force substantially. In fact, after a slow start that some commentators attributed to excessive registration and certification

---

[15] In 2004, book reserves accounted for over 58 percent of the total reserves of the five types of occupational pensions (Oster 2006).

requirements and limited distribution options, about 11 million personal "Riester" pensions – about half the number of employees covered by occupational pensions and one-quarter of the labor force – had been contracted by end-2007. The data do not permit a breakdown of members of employer-provided pension plans by the type of plan covering them.

The quite respectable growth in the number of personal pensions and any inroads into occupational pension coverage that defined-contribution pensions have made owe a lot to tax incentives, however. Both the personal and corporate forms of the defined-contribution pension enjoy a tax reduction *cum* subsidy that, for low-income workers, can practically equal the contribution. It remains high even for the better paid (Börsch-Supan and Wilke 2006, 596). This feature of the German reform contrasts distinctly with Japan's tax treatment of contributions to defined-contribution plans. Another very important difference is that personal Riester pensions are mostly not replacing, but supplementing, the older forms of occupational pensions. In sum, apart from the impact of the highly favorable tax treatment of the new pensions, recent changes to the regulatory framework do not appear to be tilting the playing field in favor of defined-contribution plans in Germany.

In the Netherlands, the existing regulatory framework was reinforced by the introduction of a risk-based approach to the financial supervision of pension plans in 2007. The key features of the new approach, which were described in Chapter 4, are a solvency test, and a "continuity analysis" in which funds are expected to project their financial position over a period of 15 years (OECD 2005, 34–5).

A policy of unconditional indexation of pensions requires that the tests be conducted with a measure of liabilities in real terms, that is, discounted using a real rate of interest. With a policy of conditional indexation, a nominal discount rate may be used. This means that funding requirements for a plan that does not guarantee that pensions will be 100 percent indexed can be significantly smaller than those of a plan where full indexation is automatic (OECD 2005).

The impact of the new regulatory framework on the relative attractiveness of defined-benefit and defined-contribution plans must depend on the stringency of the solvency test and on the willingness of active and retired plan members and their representatives to accept less than full indexation. The Netherlands' pension plans tend to maintain a high solvency ratio, but given the lack of experience with the new framework, it is premature to draw definite conclusions. If plan parameters are, in fact, flexible, the risk to employers of sponsoring a defined-benefit plan is undoubtedly reduced.

In Canada, the regulatory framework for occupational pensions has changed little in two decades. The changes to the defined-benefit legal framework introduced earlier may not have been revolutionary in their impact, but could still have contributed to the slow but steady growth of the share of defined-contribution plans in the private sector, especially among smaller employers. This said, the features that the law requires – such as a survivor pension and rights to a deferred pension – are fairly standard, and many plans would undoubtedly have already incorporated them. Canada's tax system treats defined-benefit and defined-contribution plans (and private saving) equally, and there are no nondiscrimination laws to comply with.

More recently, the issue of the *ownership* of plan surpluses has come to the fore. The way this issue is resolved may well affect the attractiveness of defined-benefit plans to sponsors. The relevant law stipulates that surpluses exceeding the statutory requirements are to be shared with plan participants (Tuer and Woodman 2005). Excess surpluses are also subject to tax. In 2004, a Canadian Supreme Court ruling on the disposition of a surplus upon a partial windup of a plan may have heightened concern among some employers about what has been termed "asymmetric" risk, which applies when plan sponsors are solely responsible for plan deficits, but must share surpluses. Its significance may become clearer in the next few years. Its impact on plan sponsors would depend in part on how likely an event partial windups are. On balance, this unresolved issue would tip the balance slightly in favor of defined-contribution plans.

In Sweden, the major changes to the Swedish regulatory framework have been the move to a prudent-person rule, and the adoption of a risk-appraisal system based on a "traffic light" model. The latter was adopted in 2006, and has undergone some modifications since then. These changes would not seem to tip the balance for or against defined-benefit plans. The swing away from defined-benefit plans dates from the reform of the public pension system, which introduced a notional (nonfinancial) defined-contribution system with a genuine individual-accounts component.

Of the three remaining countries, where defined-contribution plans are dominant, the regulatory and supervisory framework has changed the most in Australia. The implementation of the Superannuation Guarantee in 1992 led to a huge increase in the coverage of occupational pensions, prompted the passage of new laws that revamped the regulatory framework, and assigned responsibility for regulation to the Australian Prudential Regulatory Authority (APRA), which oversees the whole financial system. The debate preceding the passage of the new regulations addressed very basic issues, such as the role and responsibility of trustees and the need for regulation of investments. The security of individual accounts and the adequacy of financial literacy, given the role of self-directed investment, are major concerns. The new framework would not have tilted the playing field against defined-benefit pensions, although the more recent move to international accounting standards might conceivably have reduced the attractiveness of those defined-benefit plans that remain.

In Switzerland, no major change in the structure of occupational pensions has taken place in the past two decades, and recent reforms to the regulatory and supervisory framework have been incremental. In 2004, for example, reporting from and disclosure by pension funds and foundations was improved, and, in 2005, IAS 19 accounting rules were adopted for all internationally active companies (International Monetary Fund 2006). These revisions would not have affected the relative attractiveness of defined-benefit plans. In Denmark, too, the regulatory landscape has not changed significantly in the past 10–15 years.

In sum, the tide of regulatory reform has contributed to the decline of the traditional defined-benefit plan in the United States and the United Kingdom. It probably has had a marginal impact in the same direction in Canada. In the other countries, apart from Germany, where the very favorable tax treatment of the new defined-contribution pensions has undoubtedly boosted their popularity, regulatory change has not had a discernable impact on the relative importance of defined-benefit plans.

Pension Insurance

This section deals with the question of how the design of a guarantee on a defined-benefit pension and its financing might affect the behavior of plan sponsors and members. It concentrates on the experience of the U.S. Pension Benefit Guaranty Corporation (PBGC), which is the longest and best documented of the group.

Any insurance scheme entails a potential problem of moral hazard, and the PBGC is no exception. For single-employer plans, the annual fee has two parts: a levy of $34 per plan member, and $9 for each $1,000 (both as of 2009) of unfunded vested benefits. The second, risk-based component implies that a plan sponsor pays a penalty of 0.9 percent on its unfunded liabilities. At this level the rate creates little disincentive against underfunding or risk taking. Consequently, the PBGC's insurance can be compared (with pardonable exaggeration) to a car insurance policy that charges good and bad drivers alike the same premium. In addition, as Wilcox (2006) points out, the member-based component favors generous pension plans, adequately funded or not, as well as older plans.

The member-based fee is effectively a tax on sound plans, albeit, at about 0.1 percent of the average economy-wide salary, not an onerous one. In principle, it would tend, other things equal, to discourage sound plans – which would regard the premium simply as a tax – and increase the risk of insolvency of remaining plans. This said, the cap placed on the value of the benefit that the PBGC will replace ($54,000 in 2009) creates strong incentives for the better-paid members of a pension plan to police its investment policies, a task that would be made easier if plan members were unionized.

It is not possible to run a counterfactual experiment to determine what the rate of plan insolvencies in the United States since the creation of the PBGC would have been without any guarantee, or with one that was differently structured. Nonetheless, some tentative conclusions may be drawn from the PBGC's record. The pattern of plan claims on the PBGC is highly skewed and very concentrated by industry. A comparatively small number of plans in the air transport and primary metal products industries accounts for a disproportionate share of total claims. Specifically, during the first 33 years of the PBGC's existence (1975–2007), these two industries accounted for almost three-quarters of the total gross claims of $35 billion made under the single-employer program during the period (PBGC 2007). Pension plans from other sectors of the economy made claims during this period of $9.2 billion, or about $280 million per year. This amounts to a tiny fraction of the assets of the plans of the sectors concerned, even when the PBGC's figures are converted from nominal to constant dollars.

Some of these claims on the PBGC may have resulted from overly risky investing and a failure to match assets with liabilities, which the PBGC's insurance may have encouraged. However, in light of the cycles that the U.S. economy traversed during this period, many claims must have been the result of plan-sponsor bankruptcies that had nothing to do with the plan's management or its investment strategy. The skewed pattern of claims by industry could have been expected, given the difficulties experienced by the airlines and steel manufacturers, but the size of the claims made by the rest of the economy raises some doubts as to the significance of moral hazard.[16]

Cost Pressures and Technological Change

The consequences of globalization for manufacturing in the industrial countries have been the subject of heated, if not always enlightened, debate.

---

[16] The existence of the PBCG, even if it does not promote unsound pension-plan investing, does make the taxpayer a partner in bankruptcy. Campbell and Viceira (2006) note the analogy between the PBGC and an option for the sponsor to sell the plan's assets.

There is little doubt, however, that the competition from China and other emerging-market economies has put pressure on manufacturing companies in the industrialized world. Another source of pressure peculiar to American companies has been the seemingly inexorable increase in the costs of health care. Health-care costs are also rising in other countries but they are not as high to begin with and are largely financed through the tax system. The effect of rising health costs on producers' costs in Europe and elsewhere is, as a result, less direct than it is in the United States.

Taking the hypotheses of globalization-related competitive pressures and rising health-care costs at face value, the question to pose is why these pressures would affect pension plans, and defined-benefit plans in particular, more than they would affect other fringe benefits or take-home pay. One plausible answer is that workers are concerned first and foremost with their current standard of living. Preserving health-care benefits at the expense of pensions entails no immediate sacrifice if the pensions of workers nearing retirement are not affected: It does not reduce take-home pay.

Cost pressures could also increase the relative attractiveness of defined-contribution plans. Rather than change the parameters of a defined-benefit plan to reduce its costs to the employer, a company trying to cope with intensifying cost pressures may find it less contentious to freeze its existing defined-benefit plan (to new if not to tenured employees), and create a new hybrid or defined-contribution plan. Depending on the new plan's parameters (contribution rates, accrual rates, the terms of survivors' pensions, etc.), a company that switches its new employees if not all employees to a defined-contribution plan can reduce the costs of its pension plan without affecting a worker's take-home pay. Even if the employer's average contribution to the plan is unaffected, the switch reduces the corporation's exposure to longevity, investment, and interest risks at a stroke. This is exactly what has happened in the United States, the United Kingdom, and, to a lesser extent, in Canada.

It is technically feasible to reduce the cost of defined-benefit plans by changing their parameters, provided the changes have prospective and not retroactive effect. This more direct tactic would, however, make the reductions in benefits more apparent than they would be when new or even tenured employees join or move to a defined-contribution plan. It is worth pondering whether the consequences of the indirect approach are well understood by all plan participants.

The Risks Posed by Basic Uncertainty

The discussion to this point has been concerned with specific supply-side influences. However, the decline of the traditional pension has also been influenced by more general forces. The terms of a traditional pension cannot, as previous chapters have stressed, be modified easily. A plan's liabilities cannot be scaled back just because its sponsor's profit margins and market share are eroding. The costs of a traditional plan are both largely fixed and unpredictable.

The experience of General Motors seems an object lesson in the perils of overly costly pension plans, not to mention corporate hubris. Although the cost of its pensions had been steadily increasing with increases in the longevity of its employees, General Motors adopted a very generous early retirement program in 1973 and then raised pensions across the board in 1979. In the ensuing years, General Motors found that it had saddled itself with substantial additional labor costs that undermined its ability to compete (Lowenstein 2008, 40).[17] Escalating health-care costs were also taking a toll. As long as General Motors was the biggest member of an oligopoly, it could pass on most of its cost increases to its customers. By the 1980s, such behavior was no longer possible. Similar stories can be told of other large companies in troubled economic sectors, although other companies may not have increased benefits to the same extent. The risks these companies faced simply could not be hedged.

It is not surprising that a troubled corporation might come to see its pension plans as a financial albatross that would bring the whole company down if they were not closed. But what about companies with a healthy bottom line: Would established companies want to close their traditional plans, and would new companies decide not to open plans in the first place? For a thriving company, freezing its plan or adopting a defined-contribution plan rather than a defined-benefit plan could be viewed as a sensible precaution, to avoid giving hostages to fortune. This being said, business has always been uncertain, which raises the question of why the wave of plan closures is happening now, rather than 30 years ago?

The argument based on general uncertainty about what the future will bring can explain some of the shift away from traditional plans, especially those of established businesses facing a serious competitive threat. An established company may have difficulty scaling back a traditional pension, and will instead opt to freeze it. This is not true of a young and expanding company, which could protect itself from excessive risk by introducing a traditional plan with a modest target replacement rate, and complement it with

---

[17] Lowenstein (2008, 47) cites a 1981 study by an independent actuary that concluded that benefits had increased much faster than basic wages in the auto, rubber, and steel industries. In the case of the Ford Motor Company, benefits were estimated to have increased tenfold since 1950, while wages increased fivefold.

a defined-contribution plan. It could also introduce a defined-contribution plan with guarantees. Depending on the extent of the guarantee, this would reduce the sponsor's risk but give plan members some of the benefits of a traditional plan.

The shift away from traditional plans has occurred in both expanding and declining industries, and in both profitable and struggling companies, which suggests that the inflexibility of traditional plans in the face of basic changes to the economic environment is not the whole story.

The Employment Bargain from the Employer's Point of View

As Chapter 2 discussed, pensions, in the eyes of their sponsors, have always been more than just a means of promoting their employees' long-term welfare by obliging them to save for retirement. Some economists have claimed that changes in the organization of work have reduced the motivational utility employers perceive in a traditional standard pension plan. Workers these days are viewed as accumulating technical know-how that is less specific to their particular employer. In other words, technical knowledge that may be useful to many employers is becoming more marketable than know-how specific to one firm, and consequently of limited usefulness to other firms. Friedberg and Owyang (2005) test a model of labor market developments in the United States and conclude that a trend to less "firm-specific" human capital formation explains part of the declining role of defined-benefit plans.

Analysis of the Demand-Side Influences

Declining Tenure

The changing workplace relationship and the decline in long-term employment have probably reduced the attractiveness of the conventional form of the defined-benefit plan to employees as well. The typical final- or average-salary plan is designed to penalize plan members who do not stay until retirement. As Chapter 2 discussed, the ultimate value of the benefit that a departing worker takes away will likely be substantially less than the benefit he or she would have earned for the initial years of service had the worker stayed on. Consequently, an increase in the risk of being laid off would diminish the attractiveness of defined-benefit plans. Even if the risk of being laid off has not increased, a deliberate strategy of changing employers could, for many, be a more efficient way of increasing their skills and marketability than staying put with the same employer.

The changing composition of the labor force may also be playing a role. Aaronson and Coronado (2005) find that that the increase in the number of women in the labor force – in particular, women in dual income couples or women with children – in the United States will have increased the attractiveness of defined-contribution plans to employees, since these workers are likely to be more mobile and to have shorter employment spells. Munnell (2006) cites several U.S. studies from the 1990s that find that changes in industry composition, firm size, and unionization (see the following) account for a large share of the shift away from defined-benefit plans.

Long-term tenure – as measured by the share of employees of a given age group who have worked for ten years or more with the same employer – has been on the decline in the OECD's industrial countries for some years, and the differences among countries in the share of the workforce with long tenure is striking (Table 6.2).[18] Long-term tenure is lowest in the two economies that have experienced the most substantial erosion in the share of defined-benefit plans. The United States is a clear outlier, with less than one-third of the workforce aged 25 to 54 having worked for their current employer for ten years or more. About two-thirds of the workforce aged 55 to 64 had long-term tenure (at least ten years), but this ratio has also been declining. Long-term tenure is pretty much the rule in the United Kingdom, with some 64 percent of the workforce aged 55 to 64 having worked for the same employer for ten years or more, but it is becoming less common. Long-term tenure is even higher in continental Europe, especially Germany where it actually increased between 1996 and 2005. Tenure rates in Canada, where the share of defined-benefit plans in coverage has not declined as much as it has in the United States and the United Kingdom, are also high.[19]

Interpreting these figures is not straightforward, although they appear to bear out the importance of long tenure for traditional pension plans. Declining tenure undoubtedly makes these plans less attractive to their participants, but it also improves the financial position of the plan, other things equal, given the penalty that early separation imposes on participants. Interpretation is also complicated by the fact that the closure of

---

[18] The OECD's database, from which Table 6.2's estimates are drawn, did not have estimates for Australia or Japan.

[19] Some economists have relied on a measure of average tenure. In the United States, average tenure has not declined in recent years (Copeland 2007). A stable average is consistent with declining long-term tenure if the share of the workforce with a shorter period of tenure, such as five years, is increasing at the expense of very short tenure. Arguably, the prevalence of long tenure is a better indicator of the attractiveness of defined-benefit pensions.

Table 6.2. *Selected OECD countries: Percentage share of employed persons by age with tenure of ten years or more*

	Age group	1996	1998	2000	2002	2004	2005
Canada	25 to 54	58.2	61.0	64.9	65.2	61.7	59.8
	55 to 64	78.2	78.6	79.3	79.1	78.1	77.1
Denmark	25 to 54	53.2	52.3	49.5	46.3	43.2	42.3
	55 to 64	76.9	80.6	76.1	76.9	75.1	76.0
Germany	25 to 54	50.3	50.3	54.4	56.9	55.4	54.9
	55 to 64	77.8	76.7	78.7	81.2	81.5	80.3
Netherlands	25 to 54	50.4	53.1	54.7	53.3	46.4	46.2
	55 to 64	81.2	84.7	83.5	83.5	79.9	79.4
Sweden	25 to 54	54.1	59.5	61.4	54.8	49.9	48.9
	55 to 64	80.3	82.1	84.1	81.2	79.7	77.4
Switzerland	25 to 54	44.8	44.6	50.4	52.6	48.1	47.2
	55 to 64	74.9	76.7	78.3	77.6	76.9	76.1
United States	25 to 54	29.8	29.2	29.3	27.8	27.2	...
	55 to 64	53.1	53.5	53.1	52.3	50.5	...
United Kingdom	25 to 54	49.8	48.9	50.7	48.8	45.5	44.4
	55 to 64	68.5	66.6	67.4	66.1	64.4	64.0

Source: OECD, U.S. Bureau of Labor Statistics.

pension plans might lead to early separations, so that the causality runs in both directions.

Whatever the precise relationship between tenure and the choice of pension plan, it is pretty clear that in the United States, reliance on a series of traditional defined-benefit plans, if that were feasible, would substantially penalize many in the labor force even with the improved vesting that ERISA introduced. This problem is not as acute in the other countries.

Shortsightedness of Plan Participants
Shortsighted people discount the future at a high rate, and there is solid evidence that many people are shortsighted. One study, by Warner and Pleeter (2001), is particularly telling. It analyzes the decisions made by a group of downsized U.S.-government employees among various possible severance-benefit packages. The study finds that their choices between lump-sum packages and term annuities implied a discount rate of as high as 17 percent. Other studies, including Laibner (2006) and Frederick et al. (2002) draw similar conclusions.

As noted, a high discount rate can influence the choice between defined-benefit and defined-contribution plans when there are differences in the timing of payment of the benefits, or in the range of permissible contribution rates. With a defined-contribution plan, the benefit is typically a lump sum, and with a defined-benefit plan, it is an annuity (although a lump sum may be an option). Faced with a choice between two plans with the same contribution rate and the same expected present value of benefits when these are discounted at a market rate of interest, the short-sighted person will pick the defined-contribution plan, because he or she will discount future benefits at a subjective rate of discount well above the market rate.

For our purposes, however, the key question is whether shortsightedness helps explain the erosion in the position of defined-benefit plans. If shortsightedness is no more common than it was 20 years ago, the answer might seem to be no. It is difficult enough to measure subjective rates of return, let alone measure changes in them. Anecdotally, one can point to the consumerism that marks (or mars) every industrial country, and to a general decline in saving rates. It is, however, possible to explain the decline in saving rates without having to drag in shortsightedness.[20]

Nonetheless, some of the shift away from defined-benefit plans might result from the interaction of shortsightedness and changes in the options available to plan participants. In Germany, there is relatively little choice regarding the annuitization of the balances in an occupational, hybrid pension or a personal pension: A minimum of 70 percent must be annuitized. In the United States, participants in 401(k) plans typically can take the whole of their accumulated balance as a lump sum, and some access to the balance is possible before retirement, which is not the case with the new German personal pensions. The flexibility of arrangements in the United States suggests that shortsightedness may have a bigger role to play there than it does elsewhere.

Falling Rates of Unionization

Declining rates of unionization might also have worked to reduce the prevalence of defined-benefit plans. Ghilarducci (2006), in an analysis of developments in the United States where the rate of unionization has been declining for some time and is the lowest of the group of ten countries, argues that the group processes that unions foster work to overcome shortsightedness and

---

[20] For example, see de Serres and Pelgrin (2003).

denial (of the need to make provision for the future). Union management would also tend to prefer defined-benefit plans to the extent that union representatives or staff help manage the plans. The impact of the decline of unionization would extend beyond the companies directly concerned, because it would reduce the pressure on nonunionized firms to match the fringe benefits their formerly unionized competitors would offer.

The higher rate of unionization in Canada – including the public sector, the rate in Canada was about 30 percent in 2006, compared with 12.5 percent in the United States in 2005 – may help explain the greater staying power of defined-benefit plans (Brown and Liu 2001, 75). Brown and Liu maintain that Canadian unions emphasize employment security and defined-benefit coverage. The rate of unionization in Canada now slightly exceeds the rate in the United Kingdom, where it has been falling rapidly.

There is no straightforward relationship between the strength of the union movement and the role of the defined-benefit plan in other countries. In Denmark, for example, the union movement is relatively strong despite the apparent dominance of defined-contribution plans; the same is true of Sweden. In both countries, however, the rate of coverage of the occupational pension system remains high, and the national pension system is relatively generous. In addition, and as already noted, a guarantee feature gives Danish plans a definite defined-benefit cast.

Distrust of the Employer

Saying anything concrete about attitudes of trust or distrust is extremely difficult. One recent U.S. opinion poll does suggest that there is much distrust either of the institution of a defined-benefit plan or of the employers who sponsor them. The poll, which was conducted in August of 2006, asked respondents whether they would prefer a defined-benefit plan, where the employer managed the money and promised a "sum certain" upon retirement, or a defined-contribution plan, like a 401(k) plan, that would be self-managed. Some 79 percent of those polled chose the defined-contribution option. In response to a question regarding sources of income in retirement, only 4 percent of respondents aged 18 to 34 stated that they would rely most on an "employer-based" pension (*Wall Street Journal*, Personal Finance Poll 2006). Of respondents aged 45 to 54, 16 percent would rely most on an employer-based pension. The huge losses suffered by defined-contribution plan members since 2008 might well cause these preferences to change.

In the United Kingdom, a study for the Pension Commission of general knowledge and attitudes toward pension and pension reform found that there was widespread distrust of employer-provided and private pensions

(Bunt, Koroglu, and O'Donnell, n.d.). Whether such mistrust would reduce the attractiveness of defined-benefit plans more than defined-contribution plans is very hard to say. Finally, a more general survey of opinions toward globalization and related economic issues in the United States and five European countries, including Germany and the United Kingdom, carried out in July of 2007 found little admiration and respect for corporate leaders in any of the three countries. Such attitudes would arguably tilt wage and salary earners toward defined-contribution or personal saving plans, because of the greater degree of control over saving and investment (*Financial Times* 2007).

A Summing Up

The drastic decline in the role of the defined-benefit plan in the United States and the United Kingdom is the result of declining job tenure (more in the United States than in the United Kingdom); a complex regulatory and tax regime that burdens defined-benefit plans more than it does defined-contribution plans (especially in the United States); an uncertain regulatory environment (in the United Kingdom); a lack of flexibility in the design of defined-benefit plans that makes freezing an attractive option even when a modified plan might serve a company's workforce better than a defined-contribution plan; and a shortsighted attitude to saving combined with a misunderstanding of the properties of defined-benefit plans, which may owe something to the decline in the mediating role of union representatives.

The slower pace of decline of the defined-benefit plan in Canada results from less burdensome regulation, a more level fiscal playing field, and perhaps the greater rate of unionization of the Canadian labor market. In Japan, defined-contribution plans are spreading, but a combination of a low contribution limit and possibly the perceived low rate of return to self-investment is preventing them from spreading further. The potential veto power of labor unions with respect to plan conversions may also be having an effect. The comparatively rapid spread of both employer-provided (and personal) Riester pensions in Germany must owe something to the very favorable tax treatment they receive. In neither Japan nor Germany is the regulatory burden borne by defined-benefit plans obviously disproportionate. In addition, in both countries early distributions from defined-contribution plans are forbidden, and in Germany a minimum benefit applies (Berner 2006). These features give defined-contribution plans in both countries a defined-benefit character that they do not have in either the United States or the United Kingdom. By reducing the difference between defined-benefit and defined-contribution plans, they reduce the attraction of switching from the former to the latter. Finally, the prevalence of long job tenure is much higher in both countries than it is in the United States, and higher than it is in the United Kingdom.

In the Netherlands, another country where the defined-benefit plan remains predominant, the regulatory playing field is level. The participation of unions gives flexibility to the defined-benefit plan that it does not have elsewhere. Sweden looks like an anomaly; it has a high rate of unionization, a high percentage of workers with long tenure, and no obvious regulatory bias against defined-benefit plans. Its move away from them in the past ten years may seem curious. This may simply reflect the government's success in convincing unions of the merits of the reform of the national pension system. In addition, the private sector is covered by only two occupational plans, and when one of them converted to defined-contribution, a demonstration effect might have been created. Palme (2005) argues that it is "… potentially very expensive to run defined-benefit plans on top of defined-contribution."

Switzerland's situation may be tougher to decipher, because the share of defined-benefit plans has undoubtedly fallen substantially, and it may not be obvious why. Regulatory complexity has not been an issue, and average job tenure is not low. Some, if not all, of the mystery may be resolved when we remember that two features of Swiss occupational pension plans give them a distinctly defined-benefit character. These are the minimum guarantee on earnings of accumulated contributions, and the state-prescribed rate of conversion of account balances into annuities, which applies to the entire balance. It is not facetious to say that the move away from defined-benefit plans in Switzerland was not so great a move after all.

7

Policies to Address the Decline of the
Traditional Pension

Introduction

This chapter has two parts. The first and longer part addresses the policy implications of the decline of the traditional pension. The second part evaluates recent reforms of first-tier coverage and briefly discusses the need for reform of employer-provided public-sector pensions.

The first part begins by considering how the traditional pension might be partly revived by reducing its scale or by making changes to its structure. It then examines the potential role of hybrids as alternatives. With the analysis presented in Chapter 2 of the consequences of do-it-yourself longevity insurance as a benchmark, this chapter then assesses the potential value of two "add-ons" to defined-contribution plans developed in the United States that aim to address the shortcomings of these plans at the distribution phase. It also discusses the issues surrounding the setting of defaults on the annuitization of the account balances of defined-contribution plans.

The preceding chapters have chronicled the pressures assailing the traditional pension in the Anglo-Saxon countries, and the growing role of defined-contribution plans in the others. The decline of the traditional pension has so far been confined to the private sector. However, the finances of many public-sector employer-provided pensions have become seriously unbalanced, and the political pressures to freeze or close these plans may intensify if they come to be seen as an unjustified privilege of government employees.

Although the traditional plan may not have been the perfect vehicle for the second tier of the pension systems of the Anglo-Saxon countries, it provided valuable longevity insurance and boosted the standard of living in retirement of tens if not hundreds of millions of workers. Policies that might reverse some of the decline of the traditional pension, encourage hardier versions of it, or develop alternatives to it are undoubtedly necessary.

The Traditional Pension Plan's Role in Broadening Second-Tier Coverage

Policies to deal with the consequences of the decline of the traditional pension need to be seen as part of a broader policy that tackles the inadequate coverage of the second tier. Even if the traditional pension, possibly modified in certain respects, or an acceptable substitute for it could regain all or more than all of the ground it has lost in the low-coverage countries, the coverage of the second tier in these countries would still be a long way from universal. In the circumstances, policies aimed at reviving the traditional pension or finding a suitable substitute should not be drawn up without considering their implications for the broader issue of second-tier coverage.

The precise scope and content of policies to restore the traditional pension to its former role must depend on the approach taken to the objective of broader second-tier coverage. Speaking rather generally, second-tier coverage can be broadened in one of three ways: making coverage mandatory, encouraging broader coverage by means of default setting, and enhancing the tax preferences given to contractual saving. These strategies are not mutually exclusive. Even if plan participation is not voluntary for most employees, tax preferences can mitigate the sacrifice that some employees would see themselves obliged to make. Favorable tax treatment would be an added attraction with a policy that relies on default setting.

Mandatory Coverage

Australia and Switzerland implemented broad coverage by requiring employers to offer their employees a pension plan that satisfied certain requirements, including a minimum contribution rate or a range of rates. These conditions do not have to rule out any particular plan type, and both countries permit defined-benefit as well as defined-contribution plans. The type of plan that qualifies could be limited, however, to the traditional pension plan and other defined-benefit plans, to defined-contribution plans, or to a type of hybrid.

There is no instance as yet of a country with mandatory second-tier coverage that limited the qualifying plan type to a defined-benefit plan. The limited evidence of countries with mandatory second tiers together with certain features of traditional plans suggest that mandatory coverage would probably not be successful if only traditional plans could qualify. Traditional plans would be very costly for small employers, unless they were to be heavily subsidized or unless their employees could join multi-employer plans. This might work well for some occupations and industries and not for others. Even large employers in the low-coverage countries, as previous chapters have emphasized, have been moving away from the traditional pension. Making the traditional pension the required form of pension would also be politically contentious. It might have supporters among working people, but would face stiff opposition from employers.

A more promising approach would be for the government to require employers to offer at least one of either type of plan while leaving the choice of plan to the employer. If employers were to choose to offer a traditional plan, it would be necessary to have some way of ascertaining that the plan offered the same potential benefits as defined-contribution plans. Parity of benefits could be achieved in two ways: (1) by requiring that the sum of the rates of employee contributions and *regular* contributions from the employer at least equaled the contribution rate set for defined-contribution plans and (2) by requiring that plans achieve a minimum replacement rate.[1] In addition, there would have to be safeguards to ensure adequate portability, speedy vesting, and benefit preservation. Meeting these requirements would be less onerous for employers in some countries than others. The experience of Australia suggests that the defined-contribution plan would be likely to crowd out the traditional plan. Simply suffering the existence of traditional plans would not necessarily lead to their revival. Other policies, discussed in what follows, would be necessary for that.

The guaranteed retirement account (GRA), a recent proposal by Professor Ghilarducci to introduce a compulsory second tier in the United States, explicitly provides for traditional pension plans.[2] Its design would actually encourage the adoption of defined-contribution plans rather than traditional plans. The plans adopted under a GRA arrangement would be effectively hybrids, with some similarity to Swiss plans. The GRA would be funded by a 5 percent contribution rate that could be split between the employer and the employee. The government would guarantee a minimum rate of return on the accounts of 3 percent. A traditional pension plan would qualify if the combined contribution rates were at least 5 percent.[3]

---

[1] Achieving parity also requires that the two plan types are treated equally for tax purposes.

[2] See Forman (2006, 242) for an account of this proposal's antecedents.

[3] Ghilarducci (2008) does not explicitly address the issues of portability, benefit preservation, and vesting. If the benefits earned by participants in traditional plans are to be on

If a reform along the lines of the GRA were ever introduced, it might well prompt further freezes of traditional plans, because in key respects it is closer to a defined-benefit than a defined-contribution plan.[4] In particular, the GRA would offer an indexed annuity, provided by the Social Security Administration (SSA), and the guarantee feature would reduce the advantage that traditional pension plans have regarding investment risk.

Although it would be very difficult to build a compulsory second tier around a traditional defined-benefit pension, Switzerland provides a precedent for a mandatory second tier built around a hybrid. The cash-balance plan might also work well. For the reasons set out in Chapter 2 and to be elaborated later in this chapter, this plan would probably appeal more to employers than the traditional plan. Determining whether they qualify would be easier than it is for the traditional pension: The law could establish a minimum contribution rate and an interest credit, with which each plan would have to comply.

The compulsory extension of coverage could reduce the take-home pay of workers who were not already covered by a plan with a rate at least as high as the universal plan. These reductions could spell hardship for some workers, especially the low paid. A decision would need to be made about the feasibility and desirability of providing relief, possibly through a tax credit or subsidy scheme.

Default Setting

Another route to broader, if not universal, coverage is through default setting. Employers with more than some specified number of employees would be required to offer their employees a specially designed plan if their employees were not already enrolled in an existing plan. The employees would not have to join their employer's plan, but they would be enrolled automatically unless they explicitly declined to join. There is mounting evidence that default setting has a powerful influence on behavior.[5]

In the United States, a default setting that encourages enrollment is a feature of many established 401(k) plans. In addition, the auto-IRA proposal

---

   a par with those of other accounts, they would need to be completely portable and vest immediately.

[4]   The GRA addresses some of the problematic aspects of the 401(k) and other defined-contribution plans. Investment fees would be reduced by drastically limiting the funds in which account holders could invest, and by the practice of wholesale investing. The GRA would freeze the creation of new 401(k) plans, and would end the favorable tax treatment of existing plans. Plan participants would all receive a refundable tax credit of $600, which is intended to defray the costs of the 5 percent contribution paid by low-income workers.

[5]   For discussion, see Thaler and Sunstein (2008, 2009), especially 109–11.

mentioned in Chapter 4 has been developed to take advantage of the power of default setting, and to expand the pension coverage offered by small employers. Despite its name, the auto-IRA is closer to an employer-provided pension, except that the employer acts as a conduit for contributions by its employees to investment accounts, with no fiduciary responsibility. The scheme has been designed to minimize the costs to small employers, because coverage of their employees by any kind of pension is very low.

Default setting would not be an efficient way of increasing the coverage of the traditional pension plan. To avoid adverse selection, the members of a traditional plan are normally employees of the plan sponsor, for whom participation in the plan is a condition of employment. Making membership of a traditional plan voluntary would not work.

Does a strategy of default setting to encourage the expansion of coverage of a plan like the auto-IRA dovetail with a strategy to revive the traditional pension? Although the traditional pension's coverage cannot be efficiently increased through default setting, there is no reason why a policy like the auto-IRA, which is really aimed at small employers, would frustrate measures to increase the coverage of the traditional pension, such as streamlining regulation or developing new financial instruments that can enhance a traditional plan's abilities to hedge its liabilities. Similarly, promoting the auto-IRA is fully compatible with the development of hybrid or other alternatives to the traditional pension. The traditional pension might continue to serve certain niche markets or select groups of employees in firms where the majority of employees were enrolled in another type of plan.

Tax Incentives

This brings us to tax incentives. The current structure of incentives in the Anglo-Saxon countries favors pension-plan members who are better off, because the deductions from income they provide make tax relief a function of the marginal rate of tax on income, as Chapter 2 discussed. In the United States, the tax expenditures entailed by the favorable treatment of contractual saving are very costly; the Office of Management and Budget (OMB) estimates their cost in foregone tax revenues in the 2010 fiscal year at $97 billion (Office of Management and Budget 2009, 308). It is doubtful whether they cause a big increase in private saving. A switch away from deductions to refundable tax credits might increase the participation of lower income workers in some kind of retirement saving or pension plan, by increasing the tax relief enjoyed by these workers. Germany instituted a subsidy system, which functions effectively like a tax credit, to level the playing field for the well paid and the less well paid, and to encourage the take-up of the pensions introduced in 2001–02 (see Appendix 1, Germany). The Saver's Credit available to low-income taxpayers in the United States has a similar intent. Unless tax preferences were deliberately fashioned to favor nontraditional pension plans, however, more favorable tax treatment or a redistribution of tax expenditures toward low-income workers would not affect the relative attractiveness of the traditional pension plan.

To sum up the discussion of the compatibility of measures to promote broader coverage with a program aimed at reviving the traditional pension: A policy of compulsory coverage would be at odds with the goal of reviving the traditional pension, but not with a policy of promoting hybrids. Default setting with an instrument like the auto-IRA would be compatible with the goal of reviving the traditional pension, and so would a strategy of favorable tax treatment.

Addressing the Decline of the Traditional Pension

As Chapter 6 argued, no single culprit can be blamed for the decline of the traditional pension. Policies aimed at stemming its decline confront the daunting task of reversing the impetus of many social and economic forces, and it is doubtful whether anything short of outright subsidization could really boost its coverage. Most of the causes of decline that Chapter 6 identified would be very hard to reverse. Lack of trust by workers in the employer's promise to honor the obligations of a defined-benefit plan might dissipate in the light of the severe losses endured by workers with defined-contribution plans, but it would be foolish to expect confidently that this would occur. Similarly, unions might regain some of their former power and influence, but it would be rash to assume that legislation could bring that about.

The only obviously reversible cause of decline that Chapter 6 pinpointed assuming no significant political opposition, is heavy-handed regulation. How much of a reviving effect that would have on traditional pensions is hard to say.[6] Financial markets may become more stable once the global economy recovers from the crash of 2008, and conceivably improved

---

[6] Some of the changes to the traditional pension in the Anglo-Saxon countries were intended to deal with disparities in treatment that liberal societies no longer thought were justifiable. Although the impact on plan costs of these changes could be offset by changes in accrual rates and other plan parameters, the changes would reduce the implicit rate of return of plan membership to the average member. In these circumstances, it might be easier for the employer simply to close the plan, especially if a defined-contribution alternative were popular with the workforce.

regulation might make plan sponsors less unwilling to go on sponsoring a traditional plan, but it would be wishful thinking to believe both that regulatory reform would come to pass and that it would have a stabilizing effect. Some streamlining of the regulatory framework for the traditional pension could help preserve it in those industries and occupations for which it is well suited, however. This said, efforts to peel back excessive layers of regulation might be stymied by a general distrust of financial deregulation, in light of its apparent role in the financial crisis.

A more promising approach might be to alter the scale or design of the traditional pension to make it more attractive to sponsors and plan members. If the decline in the traditional pension reflects an increase in the risk aversion of plan sponsors, that might be addressed by reducing the size of the plans, or by greater risk sharing by plan sponsors with plan members. For example, the traditional pension might be modified so that aggregate longevity risk could be borne partly by plan members instead of being borne entirely by the sponsor. A change like this would not amount to a really substantial structural change in the traditional pension. The new model would still preserve key features of the traditional plan, namely, the sponsor's assumption of investment risk and individual longevity risk, and a benefit taking the form of an annuity.

Yet another approach would be to adopt other forms of the defined-benefit plan, such as a version of the cash-balance plan found in the United States. As Chapter 2 explains, a cash-balance plan can be designed so that participants bear no investment risk, although they will normally bear longevity risk. Another – and in some respects more radical – approach would be to recognize that defined-contribution pensions are unlikely to give up the ground that they have won at the expense of the traditional pension, and to adopt a variant of the defined-contribution pension with features that address its shortcomings. A related policy is reliance on default settings to encourage the annuitization of a part of a defined-contribution plan's account balance.

Patching Up or Replacing the Traditional Pension

Altering the Parameters or the Design of the Traditional Pension
One way of reducing the risk that employers assume when they sponsor a traditional pension, and of making them more willing to stick with the traditional plan, is to reduce its scale. The sponsor need not change the plan's basic structure but simply shrink it. Unlike some of the other approaches for sharing risk that the chapter discusses, this approach is not based on any

adjustment mechanism, and it does not specifically pinpoint one risk, as longevity bonds or adjustments for increased life expectancy do. It involves instead a once-off (or infrequent) change to the parameters of a traditional pension plan.

For example, a plan financed with equal contributions of 8 percent from the employer and employee and an accruals rate of 2 percent could be transformed into a plan with contribution rates of 4 percent for both employer and employee and an accruals rate of 1 percent. (The saving in combined contributions of 8 percentage points would be passed on to the employee in a higher take-home pay.) This stratagem should not alter the expected implicit rate of return of the plan, and employees would be free to save the increase in their take-home pay.[7]

Assuming that the scaled-down plan allocated its assets in the same way as the original plan did, the impact on the smaller plan of a given financial market shock should be half the impact it was on the original. As well, the exposure to financial risk entailed by the scaled-down plan is much less than the exposure entailed by the original plan. Scaling back a traditional plan, in other words, could make the sponsor more willing to maintain it.

Another and obviously more contentious approach would be to alter a plan's parameters in order to reduce its expected rate of return to members and the potential risk borne by the sponsor. This could be done in any number of ways, some of them less obvious in their effect than others would be. As an example of a less obvious approach, a final-salary plan could be converted gradually into a career-average plan, but with less than a fully compensating change in accrual rates. This revision to the plan would reduce pension payouts because average salaries would (on average) be less than final salaries.

Because a plan cannot change its accrual rates and its other parameters retroactively, a whole generation would pass before the accrued benefits of new retirees were completely scaled down. There would be a long transition period during which new retirees would receive a pension that was a weighted average of the pension available under the old and new plans. The weights would be determined by the number of years each cohort of retirees served under each of the two plans. Even if the revised plan parameters applied henceforth to both the existing workforce and new hires, the plan

---

[7] Strictly speaking, for this approach to be neutral, the additional private savings financed by the reduction in contribution rates would have to be treated by the tax system in the same way as plan contributions were treated. If private (third-tier) saving is treated less favorably, the plan member who would have voluntarily joined the original plan would be worse off.

sponsor would be required to maintain adequate funding for the benefits accrued and pensions payable under the original plan. The adoption of a different plan form, like a self-directed defined-contribution plan, would be subject to the same constraint, however. Converting to a new type of plan cannot affect the accrued or legacy costs of the old plan.

In the countries where the decline of the traditional plan is most advanced, the traditional plan, rather than being made over as a smaller image of itself, is being effectively phased out, with a new type of plan taking its place. Employers have chosen the latter approach to dealing with the problems of their traditional plans for several reasons. First, and somewhat paradoxically, if a plan has been collectively bargained, scaling it down may be more time consuming and contentious than simply freezing or closing it and starting up an entirely different plan for new employees or both new and old employees. Second, the kind of reduction in the plan's generosity that would make employers happy to go on sponsoring it might make it unappealing to plan members. Third, the reduction in fringe benefits entailed by reducing the benefit the existing plan provides is much more obvious than the reduction that could be achieved by adopting a defined-contribution plan, even one with a lower implicit rate of return to its participants.[8] Fourth, adopting a new plan may ultimately reduce the costs of plan administration. Maintaining a plan but reducing its generosity without actually reducing the number of active or retired plan members may not save the sponsor much if the variable element of administrative costs depends mainly on the number of plan members.

Another way of saving the traditional plan is to modify it by introducing an adjustment mechanism that permits the sponsor to alter the plan's parameters when underfunding threatens. This is the approach of the Dutch employer-provided pension plans. The policy of conditional indexation allows a plan to temporarily adopt a policy of less than full indexation (see Chapters 1 and 4, and Appendix 1, the Netherlands). This gives pension plans extra room to maneuver when financial shocks cause plan assets to drop below the minimum value they are expected to maintain relative to liabilities.

Conditional indexation is feasible in some countries but not in others. In the United States, indexation of pensions is very rare in the private sector, as is indexation of the accrued benefits of separated workers. Exclusive

---

[8]   Comparing the ultimate benefit that a defined-contribution plan can finance with the benefit of a traditional plan is difficult. Knowing the current balance of a participant's plan (a stock) does not allow the participant to convert it into a sustainable income flow.

reliance on conditional indexation as the adjustment mechanism would not be feasible even in countries where pensioners are prepared to bear part of the cost of adjustment, because such a policy would impose 100 percent of the costs of adjustment on pensioners when a plan is underfunded. Consequently, conditional indexation as practiced in the Netherlands must encompass the adjustment of other plan parameters, like the accrual rate. Making the accrual rate a function of a plan's finances shifts some of the burden to active plan members. As noted in Appendix 1, the Netherlands, one large Dutch plan announced an increase in contribution rates of 1 percentage point in response to the underfunding that emerged in late 2008.

Another possible adjustment mechanism is to make the pension benefit vary inversely with the life expectancy of each cohort of retiring workers. Under such a mechanism, the benefit could be adjusted to maintain as a constant the expected present value of the pension at retirement. Increasing life expectancy at retirement would then entail a decline in the value of the annual pension.

As Chapter 5 discussed, a number of national governments have already adopted mechanisms like these. Because it is not feasible to develop measures of the life expectancy of the retiring workers of particular employers, a national or perhaps a sectoral measure of life expectancy would have to do. Further, to give retiring workers adequate notice in advance of the pension they could expect to receive, the life expectancy of each cohort would have to be projected some years before the cohort reached normal retirement age. Ideally, the projections would be made by an independent agency of the central government. The projections would be updated periodically, although not necessarily annually.

The adjustment just described is a way of dealing with the impact of increasing longevity on a plan's finances, whether the increase is predictable or not. Financial instruments – longevity bonds – are being developed to specifically address the problems entailed by aggregate longevity risk. One type of longevity bond makes a series of payments over a specified period such as 30 years, and the payments decline proportionately with the survival rates of a specified age cohort – for example, all German males who turned 65 in 2009. If the initial payment is €50 million, and in 2014 the survival rate of the benchmark population is 90 percent, then the payment in year five will be €45 million. Box 7.1 illustrates how this type of longevity bond works. Longevity bonds can take other forms, and it is also possible to construct derivatives, the value of which depends on the survival rates of particular cohorts of a specified population that can be used to hedge aggregate longevity risk (Blake et al. 2006d).

Box 7.1.   Hedging against unexpected changes in longevity

The table below illustrates how deviations in survival rates from the rates assumed by a plan's actuaries (referred to as assumed survival rates) affect plan costs, and how a longevity bond such as that described in the text could serve as a hedge. Actual survival rates are assumed to be higher than the assumed rates shown below by 0.003 per year. With longevity bonds, where each payment is proportional to the actual survival rate of a benchmark population, and assuming that survival rates of the benchmark population behaved exactly as survival rates of the plan's pensioners, a plan could completely hedge its liabilities against unexpected changes in longevity. Holders of longevity bonds would, however, expect a rate of return higher than that of a conventional bond for taking on this risk.

The size of the unexpected increase in survival rates assumed in the table is large. At age 95, the proportional increase in survivors is almost 50 percent (28 survivors of an original cohort of 100, compared with the actuarially assumed figure of 19). The increase in the present value of pension costs is 6.8 percent.

Age of cohort in years	70	75	80	85	90	95
(Payouts in millions of euros)						
Assumed survival rates	0.89	0.83	0.73	0.65	0.42	0.19
Actual survival rates	0.91	0.86	0.78	0.71	0.50	0.28
Impact of difference on payouts	0.60	1.20	1.80	2.40	3.00	3.60
Discount factor	0.86	0.74	0.64	0.55	0.48	0.41
Discounted impact	0.52	0.89	1.16	1.33	1.43	1.48
Present value of impact on payouts of higher than projected survival	6.8					
Present value of payouts with assumed survival	100.0					
Initial payout	40.0					
Annual discount rate	3.0%					
Quinquennial discount rate	15.9%					

Note: Pension payouts are made every 5 years, and are constant in nominal terms.
Source: Author's calculations.

The widespread use of longevity bonds or derivatives could reduce some of the risk that traditional pension plans confront, and might reduce the need for the kind of adjustment in pensions just described. These instruments will never be a panacea for risk in general, however, because aggregate longevity risk is only one of the risks plans confront, and may not be the biggest (Balevich 2009). As Chapter 6 discussed, aggregate longevity risk is certainly a fact of life, but it is difficult to prove conclusively that it has increased.

The goal of developing a thriving market for longevity bonds confronts a number of obstacles. One of these is *bias risk*, the risk that the survival rates of the population on which the bond's payments are based are not closely correlated with the survival rates of the pension plan's members. Another is uncertainty regarding the likely spread between longevity and conventional bonds. Because a market has yet to develop, the premium on the expected rate of return that bondholders will demand is uncertain. Insurance companies and other investors who use longevity bonds to hedge their own exposure to longevity risk might be happy to receive a discounted rate. The average risk-averse investor would expect a premium over the risk-free rate. Several students of the market have argued that the premium will not be especially high, because fluctuations in survival rates are not closely correlated with financial market returns. That remains to be seen.[9] One day, a financial instrument might be developed that was indexed to both wages or prices and survival rates, like a longevity bond. Such an instrument would hedge the risks confronting a pension plan more comprehensively.

Hybrids

The cash-balance plan, which was analyzed in Chapter 2, is more removed from the traditional pension plan than the modified versions of the plan that this chapter has just discussed. The cash-balance plan and its cousin, the pension equity plan, have an obvious, albeit not universal, appeal to U.S. employers, and might have a similar appeal elsewhere. In particular, investment risk is limited, and the employer bears no longevity risk.

The longevity risk that employees must bear is arguably the major drawback of the plan for them, along with interest risk at the annuitization stage. Nonetheless, cash-balance plans are a superior plan form in some

---

[9] Friedburg and Webb (2006) use the capital-asset pricing model to estimate the risk premium that longevity bonds could be expected to bear, and find the risk of holding them in a diversified portfolio to be quite small.

respects for employees over the traditional pension plan (and also over defined-contribution plans). In particular, the cash-balance plan is readily portable, and as Chapter 2 explained, its benefits accrue much more evenly over a participant's period of service. This becomes an important feature when vesting requirements of traditional plans are strict and their portability is limited.

A further advantage for some observers is the superior transparency of cash-balance plans, owing to regular reporting of the balance accumulated to date.[10] Like the traditional pension plan, the cash-balance plan mitigates the risk of inadequate saving, because plan participants do not set the pay-credit percentage or the interest rate. A hybrid plan also mitigates the risk of poor investment returns, because the choice of a government bond-related rate would reduce investment risk below that of a self-directed defined-contribution plan with a more aggressive asset allocation. That said, a hybrid plan cannot offer a rate of return that is both high and secure unless the plan sponsor is willing to assume substantial investment risk.

The weak link of a cash-balance plan is the distribution stage. In the United States, annuitization is a required option but is not mandatory, and the premium per dollar (the annuitization factor) can still vary substantially from year to year. The effect of this variability on annuity income can be partly offset by buying annuities in installments, and by replicating the immunizing portfolio strategies of insurance companies. These are relatively sophisticated strategies, however, and may be costly for people with small balances. The approach of the in-service annuity described in the following, which has been developed for defined-contribution plans, might conceivably be adapted to the needs of the cash-balance plan. One way of introducing longevity insurance in the typical cash-balance plan could be to insert a default setting at the distribution phase, stipulating that some minimum share of the balance will be annuitized subject to certain safeguards and conditions unless the plan member expressly chooses another option. This possibility is taken up again in the following.

Two Add-Ons to Defined-Contribution Plans for Longevity Insurance
Two financial products now available in the United States may enhance the ability of defined-contribution plans there and in other countries to address the risk of a retiree's outliving his or her resources. The first of these grafts a variable annuity with a guaranteed minimum withdrawal benefit (GMWB) onto a 401(k) plan. The insurance companies that provide this instrument

---

[10] This advantage may be more apparent than real. See footnote 8.

guarantee a minimum rate of withdrawal expressed as a specified percentage of plan assets measured at one or more past dates (like the highest balance achieved to date). Provided the insurance company can make good on its promise, the plan member is guaranteed some income for life.

The variable annuity with a GMWB that is embedded in the instrument is a risk-sharing arrangement that should provide a retiree with a rate of return that is higher on average than the rate he or she would obtain from investing in safe, low-yielding assets. It is not a life annuity and there is no pooling of longevity risk, because the account balance may be bequeathed upon the holder's death. The guarantee of lifetime income is financed by a separate fee levied on top of an investment fee. Because the guarantee is expressed in nominal terms, the level of guaranteed income in real terms tends to decline over time in a down market.

The second product is the in-service annuity. This type of instrument, which is still uncommon, effectively exchanges a contribution to the plan as it is made for a stream of lifetime income that begins at retirement, in the same way that a traditional defined-benefit plan does. Rather than purchase one annuity at retirement or several in the approach to retirement, the in-service annuity entails the purchase of a small annuity with each contribution (or perhaps several contributions bundled together).

A 401(k) Plan with a Guarantee

Defined contribution plans with income guarantees are intended to attract the assets in 401(k) plans as their holders approach retirement, and also to attract IRA holders nearing retirement (or actually retired) who are looking for some degree of income security in retirement, as well as defined-contribution plan members more generally. It has an accumulation as well as a distribution phase, but because the insurance companies are targeting workers who are contemplating retirement (for example, by imposing a minimum age on participants, such as 50 years of age, as a condition of eligibility), the former phase is likely to be shorter than the latter. We refer to it as a defined-contribution plan with a guarantee feature, or a DC_G plan.

The mechanics of a prototypical DC_G plan are as follows.[11] Participants are offered a choice of investment funds, with asset allocations that might range from somewhat conservative (more bonds than stocks) to aggressive, where most of the portfolio is invested in growth stocks. Participants continue to maintain an account with investments in these funds when they

---

[11]   This plan's broad features are similar to those of investment vehicles with a guarantee feature that are offered by a number of U.S. insurance companies.

elect to begin drawing their guaranteed income, and if they wish may elect to change their portfolio's asset allocation during the decumulation phase.

The amount of income that is guaranteed depends on the performance of the account holder's investments and the formulation of the guarantee. In the example presented here, the guarantee is assumed to be determined by applying a fixed percentage, such as 5 percent, to the highest nominal value attained in the postretirement period. The way that guaranteed income is determined means that its real value may either rise or fall over time; it is not indexed. It is likely that the real value of the guaranteed benefit will have a procyclical pattern, rising during rising equity markets and vice versa. Account holders/participants can always supplement the guaranteed income by making an additional drawing. Doing so reduces the account value from which the guaranteed income will be derived in the future, however.[12]

The DC_G plan has its performance analyzed under two different withdrawal rules, and their success in maintaining a stable income stream is examined using the Monte Carlo simulation technique of Chapter 2. The only difference is that these simulations are conducted with nominal, not real values, and a certain rate of inflation is assumed (see Box 7.2).

With the first rule, withdrawals never exceed the guaranteed income. With the second, withdrawals are allowed to exceed the guaranteed income when that is necessary to maintain the initial purchasing power of the withdrawal. Under either rule, a participant's assets are invested in two funds, as with the phased-withdrawal simulation experiments – one composed of large capitalization stocks and the other composed of long-term government bonds – and the initial proportion of stocks and bonds is maintained by rebalancing the portfolio each year. The fees that participants pay for the management of their portfolios amount to 1 percent of its outstanding value. In addition, the DC_G plan charges an additional 1 percent for the guarantee it provides. As with the tests of the do-it-yourself approach in Chapter 2, participants confidently expect to live until the age of 90. This assumption allows us to focus on investment risk.

The Guaranteed Income Approach[13]

Under rule 1, the income that the DC_G plan generates can fluctuate substantially from one period to the next, because of the potential volatility

---

[12] As an example, suppose that the guaranteed income base is $480,000. With a guaranteed withdrawal rate of 5 percent, guaranteed income is $24,000. An additional withdrawal of $40,000 would reduce the guaranteed income base by that amount and the guaranteed withdrawal by $2,000.

[13] The monetary amounts in this section are expressed in real terms (2009 dollars).

Box 7.2.   Assumptions used in Monte Carlo simulations of the DC$_G$ plan

Financial parameters[a]	
Rates of return (in percent)	
Large-cap	12.3
Long-term bonds	6.2
Standard deviation (in percent)	
Large-cap	20.0
Long-term bonds	8.4
Initial balance	$500,000
Equity-bond mix (in percent)	50–50
Initial withdrawal rate	5% of capital
Marginal and average tax rate	15%
Fees covering all services (except the guarantee)	1.0% of capital
Charge for guarantee	1.0% of capital
Annual rate of inflation	3.1%

[a] The distribution of returns is assumed to be lognormal (i.e., with the return – the increase in the value of the asset – denoted by r; log $(1+r)$ is a normally distributed random variable). The rates of return and standard deviations are based on the performance of U.S. stocks and long-term government bonds over 1929–2007.

Source: Morningstar (2008).

of the guaranteed income withdrawal. Moreover, because the guarantee is set in nominal terms, the guaranteed withdrawal in real terms will decline over time unless the nominal value of the portfolio is rising at least as fast as the inflation rate. The presence of the guarantee does place a floor on how low withdrawals can go, although average income in the last five years drops to $16,200 (Table 7.1). Under rule 1 of the DC$_G$, the actual balance can be reduced to zero and withdrawals can still be positive. Consequently, the DC$_G$ does give the account holder some, albeit highly unpredictable, protection against the hardships of an unexpectedly long life. The price for that insurance is a lower average withdrawal (see Table 7.1), about $4,000 less than under phased-withdrawals rule 1, and over $9,000 under phased-withdrawals rule 4, which also provides some protection from complete penury.

Table 7.1. *Comparative performance of a defined-contribution plan with guarantee (DC$_G$) (in thousands of 2009 dollars except where noted)*

	Rule 1	Rule 2
Average withdrawal		
Mean	20.1	23.2
Standard deviation	3.0	2.3
Average final 5 years' withdrawal		
Mean	16.2	17.4
Standard deviation	4.5	8.8
Final balance		
Mean	180.0	77.7
Standard deviation	141.0	161.7
Probability of exhaustion (in percent)	0	0

Source: Author's simulation model. For assumptions, see text.

The application of rule 2 allows us to test the ability of DC$_G$ to sustain constant real withdrawals. The risk with such a strategy is that when withdrawals systematically exceed the guaranteed amount, the guaranteed amount will decline so low that it will provide virtually no protection. Rule 2 does impart some stability to income withdrawals. About 50 percent of the time, they maintain themselves at their initial real level. In spite of the guarantee feature, however, there is about a 30-percent chance that withdrawals will fall to $10,000 or below in the last five years. Under either rule, the DC$_G$ does not perform better on the whole than a sophisticated phased-withdrawal strategy, such as rule 4. It does have two selling points, however. First, when rule 1 applies it will keep paying some amount (determined in nominal terms), as long as the account holder is alive. Second, the account holder or plan member will know upon retirement that he or she can draw a nominally fixed income equal to a fixed proportion (5 percent in our example) of the value of the assets in the account upon retirement. To sustain this constant nominal income, the account holder must follow rule 1, and not adopt rule 2.

The In-Service Annuity

The in-service annuity (ISA) is the most novel of the alternatives to a traditional pension plan, and at the same time its resemblance to the traditional plan is greater than the other alternatives. The ISA is novel in two ways.

First, it reduces or eliminates investment risk by minimizing – effectively eliminating – the time that elapses between a contribution and its conversion into a stream of deferred fixed income. When distributions from a retirement savings account take the form of an annuity, the conventional approach is to convert the accumulated balance of a retirement savings plan into a single annuity or perhaps several annuities in the last few years prior to retirement. That approach keeps the retiree exposed to investment risk throughout the accumulation phase. With the ISA, the conversion takes place more or less continuously during the latter half of a plan member's working life.

Second, the ISA reduces income risk by annuitizing savings in many installments rather than in just a few. In this respect, the ISA works in a similar way to the dollar cost averaging technique applied to purchases of equities. By converting savings gradually over time into a stream of future income rather than doing it all in a single or small number of installments prior to retirement, there is less risk of the investor being obliged to annuitize at a high premium because interest rates happen to be low during his or her last few years of work. An additional advantage is that gradual annuitization is less daunting than annuitization in one go.

Finally, early annuitization of savings means that, provided the plan member does not require a guarantee of principal or continued income upon his or her death, the deferred income stream purchased by a given amount of savings prior to the start of the annuity payments is greater than it would have been had the savings been invested in conventional fixed-income instruments until the member retired and annuity payments began (see Box 7.3 for further discussion).

Whether an ISA could prove to be a good alternative to the traditional career-end annuity depends on both the average replacement rate it would generate and the variability of that rate. The model used here assumes, for simplicity, that the plan member buys a deferred annuity once a year, with payments from all the annuities thus purchased to begin at age 66.[14] The premium per dollar of annuity income depends on how far in advance the annuity is purchased as well as on the rate of interest prevailing the year the annuity is bought, and the plan member's life expectancy. It is assumed that the plan member begins contributing at age 45. Consequently, the first annuity he or she purchases is deferred for 20 years, the second for 19, and so on. These assumptions allow us to derive

---

[14] This assumption is tantamount to assuming that the premium is set once a year. In practice, premiums might be set more frequently than that.

Box 7.3.   The pricing of deferred annuities

Suppose that saving in the amount S_{65} at age 65 can purchase an annuity with a lifetime income stream of A dollars per year beginning at age 66. With a constant interest rate of r and costless financial intermediation, it should be possible to purchase the same income stream at age 55 for the sum $[S_{65}/(1+r)^{10}]$ with a guarantee of return of the purchase price plus interest. But if there is no guarantee should the annuitant die before age 65, then the cost of a deferred annuity (C_{DA55}) at age 55, where SP_{55-65} stands for the probability that the annuitant survives from age 55 to age 65 is given below:

$$C_{DA55} = (S_{65}/(1+r)^{10}) \cdot SP_{55-65} \qquad (7.1)$$

As the contributor ages and the period of deferral diminishes, the cost of the deferred annuity increases at a rate that exceeds the rate of interest. If the insurance company providing the arrangement offers a guarantee of principal or some similar guarantee in the event of the annuitant's death preretirement, then the cost of a deferred annuity will be higher than C_{DA55}. However, if the guarantee is for the nominal value of the contribution, the insurance company should be able to offer a price that falls between C_{DA55} and $[S_{65}/(1+r)^{10}]$.

an average premium per dollar by adding up the estimates for each year and dividing by the length of the contribution period in years. We assume that the yield on Treasuries is a normally distributed random variable that together with life expectancies at different ages determine annuity premiums, and use Monte Carlo simulation to determine the variability of the average premium. A section in Appendix 2 describes the model used in the simulations in more detail.[15]

The average premium will also depend on the intermediation costs of deferred annuities, which are likely to exceed the costs of immediate annuities. A longstanding problem with the pricing of deferred annuities has been the difficulty of matching the duration of the annuity income flows with that of a long-term bond. As an example, if an insurance company offers a deferred annuity to a cohort of 50-year-old women, with payments beginning at age 66, the company is making a commitment to provide income at least 50 years into the future, because some of the cohort's members will live to be 100 or more years old. Matching this distant liability with income from a long-term bond is not possible if the longest bond maturity is 30 years.

---

[15] With the exception of the United Kingdom, indexed annuities are not common as yet in the survey countries, and the annuity the text models is in nominal terms. An in-service "real" annuity would also damp down the variance of annuitized income.

In practice, the survival rates at advanced ages of the cohort's members may be sufficiently low that little risk is entailed by backing the long maturity claims with shorter maturity assets. However, even the principal repayment on a 30 year bond has a duration of only 30 years. In recent years, the mismatch problem has been mitigated by the development of a swap market, in which, as Chapter 3 noted, a floating-income stream may be swapped for a 50 year fixed-income stream.[16] It is uncertain, however, whether the counterparties to such transactions can really guarantee the payment of a fixed income for so long a term

The need for insurance companies to take account of the risk of a maturity mismatch (or the extra cost entailed by hedging in the derivative market) would increase the premiums paid by a plan participant for a given level of interest rates, but by an amount that would be difficult to gauge. The modeling exercise that is described in the following concentrates on the impact of interest-rate variability on the variability of average premiums and the replacement rate. The exercise assumes costless financial intermediation and does not try to predict the impact of these extra costs or other costs on premiums.

The simulations imply that annuitizing gradually but steadily can substantially reduce the variance of the premium. The mean value of the simulated average premium per dollar of income is $4.63.The premium exceeds $5.15 in only 2 percent of the simulations, and stays within the range of $4.33 and $4.92 in 800 of 1,000 simulations. By comparison, the variance of the premium per dollar for a single annuity contract is much higher. For example, the simulated value of the last premium ranges from $7.59 to $9.93 in 800 of every 1,000 simulations (see Table 7.2).

Calculating an average premium in the way just described has the undoubted merit of simplicity. However, the measure needs to be used with caution, both because it adds up premiums paid in different years without discounting them, and because it takes no account of the amount of contributions made each year. To some extent, these errors offset one another, because contributions would typically grow over time, offsetting the impact of the discount rate. Nonetheless, by making assumptions about the contribution rate and the rate of growth of salaries, it is possible to derive estimates of the replacement rate that an in-service annuity would provide, and to simulate its variability.

[16] In other words, the insurance company selling annuities invests its premium income in an instrument with a rate tied to an interbank lending rate or some other short-term rate. It then swaps the income for a fixed stream of 50-years maturity.

Table 7.2. *Frequency distribution of average and single premiums*
(premium per dollar)

Percentile	0	10	20	30	40	50	60	70	80	90	100
Average	4.07	4.33	4.44	4.50	4.56	4.62	4.67	4.73	4.81	4.92	5.59
Single (last)	6.32	7.59	7.93	8.18	8.42	8.64	8.87	9.15	9.46	9.93	12.57

Source: Author's calculations. For assumptions, see text.

Table 7.3. *Frequency distribution of replacement rate (ratio of annuity*
payment to average contributory income)

Percentile	0	10	20	30	40	50	60	70	80	90	100
Salary growth (in percent)											
3.5	0.42	0.49	0.51	0.51	0.52	0.53	0.54	0.55	0.56	0.58	0.69
4.0	0.41	0.48	0.50	0.51	0.52	0.53	0.53	0.54	0.56	0.57	0.68
4.5	0.41	0.48	0.49	0.50	0.51	0.52	0.53	0.54	0.55	0.56	0.66

Source: Author's calculations. For assumptions see text.

The approach used to generate replacement rates is further explained in Appendix 2. As with the simulation of the average premium, the concern is with the *variability* of the replacement rate, rather than with its *level*. The results of exercises simulating the replacement rate of a hypothetical plan member are similar to the results of the earlier set of simulations with the average premium (see Table 7.3), in that their variance is moderate and they are not particularly sensitive to the assumed rate of salary growth.

Qualifications

Any judgment at this stage about the suitability or appropriateness of an ISA needs to be tentative, given the lack of experience with these products to date. The discussion has already noted two features of the product about which more needs to be known. These are the ability of insurance companies to hedge against longevity risk, and the cost of financial intermediation.

The ISA, if it can be efficiently supplied, should provide retirees with a steady and relatively predictable source of income. Whether it is appropriate for any particular retiree depends on their particular situation – notably, the extent to which their wealth is already annuitized – and their taste for risk. Recall that the conditional rate of return on an annuity – that is, the rate of return earned by an annuitant who lives to the maximum age – is determined by the yield on the bonds that back it and by the annuitant's life expectancy. With an efficient market for annuities, the conditional yield should exceed the yield on bonds by a noticeable margin, which increases as the annuitant's age upon contracting the annuity increases. However, the conditional rate of return may well fall short of the expected rate of return of a portfolio that includes stocks as well as bonds.

Some retirees, particularly those who are good at managing their money and establishing and sticking to withdrawal schedules, might prefer to leave their savings in a fund with a variable but guaranteed minimum rate of return. Similarly, retirees with a high share of their wealth already in annuitized form, like someone with both a first-tier pension and an employer-provided pension that combined produce a suitably high replacement ratio, would be likely to steer clear of another annuity of any kind.

ISAs also raise the contentious issue of the timing of annuitization. There are obvious advantages to deferred and gradual or continuous annuitization. One potential drawback, however, is that because of the need to minimize the risk that annuity providers will default, premiums will be invested in high quality bonds, and not in a mix of stocks and bonds. As noted, the conditional rate of return to investing in annuities may fall short of the expected rate of return on a mixed portfolio. That said, the fact that the annuity is deferred reduces its cost, which increases the share of saving that can be invested in riskier assets.

There is a certain similarity between the ISA and the advanced life delayed annuity (ALDA) that Milevsky (2006, chap. 10) describes and analyzes. Both involve gradual annuitization (multiple payments by the annuitant) during working life and a substantially deferred start to payments to the annuitant. With the ALDA, the terms are fixed at the outset, and annuity payments do not begin until an advanced age, like 85. The cost of the annuity is substantially reduced by being so long deferred, which increases the share of saving that can go to equities and other risky assets. Because payments begin at so late an age, the annuity's conditional rate of return is very high.

Default Setting to Encourage Annuitization[17]

Even if a policy of mandatory annuitization is ruled out and annuitization is not built into defined-contribution plans, there are other ways of increasing the share of defined-contribution account balances converted into an annuity. Specifically, a default setting can be devised that will encourage

---

[17] This section deals mainly with U.S. experience with policies to encourage annuitization. Its lessons have application to at least some of the other nine survey countries, however.

annuitization, and annuitization can be made more appealing to potential annuitants by lowering annuity premiums and dispelling irrational distrust in the product. Not all such distrust is irrational, but economists have long argued that the welfare of many retirees would be increased if more of their wealth at retirement were in annuitized form.

Behavioral studies have found that the perceived attractiveness of annuities varies markedly with the way they are presented. Emphasizing the lifetime income they provide is more likely to interest a potential annuitant than emphasizing their role as an investment with a large up-front commitment and a risk of loss of capital (Gale et al. 2008, 8). The fact that a decision about how much wealth to annuitize is complicated will deter many potential annuitants.

A default setting can deal with both of these barriers to annuitization. As is by now well known, a default setting can overcome inertia; it appears to endorse a particular choice and, to some extent, takes the burden of decision making off the shoulders of the hesitant choice maker. The topic of default setting for annuities is less well-covered terrain than default setting for saving, and raises a number of special issues. First, the decision to annuitize can and often will involve more than one person: the potential annuitant and his or her spouse. In consequence, a default setting has to ensure that spousal rights are respected. One approach would make spousal consent to the terms of an annuity a necessary condition for annuitization. Another would require potential annuitants who were married to obtain a joint and survivor annuity on specific terms, like a survivor annuity that was at least 50 percent of the joint annuity. Second, any default setting needs to ensure that it does not entail over-annuitization. Some workers in some countries will have a substantial share of their wealth in the form of an annuity at retirement, particularly those with average or below-average incomes. A counseling service might be useful in helping some workers decide how much annuitization is enough. Third, however diligent a plan sponsor has been in devising a default setting, a retired plan member who has not opted out may come to regret the choice. The plan sponsor, especially a U.S. sponsor, will be concerned about its exposure to liability in such cases. More generally, a default setting for annuitization, if the annuitant does not opt out, has irrevocable consequences. The decision cannot be undone. Someone who defaults into a defined-contribution plan at a given rate may regret the decision, but he or she can back out of it without serious consequences.

Gale et al. (2008) propose that potential annuitants be allowed a trial period of 24 months over which they would receive a steady income. If, at the end of that time, they had no wish to annuitize any part of what is left in their account, they would be under no obligation to do so. In effect, during the trial period, the tentative annuitants are learning by doing. Instead of having to dive off the deep end, they can start by sticking their toes in the water. There is some similarity between this approach and the dollar cost averaging technique of stock purchasing.

A more purely voluntary approach has also known some success. Specifically, one specialist broker in the United States brings together insurance companies that want to sell annuities and companies with 401(k) plans who want to offer their retiring employees a steady income after retirement. Because the plan sponsors can have a relatively large number of potential annuitants, they are able to obtain pricing on a group rather than an individual basis. The issue of fiduciary liability is sidestepped by first rolling over 401(k) plan balances into an IRA (*Annuity Market News* 2007).

Remarks on Public-Sector Pension Plans

As Chapter 5 explained, U.S. state and local government plans are not in a good way. The funding ratios of most of them, even when they are calculated at a rate well above the risk-free rate, are far from what they should be. Calculated at a risk-free or near risk-free rate, some of them would clearly be insolvent. The funding gap is so large that even a substantial hike in contribution rates would not fill it.

Leaving aside the drastic option of a hard freeze, and assuming that the traditional pension plan will survive in state and local government in some form, there is no alternative to a substantial decline in benefits accrual. Whether that will reduce the amount of provisioning for new benefits will depend on whether states will choose to adopt or move toward a risk-free discount rate. Closing or narrowing significantly the funding gap will require huge additional provisions even at the current discount rate.

The fact that so many states confront the same predicament might conceivably make it easier for them to take action. A state that is planning drastic changes to its pension plans can point to the plans of other states that are in more or less the same situation to show their civil servants that the need for reform is widespread. A common approach to reform would increase the chances that it would be acceptable politically.

The alternative of imposing a hard freeze and moving all employees into a defined-contribution or cash-balance plan would have some obvious advantages from the point of view of state plan sponsors. The plan liability would become completely or highly predictable. This more drastic approach raises some technical issues, however. To preserve the value of accrued benefits in real terms, it would not be enough for existing plan members to have tenure. The value of benefits accrued at the point of the conversion to the new plan would need to be indexed in some manner. Failure to do this would mean that benefits accrued during membership in the defined-benefit plan would be below what they would have been had the defined-benefit plan not been frozen. The analysis of the effect of early separation presented in Chapter 2, which showed that it could substantially reduce a pension, applies to this type of situation as well. Moving from a traditional plan to a plain-vanilla defined-contribution plan would also shift both investment and longevity risk entirely onto the plan member.

Reforms to Tier-One Plans

The major recent innovation affecting public sector pension plans, as Chapter 5 explained, is the incorporation of an automatic adjustment mechanism (AAM). The notional defined-contribution plan comes with one built in, but these mechanisms can be and have been added to more conventional public plans.

AAMs have certain technical requirements if they are to work well. In the particular case of adjustments based on increases in life expectancy, estimates of the longevity of different age cohorts need as solid a technical base as possible. Changes in the longevity of persons who have already retired do not generally elicit a change in a system parameter. The key issue with all these plans is whether they are truly automatic or not. If adjustments can be postponed or deferred for any length of time, then the mechanism loses its rationale.

As Turner (2009) has emphasized, AAMs have important implications for the distribution of income and welfare. For example, reducing the value of the annual pension to maintain the present value at retirement of the stream of pension payments will reduce the total income of those retired persons who depend heavily on the public pension by more than it does the income of those retirees who are less dependent. Over time, the distribution of income of retirees becomes more unequal with this particular AAM. A minimum pension mitigates the effect, but only for the very poor. The U.K. approach, which aims to maintain the ratio of time working to time in retirement constant, mitigates this difficulty, because contributions should grow at the same pace as pensions.

An AAM that maintains the present value of benefits constant by raising the retirement age at which the normal pension is paid avoids this particular problem but creates another. Specifically, those workers who would find it difficult to work longer to claim the same pension may well retire at the same age as before the adjustment, but at a lower pension.

8

Summary and Conclusions

What Happened...

In the Anglo-Saxon Countries

In the United States, the United Kingdom, and Canada, the traditional pension's coverage of the workforce has suffered a serious decline, albeit less in Canada than in the other two countries. The decline has been underway for several decades, but in the United Kingdom its pace quickened alarmingly after 2005. As of 2007, the coverage of the traditional pension plan is only 17 percent in the United States, 30 percent in the United Kingdom (15 percent if only private-sector coverage is considered), and 34 percent in Canada (20 percent if only private-sector coverage is considered). High rates of coverage in the public sector help sustain overall coverage in all three countries, even in the United States, where the traditional pension plan's share of private-sector coverage is estimated to be only 10 percent.

The diminished standing of the traditional plan is associated with a decline in the overall rate of coverage of employer-provided plans in both Canada and the United Kingdom. In the United States, the overall rate of coverage has remained at about one in two workers despite the growing importance of 401(k) plans. Nonetheless, the role of annuitized pension benefits at the second tier has declined in all three countries. It is doubtful whether this decline in the role of annuitization at the second tier is compensated or offset by an increase at the third tier. The balances of voluntary private saving plans are typically not converted into annuities.

In Germany and Japan

Both countries launched major reforms of their employer-provided pensions in 2001–02. Japan's reform was particularly comprehensive, but both countries encouraged the spread of declined-contribution pensions (hybrid pensions in Germany's case). The evidence on coverage is partial, but suggests that in Germany, increases in the coverage of defined-contribution or hybrid plans have increased the overall coverage of the system.

In Australia, Denmark, the Netherlands, Sweden, and Switzerland

In these five countries, the employer-provided pension system attained high rates of coverage some time ago. Australia has a defined-contribution plan, the Netherlands a modified version of the traditional defined-benefit plan, and Sweden a mix of the two. Denmark and Switzerland offer hybrid plans. Australia moved away from the traditional pension some time ago, and its Superannuation Guarantee – despite its name – typically has no guarantee on rates of return. The Netherlands has adopted a flexible system in which the rate at which pensions are indexed against consumer price inflation can be adjusted in light of a plan's overall financial position.

A Basic Observation on Coverage Drawn from the Ten Countries' Experiences

If broad coverage of the second tier is wanted, then it should be made obligatory or quasi-obligatory. The five high-coverage countries all rely on compulsion or on a network of collective bargaining. Tax preferences, which play such an important role in the Anglo-Saxon countries, do not work; because they reward better-paid employees for doing what they would do anyway, they are a completely wasteful fiscal expenditure. Systems relying on tax preferences suffer from marked disparities in coverage by income and age. Their portability and vesting and preservation rules compare unfavorably overall with those of the broad-coverage countries.

In none of the five high-coverage countries is the traditional plan the main form of pension. The Netherlands comes the closest, in that its second-tier pension is similar to the traditional pension. However, the organization of the second tier makes more feasible the inclusion of small firms in an industry-wide defined-benefit pension plan, and the policy of conditional indexation modifies the traditional design to give the flexibility needed for risk-sharing among plan sponsors, active plan members, and retired members.

Four Issues in Funding

If the traditional benefit plan is to enjoy a renaissance, the measure of its assets and liabilities must reflect, as accurately as possible, the cost of plan service and funding. This book takes the following positions: With either an average- or a final-salary plan, the cost of accrued plan service should be measured by projecting wages and salaries to the date of retirement, and not by their current level; plan liabilities should be discounted to the present using a risk-free discount rate or a closely related rate; plan assets should normally be marked to market, assuming that there is an active market for them; and there is no hard-and-fast rule regarding the pace at which a shortfall of plan assets from plan liabilities should be eliminated, so that any quantitative adjustment rule is to some extent arbitrary. This said, regulatory forbearance (i.e., the relaxation of the applicable rule in periods when most plans have become underfunded) has to be used sparingly.

The adoption of a risk-free discount rate may discourage the traditional pension further. However, an artificial reduction in the cost of plan funding is not a viable or sensible solution to the traditional plan's difficulties.

Investing

A basic tenet of pension-plan investing is that the assets side of the balance sheet cannot be judged independently of the liabilities side. The technique of asset-liability management (ALM), which has become more popular in recent years, is the practical expression of this tenet. With ALM, what counts is the volatility of net, not gross, assets. ALM is not based on particular rules of thumb, like an asset allocation of 60 percent equities and 40 percent bonds. Its consistent implementation requires that a plan sponsor formulate a specific rule about when it will make exceptional contributions to a plan. For example, a sponsor might adopt a rule that it will make exceptional contributions to the plan any time the asset-liability ratio falls below 90 percent at a rate that would close the gap between the actual ratio and 100 percent in a specified number of years. The sponsor's objective could then be selecting an investment strategy that minimizes expected contributions given this constraint.

The standard ALM exercise uses Monte Carlo experiments to determine the plan's investment strategy, making it vulnerable to the charge that it relies on a black box. The risk of model error could be reduced by adopting a strategy of asset-liability matching, where the liabilities projected for different periods are exactly matched by assets of the same duration. Because perfect matching is not feasible, however, pension plans will be forced to rely on some form of ALM. Liability-driven investment (LDI) is a variant of ALM that recognizes that some of the risks associated with pension-plan liabilities are not well hedged by some combination of bonds and stocks alone, but instead require the use of derivatives and other investments.

Regulation of Plan Design

The regulation of pension plans is justified by their inherent complexity, the millions upon millions of people whose welfare depends on them, and their impact on capital markets. Two kinds of regulation should be distinguished: (1) regulation via the legal system, which is intended to ensure that the implicit contracts entailed by employer-provided pensions, and especially traditional ones, are honored, and (2) regulation driven by social activism. An example of the latter would be measures that boost coverage, be it among the working population at large or certain subgroups, like women or part-time workers. Another example would be placing a cap on the number of years an employee can contribute to a plan without vesting. Social activism runs the risk of creating unfunded mandates, because it imposes costs on the plan sponsor.

All countries regulate vesting requirements. A pension plan with a long vesting period effectively discriminates against short-tenured workers. Shortening the vesting period is justifiable on grounds of equity, but it does add to the costs of the plan. In principle, the increase in cost could be offset by reducing the overall generosity of the plan, although this may not always be easy to do. A similar argument applies to portability and benefits preservation. In a small number of countries, a worker who has vested and who separates will receive at retirement only the current value of his or her accrued rights as of the date of separation. If many years pass between separation and benefit eligibility, the real value of the benefit may decline drastically.

A key issue with activist regulation is whether it kills the goose that lays the golden eggs. In both the United States and the United Kingdom, measures taken since the mid-1970s to provide a more equitable distribution of benefits to participants in traditional plans may, in fact, have encouraged their decline. This is not an issue in countries where employer-provided plans are mandatory or quasi-mandatory. The problem arises when public policy can control some aspects of pension design but not others. In these circumstances, pension design faces the same challenge as someone who tries to control the amount of air in a balloon by squeezing one end of it.

With the growth in popularity of defined-contribution plans, the provision of accurate, clear, and timely information on plan balances and the performance of plan investments has become an important regulatory issue. The provision of information is especially important for self-directed plans. Plan sponsors cannot be assumed to provide all the information that they might be reasonably expected to provide – they may not have it all themselves. For the same reason, the provision of financial education is more important than ever, but must begin in the schools.

Regulation of Investments

Traditionally, pension-plan investing has been governed by the prudent-person (or prudent-investor) rule when pensions are established as a trust. In these countries and in countries where other models prevail, quantitative restrictions on asset allocation have also applied.

A more recent approach to investment regulation, known as risk-based supervision (RBS), starts from the premise that pension plans ought to be treated, for regulatory purposes, like financial institutions, and that their investment policies ought to be judged by the systemic risk they pose. This approach is congenial with ALM, because both are concerned with the impact of deviations from the projected outlook on plan balance sheets. In neither case would a pension plan's investment strategy receive a passing grade just because assets were roughly in alignment with liabilities.

The Netherlands is the foremost practitioner of RBS. RBS is not light regulation; the resources it requires of both the regulator and pension plans are substantial. It is most feasible when pension plans are relatively large, given the economies of scale that characterize both the regulatory function and the investment function of pension plans. It is best suited for countries where industry-wide plans are prominent or the scale of business enterprise is large. Despite the important role played by modeling techniques in its application, RBS requires a substantial element of judgment. If this approach is not feasible for a country relying on a version of the prudent-investor rule, it will be vital that the rule take due account of the need for asset-liability matching.

Why Did the Traditional Pension Fall from Favor?

As the introduction forewarned, no single cause lies behind the decline of the traditional pension in the three Anglo-Saxon countries. Both demand-side and supply-side forces have been at work. On the supply side, the evidence does not support the view that financial instability significantly reduced the willingness of employers to offer traditional plans, at least through 2007. Similarly, aggregate-longevity risk may be significant, but the evidence on whether it has worsened in recent years is not conclusive.

Revisions to the regulatory framework, including the practice of social activism have played a role in the United States and the United Kingdom in depressing employers' interest in offering or maintaining traditional pension plans. In the former country, pension law has favored the 401(k) plan over the traditional pension plan, while in the latter, the frequency of regulatory change has discouraged the maintenance of traditional plans. The impact of regulatory change in Canada is less clear. The large size and inflexibility of many traditional plans has undoubtedly contributed to their decline in troubled industries.

Several influences have been at work on the demand side. In particular, declining tenure – a phenomenon particularly pronounced in the United States – would have reduced the attractiveness of the traditional pension to potential plan members. Even when tenures are long enough to make workers vested, the limited portability of the benefit makes belonging to a traditional plan less attractive than belonging to a defined-contribution plan. The less attractive the benefit to the worker, the more likely a plan will be closed.

The slow secular decline in unionization has also had an impact, probably because union leadership could play an effective role in educating the rank and file regarding the benefits that a traditional plan bestows. For this reason, a unionized workforce is more likely to be a far-sighted workforce. Some of the attraction of defined-contribution plans, particularly plans where annuitization is optional, is that the account balance upon retirement will be valued more than the stream of annuity income it could finance. Although workforces in the United States and elsewhere may be no more shortsighted than they used to be, the increasing availability of plans where annuitization is only an option opens the door to shortsighted decisions. A lack of trust in employer-provided plans where workers have no control over the allocation of plan assets may also be playing a role.

What Needs to Be Done

Measures to revive the traditional pension plan need to be consistent with a country's program for increasing the coverage of the second tier. Should a country opt for mandatory coverage to enlarge the second tier, it must decide what types of plan an employer may be allowed to sponsor. The international experience, admittedly limited, suggests that restricting the qualifying type of plan to the traditional pension plan would not work. Some revival of the traditional pension could be a part of a campaign to broaden second-tier coverage via the technique of default setting, a strategy that has been proposed for the United States and is an integral part of the United Kingdom's future reform.

In principle, the declining role of the traditional pension can be partly but not wholly reversed by addressing those causes of the decline that are themselves reversible, by scaling plans back, or by making relatively minor changes to the structure of the traditional pension to reverse whatever increase in risks has occurred to discourage employers from offering them or counteract the influences that have discouraged plan participation. A more radical approach entails endowing defined-contribution plans with features that make them more like traditional plans. Developing products with longevity insurance or finding appropriate means of encouraging annuitization should be a priority.

Whatever reforms are adopted, most countries need to improve the statistical framework that applies to the second-tier pension. At a minimum, all countries should have accurate statistics on coverage by type of pension plan.

The Range of Possible Policies

What Can Be Changed, and What Cannot

Of the various influences that have reduced the role of traditional pensions, excessive regulation would be most easily reversed, technically if not politically. In practice, undoing the changes to pension law that social activism inspired could be politically contentious. The declining rate of unionization might also be reversed, although the link between such action and some reversal of the declining coverage rate of traditional plans is not very direct. Some of the mistrust of traditional plans might be lessened through appropriate programs of financial education, but financial education programs have not as yet proved particularly effective. They have been more successful in improving their subjects' basic understanding of financial concepts than in leading them to make more savvy and prudent choices.

Although the financial collapse of 2008 cannot explain the secular trend to decline in the share of traditional plans, it arguably would make many employers even more reluctant to offer traditional plans, at least to the extent that a large share of assets continues to be invested in equities. The same event would presumably increase employees' interest in traditional plans, or in plans that shared attributes of the traditional pension.

Measures that Do Not Require a Change to the Design of Traditional Plans

One way of reducing the risk borne by the sponsors of traditional plans is to scale back their size. As a result, a plan member remains protected, but to a lesser extent, from the three basic risks to retirement security. Simply reducing the scale of a traditional plan will reduce all the risks the plan sponsor bears. In practice, plan sponsors in Anglo-Saxon countries have not taken this route. It is apparently easier to freeze an old plan and introduce a new one than scale back the old plan, particularly if the sponsor wants to reduce the plan's generosity.

Measures that Would Require Minor Changes to Plan Design

The development of new financial instruments, like longevity bonds or bonds that are specifically designed to serve as hedges for the liabilities a plan sponsor assumes, would go some way toward reducing plan-sponsor risk. They would not require a change in plan design or a plan freeze and the adoption of a new kind of plan, although both kinds of instruments would increase funding costs.

Some risk can be shared between plan sponsor and plan members with only a minor modification to a plan's design. In particular, private pension plans could share aggregate-longevity risk. The plan would assume specific survival rates, and the increases in pension costs resulting from actual survival rates being greater than those assumed by plan actuaries could be borne at least in part by plan members. The sharing of investment risk, which has a bigger impact on a plan's funding ratio, poses more of a challenge.

Measures that Would Require Major Changes to Plan Design

A defined-contribution plan that shunts all risks onto plan members is by no means the sole alternative to the traditional plan. That said, sharing investment risk requires more significant changes to a traditional plan's design, or the creation of a supplementary plan. For example, investment risk can be shared by combining a scaled-back version of a traditional plan with a defined-contribution plan, possibly with a guarantee feature. The scaled-back version of the plan might also share longevity risk in the way just described. Hybrid plans like the cash-balance plan can be designed to leave the sponsor with investment risk, but like a standard defined-contribution plan, they leave the plan member saddled with all of the longevity risk.

Alternatively, the traditional plan might be phased out and replaced by the type of hybrid plan found in Switzerland, or by a defined-contribution plan with an add-on that provides some guarantee that income will not be exhausted in old age. Of the two add-ons that Chapter 7 described, it appears that the in-service annuity would provide a more steady and stable flow of income.

Default Setting

A default-setting mechanism that encourages retired persons to annuitize an adequate share of their wealth at retirement could be very valuable. The nature of the annuitization decision means that a default-setting mechanism to encourage it raises more issues than default setting to encourage joining a plan or contributing some minimum percentage of income to it. One possibility may be to allow a "trial run" before a decision becomes irrevocable.

Recent Reforms to First-Tier Plans

Various mechanisms have been devised to prevent demographic forces from causing public pension plans to become financially imbalanced. The key issue with these automatic adjustment mechanisms is whether they are indeed automatic: Can they avoid being overridden by the political process, or are they able to prompt a timely political decision? There is no such thing as a completely automatic mechanism of adjustment of pension-plan balances. Rules can always be changed or suspended.

Public-Sector Employer-Provided Plans

The arguments advanced for special treatment of second-tier public-sector plans do not stand up to critical examination. Employer-provided plans in the public sector should be subject to the same regulatory framework as their private-sector counterparts. Given the enormous adjustment that plans in North America may face, a move to a private-sector framework will need to be gradual.

Final Thoughts

Chapter 7 has discussed a broad range of alternative second-tier pension arrangements. The discussion could have been broader still. No one alternative to the traditional pension will please everybody. Whatever shape it may take, a good second-tier pension will need to mitigate effectively all three of the major risks to retirement security that *The Decline of the Traditional Pension* has used as a touchstone. Of the alternatives to the traditional pension in the countries the book has surveyed, it is clear that their biggest weakness is a failure to provide adequate longevity insurance and thereby mitigate the third risk.

There are many ways in which longevity risk could be addressed, ranging from the radical proposal of the guaranteed retirement account (GRA), to measures to make the annuity market more efficient, to the so-called "add-ons" Chapter 7 has examined. A GRA-type proposal entails substantial intervention by the state in the market for employer-provided pensions. It would be controversial, since it would effectively extend the public pension to the second tier (apart from the investment function). The other proposals might meet with more favor in the more market-oriented countries but might address less efficiently the failures that characterize the annuity market.

This study has sought to alert students and architects of pension policy to the serious threat to retirement security that the shift to defined-contribution pensions entails. It will have succeeded in its goal if it prompts pension experts to take a fresh look at the alternatives to the traditional pension, whether or not they have been described in these pages.

APPENDIX 1

Ten Country Profiles

Introduction

The descriptions of the ten survey countries' employer-provided pension plans in Appendix 1 are sketches that highlight those characteristics of the plans that are most relevant to this study. They focus on recent trends in and the current state of coverage of the labor force, the structure of benefits and plan financing, the relationship of the employer-provided pension tier with the public pension, and such current issues as financial literacy, regulatory reforms, and funding shortfalls. They are not intended to be encyclopedic accounts.

Australia

The Australian employer-provided pension system stands out from other industrial country systems in two respects: Its coverage has more than doubled in the past quarter century (among employed persons, coverage is close to universal) and the dominant type of pension, having been defined benefit, is now defined contribution. The new system, called the Superannuation Guarantee, has been said to have accumulated enough assets to acquire all the listed companies in Australia (Robertson 2008). Notwithstanding these improvements, an issue of adequacy arises because of a means-tested first tier known as the Age Pension, the benefit of which erodes as income from the second tier and other sources increases. The Superannuation Guarantee was expected to obviate the need for the Age Pension. The share of the population receiving it is about the same as before, but its average amount is less, and there is a higher share of "part-Age Pensioners."

Historical Background

Traditionally, pensions in Australia were provided voluntarily by private-sector employers to their senior officers, and by governments and public-sector agencies to their employees. Financial institutions provided pensions to a broader range of their employees, but blue-collar workers and many white-collar workers in the rest of the private sector had no pension.

When the Australian Bureau of Statistics conducted the first survey of superannuation (the Australian term for pension) in 1974, it estimated coverage of the workforce at only 32 percent. Private-sector coverage was 24 percent, and public-sector coverage 58 percent. Coverage of men was 36 percent and coverage of women only 15 percent. As of 1982–83, four out of five plan participants were members of defined-benefit plans [Australian Prudential Regulatory Authority (APRA) 2007]. The narrow coverage of private-sector pensions may reflect the fact that most of the population was entitled to the Age Pension, which served then as now as the first pillar of Australian retirement security. As of July 1, 2008, a full Age Pension for a couple was AUD 914 (about $845) every two weeks, and equal to about one-fourth of the average wage, which means that it could not by itself provide an adequate standard of living in retirement.

Reform of the second pillar did not really get underway until after the election of a Labor government in 1983. The current system derives from the labor agreements reached in 1985 and subsequent years, approved by the Conciliation and Arbitration Commission, which was responsible for resolving collective-bargaining disputes. Under these agreements, awards of 3 percent of compensation were paid as deferred and not current income into multiemployer superannuation funds established for the purpose (APRA 2007; Robertson 2008). The Insurance and Superannuation Commission was established in 1987, with the remit of enforcing the Occupational Superannuation Standards Act (OSSA) of the same year. OSSA established various standards of governance for superannuation funds, compliance with which was a requirement for tax concessions.

The Superannuation Guarantee (SG) law, which is the basic law for the current system, was passed in 1992. The SG requires that all except the smallest employers make a contribution to a retirement or superannuation plan for each of their employees, with certain limited exceptions described below. Employees may also make contributions of their own, but these are not obligatory. An important feature of the SG regime is the *preservation age* – the age at which benefits may first be drawn – that is now 55 years, but is being raised gradually to 60 by 2025.

With the establishment of the SG, the coverage of the employer-provided tier, which had been increasing since the mid-1980s, rose to 72 percent, and continued to rise in the 15 years that followed. The contribution required of employers was raised in steps to reach 9 percent, its current rate, in 2002. One important feature of the system, which was subsequently changed, was the responsibility given to the employer of choosing the fund in which an employee's contributions would be invested. As of July 1, 2005, employees generally have the choice of any fund into which their employer pays contributions (APRA 2007).

Coverage, Structure, and Benefits

The SG's statutory coverage of employees is broad and exempts few employment categories. The most important of these are for employees earning less than AUD 450 (about $415) per month, part-time employees under the age of 18, and employees aged 70 and over. APRA classifies the superannuation funds it regulates on both a functional basis (the sector of the economy they serve) and a regulatory basis (the applicable regulatory framework). The functional classification shows that the superannuation industry is quite diverse (Table A1.1). Industry, corporate, and public-sector funds, which make up the not-for-profit sector, account for about 40 percent of total assets. Retail funds, which are somewhat like the U.S. IRA (but with the important difference that IRA contributions are not mandatory), account for about one-third and small

Table A1.1. *Australia: Superannuation assets by functional and regulatory classifications, June 2007 (in percent of total Superannuation Guarantee funds' assets)*

Functional classification	
Corporate	6.1
Industry	17.3
Public Sector	15.5
Retail	32.3
Small	25.1
Subtotal	96.3
Balance of statutory funds	3.7
Total	100.0
Regulatory classification	
Public offer super funds	47.7
Nonpublic offer super funds	13.4
Exempt schemes	9.6
Approved deposit funds	0.0
Eligible rollover funds	0.5
Small APRA funds	0.3
Self-managed super funds	24.7
Balance of statutory funds	3.7
Total	100.0

Source: *APRA Annual Superannuation Bulletin* June 2007 (March 26, 2008).

plans (i.e., plans with no more than four members) account for most of the rest. Self-managed funds – basically individual or very small group plans – account for most of this last category.

Some superannuation funds are closed to the general public; this includes public-sector funds, corporate funds, and some of the industry funds. However, many industry funds seek and advertise for members who are not employed in their sector. They are counted under the regulatory classification as public offer super funds.

Although the SG does not forbid the establishment of defined-benefit plans, virtually all plans are defined contribution. Their dominance reflects both a big expansion in coverage of defined-contribution plans and the conversion of defined-benefit plans in both the public and private sectors. Defined-benefit plan sponsors in both the public and private sectors are said to have offered inducements to workers to shift to defined-contribution plans (Ross and Wills 2002). A fairly large number of defined-contribution plans also include members with a defined-benefit plan, but there are few exclusively defined-benefit plans left. The SG is completely portable, and members incur no charge when they switch plans. They may not switch funds more than once a year, however.

Regulatory Issues

The Australian Prudential Regulatory Authority (APRA) was established on July 1, 1998, to act as the lead agency in supervising superannuation funds. It shares the regulatory function with the Australian Securities and Investments Commission, which is responsible for overseeing disclosure (e.g., the transparency of the information on investments that the funds provide to their members and prospective members) and the advice the funds give to them. The Tax Office is responsible for the regulation of what are known as self-managed superannuation funds (see the following).

Since its establishment, APRA has developed a quite sophisticated system of risk-based supervision.[1] As Chapter 4 discussed, the risk management of defined-contribution plans requires a different approach from risk management of defined-benefit plans, because defined-contribution plan sponsors do not have the same obligations to fund the benefits that plan members accrue. Nonetheless, if a defined-contribution plan can be prudently and honestly managed, it can also be recklessly and fraudulently managed. Plan trustees are bound by the prudent-person rule, which, in addition to demanding that trustees act competently and in the best interest of plan members, places a limit on the overall degree of risk taken by the plan.

In its evaluation of the overall risk entailed by a plan's operations and investments, APRA makes two distinct assessments. The first assesses the potential severity of the overall risk facing a plan by rating eight different types of risk to which a plan could be prone. The second assesses the robustness of the plan's approach to risk control. The eight risk categories are: counterparty default risk, balance sheet and market risk (volatile asset prices and interest rates), insurance risk (absence of insurance cover when it is needed), operational risk (inadequate internal controls), liquidity risk, legal and regulatory risk (consequences of noncompliance), strategic risk (resulting from change to environment), and contagion risk. This classification is quite similar to that employed by the Netherlands with defined-benefit plans. Thompson (2008) suggests that major risks for SG funds would be balance sheet/market, operational (management of outsourced contracts), and trustee fitness and propriety. Each risk is rated in two ways: how relevant it is to the plan, and how significant it is. In the case of balance-sheet risk, a fund deemed to be low risk could be expected to have well-diversified funds spread over different instruments and low exposure to return volatility.

The supervisory consequences of a given risk rating depend on how sturdy the framework for risk control is judged to be. This is the object of the second assessment, which considers eight components of that framework: quality of plan governance, quality of senior management, effectiveness of operational management (includes human resource policies), IT and financial controls (capacity to produce timely information), adequacy of risk-management systems, compliance culture, quality of external review, and assessment of systems of external parties.

Each risk or risk-mitigating factor is assigned a ranking from one (low-risk/effective controls) to four (high-risk/ineffective controls). Aggregating these rankings yields

---

[1]   The following account of risk supervision draws substantially on Thompson (2008).

an overall ranking, which then determines (or suggests) a supervisory stance ranging from normal (no changes needed) to restructure.

In Australia, the taxation of employer-provided pensions has changed many times over the years. At present, the basic rules are that employer contributions are deductible from taxable income, but are taxed at 15 percent when paid to a fund, while the taxation of pension income or lump-sum distributions depends on the age of the pensioner. Since July 1, 2007, benefits paid after age 60 are exempt whether they take the form of an annuity or a lump sum. For younger recipients, benefits are taxed favorably up to the point at which their actuarial value exceeds a stipulated value known as the reasonable benefit level (RBL). Amounts exceeding the RBL are taxed at the highest marginal tax rate (OECD 2008a, 510).[2]

Current Issues

Coverage, adequacy, and efficiency. Notwithstanding the impressive achievements of the SG, the employer-provided pension system has some problematic aspects that could compromise retirement security for many of its members. Coverage is quite broad, although it will be important that married women with little labor-force experience have an enforceable claim on their husbands' SG account balance.[3] As with any employment-based system, some part-time workers and the chronically unemployed are left out.

Pension adequacy is a more problematic issue. The SG is the second pillar of the system. However, because the first pillar is means tested (i.e., once income from other sources exceeds AUD 240 per couple every two weeks, the Age Pension is reduced by AUD 40 for every additional AUD 100 in other income), it creates an implicit tax on any income financed by an SG account (Warren 2008). This creates an incentive to opt for superannuation before applying for the Age Pension, and then to withdraw the funds from the SG account and spend them. Reductions in the Age Pension can also be avoided by investing SG payouts in home improvements (an investment that is not subject to the asset test that with the income test determines eligibility to the Age Pension), choosing investments that produce little income, sheltering the income, and stopping work once the age of eligibility for the Age Pension is reached (Schulz 2005). These stratagems may preserve the Age Pension, but they do so at the cost of reducing the income from the second tier.

Costs. Commentators have expressed concern over the high cost of retail plans. Ellis et al. (2008) conducted a study of the net rate of return to different funds, in which they controlled for asset allocation. They found that the industry and public-sector plans with a balanced-asset portfolio earned net returns that were consistently higher than the returns of the retail plans with a similar portfolio. They attribute the difference to the higher costs of the retail plans. The advertising expenditure of the industry and public-sector plans might also be lower, because they can count on a stream of

---

[2]   A combination of annuity and lump sum payments is deemed to be an annuity if the value of the annuity is at least 50 percent of the total. As of January 1, 2006, the RBL for lump sums was AUD 678,149, and the RBL for annuities was twice that amount. These limits are indexed annually.

[3]   Provisions allowing the splitting of balances between divorcing or separating spouses by agreement or by court order came into force at end December 2002 (APRA 2007, 7).

new members who are employees of the industries they serve. Similar findings have been reported by other researchers. In addition to sales costs, the cost of retail funds may be boosted by the much greater choice of investment funds they offer. In 2005, retail funds offered an average of no less than 59 investment funds, compared with only seven for industry funds and four for corporate funds (Thompson 2008, 140). As Chapter 2 discussed, extra choice, in addition to increasing the gap between net and gross investment returns, could diminish the welfare of plan members by burdening them with a plethora of choice. Achieving substantial diversification does not require many funds to choose from. The financial crisis may heighten concerns about account costs.

Cost to the government is also a concern. The tax expenditures entailed by the favorable tax treatment of SG contributions are very large, and rival the budgetary cost of the Age Pension.

Financial literacy. Financial literacy is a special concern with defined-contribution systems. Although the Australian system narrows a worker's scope for decision making by making participation compulsory and setting a minimum contribution rate, a plan member must still choose an asset allocation. In addition, the third-tier saving decisions must be made, as well as decisions regarding the distribution phase for both tiers. Studies of financial literacy among Australians come to similar conclusions as studies in countries like the United States and the United Kingdom: It could stand some improving. A low level of financial literacy or simple ignorance of the alternative investments available might conceivably contribute to the difference already noted in the net rate of return on retail funds and the not-for-profit funds.

The financial market collapse. Australians, like the residents of other countries where the defined-contribution pension plays an important or key role, have suffered large capital losses since mid-2008. In light of the critical role assigned to the SG in retirement security, the apparent vulnerability of the SG to the market might prompt some reconsideration of the design of the first tier to increase the role it can play in a secure retirement for low and middle income earners.

Canada

Canada has experienced a muted version of the trend away from the traditional employer-provided pension that the United States and the United Kingdom have experienced, but with some noteworthy differences. The overall situation of Canada's pension system is similar in some respects to that of the United Kingdom. Like the United Kingdom, Canada will need to ensure that the coverage and generosity of second- and third-tier pensions are sufficient to make up for a modest public pension. It must also address the more immediate concern of the repercussions of the funding shortfalls caused by the drop in global equity values and interest rates in the fall of 2008.

Coverage and Basic Characteristics

The dominance of the traditional pension plan, which in Canada is usually a final-salary plan, has been slowly eroding over the past two decades.[4] In the public sector,

---

4   As was the case in the United Kingdom, high inflation in the 1970s caused a shift away from career-average plans.

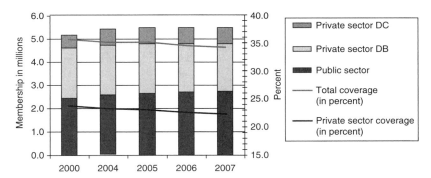

Figure A1.1. Canada: Plan membership and labor-force coverage.
Source: Statistics Canada (2009).

the traditional plan has retained its preeminence, covering over 90 percent of public-sector pension-plan members. In the private sector, its share has declined from 80 percent in 2000 to 74 percent in 2007, continuing a trend of some standing.

The increase in the share of defined-contributions plans has not been enough to prevent a slow decline in employer-provided plan coverage in the private sector from 24 percent in 2000 to 22 percent by 2007. The large share (one in five) of public-sector employees in total employment and the high rate of coverage in that sector help raise the total coverage rate to about one in three (see Figure A1.1). The skimpy coverage of the second tier is partially compensated by a thriving market for Registered Retirement Savings Plans (RRSPs), which are tax-favored personal retirement plans somewhat like the U.S. IRA.

Regulatory Framework and Related Issues
The responsibility for the regulation of employer-provided pension plans is split between the federal government and the provinces. Pension plans for employees of crown corporations and the federal government are supervised by the federal Office of the Superintendent of Financial Institutions (OSFI). Other plans, including those that cover provincial government employees are supervised at the provincial level. The applicable laws do not vary greatly across provincial jurisdictions. For example, Ontario and most of the other provinces have adopted the rules limiting certain types of investments enacted by the federal parliament. This said, the recently published report of Ontario's Expert Commission on Pension Reform expressed concern over diverging laws (Government of Ontario 2008, 198.) The province of Ontario, which accounts for about 40 percent of the country's pension-plan members, is the only jurisdiction to provide a form of insurance like that provided by the Pension Benefit Guaranty Corporation in the United States and the Pension Protection Fund in the United Kingdom.[5] Finally, the federal Income Tax Act strongly influences the amount of contractual saving intermediated by employer-provided plans through the limits it sets on deductible contributions and pensions.

---

[5]   The maximum benefit Ontario's fund pays is C$1,000 ($1000) per month, about one-fifth of the U.S. PBGC's maximum. It has not been changed since the fund's inception in 1980.

No major change in the legal or regulatory framework has taken place in the past 20 years. In the 1990s, legislation was adopted to strengthen the rights of plan members separating before retirement to the benefits they had accrued, to increase portability of accrued benefits, and to shorten the period between the start of employment and beginning of accrual of pension benefits. As a result of these reforms, Canadian pension law provides more protection to employees with short tenures than ERISA provides to U.S. workers.[6] In order to benefit from the advantages provided by the Income Tax Act, employer-provided plans must register with the Canada Revenue Agency and meet the requirements of the Act as well as the relevant federal or provincial plan legislation. Qualifying plans are termed registered pension plans (RPPs).

Canada applies the prudent-person rule – as do the United States, the United Kingdom, and most of the other seven countries – with some fairly standard restrictions on concentration of holdings. The only restriction that might impose a constraint in practice is one requiring that a plan not invest more than 25 percent of its assets in Canadian resource companies. (No similar restriction applies to foreign companies.)

All pension funds are required to undergo both a "going-concern" valuation and a "solvency" valuation every three years. The former permits some smoothing, the latter requires marking to market. The solvency valuation estimates what the plan's liabilities would be in the event of dissolution, and assumes that the plan would acquire annuities for each of the plan members from life insurance companies. The resulting estimate of plan liabilities normally exceeds the estimate plan actuaries would make, mainly because the discount rate the actuaries would use would be higher than the discount rate used by insurance companies. In the event that the asset-liability ratio falls short of 100 percent in a solvency valuation, the Superintendent may request more frequent valuations, and the gap must be amortized over a five-year period. The Canadian Institute of Actuaries disseminates guidelines on the choice of discount rate and other aspects of valuation. These guidelines give plan actuaries some degree of discretion, but most requirements of a valuation are determined by the Pension Benefits Act.

The Traditional Pension Plan in North America: Divergent Fates?

A number of features of the regulatory and legal framework of pensions in Canada may explain why the traditional pension plan's position has not eroded as quickly as it has in the two larger Anglo-Saxon countries.[7] First, unlike the United States, both employee and employer benefits are tax deductible, although the maximum

---

[6] Although there is some variation across provincial jurisdictions, full vesting is generally mandatory after no more than four years of employment or upon plan termination. Longer periods apply in New Brunswick and Prince Edward Island (with few plan members between them). In the case of termination before vesting, employees receive a return of their contributions. Benefits are portable if the new plan an employee is joining agrees to the transfer of the benefits accrued under the old plan. Two other possibilities are transfer to a locked-in retirement account (LIRA) – so-called because no access to the transferred funds is permitted prior to retirement – and transfer to a registered retirement savings plan (RRSP). Exceptions to the lock-in rule are permitted when life expectancy is short or the amount is small (OECD 2008a, 91).

[7] This discussion draws on Brown and Liu (2001).

pension – currently the lesser of 2 percent or C$2,444 ($2,440) per year of service – is much lower than it is in the United States. Taxation in Canada follows the EET principle, with pensions being taxed as ordinary income when paid. Second, benefits are typically paid as annuities, although in some provinces a specified part of the benefit may be commuted (paid as a lump sum). To the extent that annuities are perceived as attractive by plan members or their representatives, this feature would give a traditional pension an edge in any comparison with a defined-contribution plan. Third, if plan members are willing to pay additional contributions, defined-benefit plans may be upgraded to include indexation, early retirement, and death benefits (OECD 2008a, 92). Fourth, unions, which are traditionally well disposed toward defined-benefit plans, have a somewhat higher share of the labor force in the private sector. The absence of nondiscrimination rules like those that apply in the United States may also be a factor. Finally, multiemployer pension plans are relatively more important in Canada than the United States. These plans target rather than fix their benefits, so that funding shortfalls are not the sole responsibility of the sponsor, but are shared with active plan members. This reduces the risk that plan sponsors bear, although it may also make the plans less attractive to their members, who must bear more risk.

Two aspects of the regulatory framework may have worked to reduce the attractiveness to employers of the traditional pension and to increase the likelihood of underfunding. First, recent court decisions have created uncertainty about who "owns" a plan surplus – the plan sponsor or the plan members. If the sponsor believes that the membership has property rights to a surplus (over and above a right to the deferred compensation that the surplus finances), the sponsor may want to minimize transfers to the pension fund (Laidler and Robson 2007). Second, the Income Tax Act limits the transfers a plan sponsor can make to a fund when the asset-liability ratio exceeds 110 percent, and in certain other circumstances (OECD 2008a, 90). The limit will lower the average funding level that a plan will maintain.

Current Issues

Adequacy: The defined-benefit plan still covers more than one-quarter of the employed labor force including the public sector, and on present trends it will take some time for this share to drop noticeably. The more gradual trend away from defined-benefit plans may make less urgent some of the questions that arise with increased reliance on defined-contribution plans. Canadians with employer-provided pensions are more likely than their counterparts in either of the other Anglo-Saxon countries to be covered by a defined-benefit plan, and their benefits are more secure.

Nonetheless, about two-thirds of the employed labor force are not members of a plan provided by their employer. Workers earning less than C$30,000 can obtain a respectable replacement rate from the combination of the means-tested Old-Age Security and Guaranteed Income Supplement benefits, and the Canada Pension Plan/Quebec Pension Plan (CPP/QPP). Workers in the middle income range are more vulnerable.

As is the case in the United States and the United Kingdom, a third tier of voluntary saving provides additional retirement security to many. Although about 55 percent of the workforce contributed to either or both an RPP and Registered Retirement Saving Plan in 2004, about one-fifth of the workforce can be assumed to earn more than the C$30,000 that would be the maximum income at which the first tier would provide an adequate safety net alone, and to not be contributing to a second- or third-tier pension.[8,9] This hole in the retirement safety net might be addressed through a reform similar to that planned for the United Kingdom in 2010, or even a reform along Australian lines.[10]

Financial literacy. Financial literacy may be a more important issue for Canada than it is for most of the other survey countries because of the limited coverage of the second tier and the declining role of defined-benefit plans. Although participation in a defined-benefit plan does not make financial acumen irrelevant by any means, the greater range of choices of a defined-contribution system, particularly one that is voluntary, gives the issue an obvious importance in Canada. For about two-thirds of the workforce, the only source of annuitized income in old age will be the OAS/GIS/CPP/QPP. For many members of this group, making the first-tier pension their only source of annuitized income would leave them underannuitized.

Funding issues. Finally, the two problematic features mentioned in the preceding need to be addressed. The author hesitates to weigh in on a legal issue, but it is not clear why the workforce has to have property rights to a fund surplus to safeguard their right to a pension. As for the limit on the surplus of 10 percent of liabilities, the key issue is how volatile the surplus can be expected to be. If the fluctuations in equity values and interest rates exercise a swingeing effect on the ratio of assets to liabilities, the limit placed on the ratio should be set at a correspondingly high level.

According to one source, Canadian pension plans suffered a fall in assets of almost 16 percent in 2008 (thestar.com 2009). Because annuity premiums have been increasing, a large number of plans are now in deficit on a solvency valuation basis. The strictures re speed of adjustment of the shortfall of assets from liabilities under either measure were relaxed following the dot.com crash at the beginning of the current decade. In the fall of 2008, they were again relaxed. The federal government has extended the solvency adjustment period from five to ten years, and a number of provinces have followed suit. Given the fact that the drop in assets values has spared no, or very few, plans, such a policy change is unlikely to provoke moral hazard. It does, however, raise the question of whether some sort of automatic rule might govern changes in the period of adjustment, rather than ministerial discretion.

Denmark

Coverage and Structure

Although employer-provided pension plans in Denmark date from the nineteenth century, coverage did not really begin to expand until the 1950s, and only began to

---

[8] Both the share of tax filers who contribute to these plans and the average amount of the contribution are higher than the corresponding figures in the United States. Less than 10 percent of U.S. taxpayers make contributions to either traditional IRAs or Roth IRAs (see section on the United States for an explanation of these plans). The average contribution is about $2800. Part of the difference in participation and average contributions may be explained by the higher limits that apply in Canada, part by the somewhat higher marginal income tax rates that Canadians pay, and part by the tax deductibility of employer's as well as employee's contributions.

[9] The estimate of one-fifth is calculated by the author and is based on the figure for taxpayers reporting deductions for pension-plan contributions in 2004 (Statistics Canada 2007, 291).

[10] Ambachtsheer (2008) proposes a reform that is similar in some respects to the reform strategy of the British Pensions Commission.

expand rapidly in the 1990s, notably in the public sector.[11] The coverage of the second tier is estimated to be about 80 percent of the labor force and 90 percent of full-time employees. Most public-sector employees are covered by defined-contribution schemes – less than 15 percent are covered by an unfunded defined-benefit plan. Over 90 percent of workers are estimated to be covered by either the second or third tiers (van Dam and Andersen 2008, 96–7). The coverage of the voluntary personal pension plans that make up the third tier is estimated to be about 40 percent.

Most private-sector pension plans in Denmark have industry-wide coverage, and have been created by a collective-bargaining agreement. Membership in them is compulsory for all employees covered by the agreement, and most plans cover part-time as well as full-time employees. These plans can be managed by a life insurance company or a multiemployer pension plan. Some plans that cover the employees of a single company also exist, but they play a marginal and declining role. At the end of 2005, life insurance companies were managing about 57 percent of the assets of employer-provided plans, followed by pension funds with 23 percent and banks with 18 percent (International Monetary Fund 2007b, 6). Unions own the majority of the shares of some insurance companies.

Multiemployer plans are, in general, subject to the same regulatory framework as life insurance companies. The influential role of labor in pension-plan governance is evident in the requirement that at least half of the members of the board of a plan must be plan members (OECD 2008a, 219–20). In practice, unions are said to have substantial control.

Almost all private-sector plans are defined-contribution, contributory plans. The total rate of contribution in most of the new plans will be 12 percent of salary in 2009 or 2010, with employees usually contributing one-third of the total (OECD 2008a, 221). Older plans usually have a combined contribution rate between 12 and 20 percent of salary. Vesting of both employee and employer contributions is usually immediate, and portability is effectively full.

Danish employer-provided pension plans have provisions that endow them with some of the key attributes of defined-benefit plans. In particular, they provide, as Swiss plans do, a minimum guaranteed rate of return at both the accumulation and the distribution phases (Andersen and Skjodt 2007, 21). The rate, which applies to both phases, is currently 1.5 percent per annum in the case of new plans and increases in contributions to old plans, although higher rates apply when contributions are less than their level in 2000. For older plans, the guaranteed rate ranges from 2.5–4.5 percent. The extent to which plan members may choose among life annuities, term annuities, phased withdrawal arrangements, and lump-sum withdrawals varies from plan to plan. The minimum guaranteed rate of return applies to annuities and to some lump-sum and phased withdrawals, but in recent years investment-linked phased withdrawals, where all the risk is borne by the investor, have become popular. The value of lump-sum and phased withdrawals to which a guarantee applies is being capped. Unisex mortality tables must be used to calculate any annuity a plan pays, but not for members who joined the plan before June 30, 1999. The minimum retirement age is 60, but plans can establish a higher age, such as 65.

---

[11] Denmark's public pension has two elements: a flat rate paid to all older Danes and a means-tested supplement. These are complemented by the ATP, which is a defined-contribution pension with fixed contribution rates with a maximum of less than 1 percent of the average wage. Its assets are about 20 percent of the total assets of the second tier.

The return on investments is divided between shareholders and plan members. Should the results warrant it, part of the return is used to pay bonuses to plan members. Because shareholders bear more risk than plan members, their share of the total return on investment is higher than it would be if it were determined purely by share holdings and account values. To enhance intergenerational equity, bonuses paid to plan members are adjusted to reflect the fact that the guaranteed rate of return has fallen over the years. Consequently, younger plan members will receive a greater bonus per krona of account balance than members of longer standing (Andersen and Skjodt 2007, 32). If returns are sufficiently good, younger members will receive a return of 4.5 percent. What happens when returns are not high enough to pay every member a return of 4.5 percent remains to be resolved.

Regulation

The Danish regulatory framework has developed in the same general direction as that taken in other countries with well-developed financial systems, particularly those in Europe. Beginning in 1996, a gradual move to fair-value accounting took place with full implementation being achieved by 2003, and in the late 1990s the Danish Financial Supervisory Authority (DFSA) began laying the groundwork for a risk-based supervisory framework.[12,13]

In 2001, the DFSA introduced a traffic-light system to gauge the vulnerability of the balance sheets of pension plans and insurance companies to stress. The test the DFSA applies takes account of the impact of market and other risks on the asset side of the plan balance sheet, and of interest-rate risk on the liabilities side. The classification used to determine the effect of market risk on the asset side is quite aggregated, consisting of bonds and stocks/real estate. The other risks included in the model are credit risk, counterparty risk with derivative transactions, risks in subsidiary companies, and currency risks.

In the red test, share values are subjected to a fall of 12 percent, and real estate of 8 percent. In the yellow test, which was suspended during the 2008–09 crisis, share values fall by 30 percent and real estate values by 12 percent. On the liabilities side, the shock is a shift in interest rates that varies inversely with duration. With long bonds (i.e. a duration greater than 3.5 years), the shift is 1.0 percentage points for the yellow test and 0.7 percent for the red. A fund or insurance company that fails the red-light test may be ordered to take remedial action. Failing the yellow-light test normally subjects the institution to intensified supervision.

To complement this quantitative approach, the DFSA has developed a system to rate qualitative risks, such as the adequacy of internal risk control systems, the appropriateness of the staff's expertise, the quality of managerial information systems, IT risk, legal risk, and so on (van Dam and Andersen 2008). These initiatives should prepare the pension industry for full-fledged risk-based supervision.

---

[12] A change in the tax regime obliged insurance companies to value assets at market prices.

[13] Some quantitative restrictions apply to the assets that cover technical provisions. Specifically, 30 percent of these assets must be invested in low-risk investments (e.g., government bonds), while up to 70 percent of total assets may be invested in equity, with a maximum of 10 percent in shares listed outside OECD countries (OECD 2008a, 221). In practice, these limits would probably not constrain asset allocation much, as few pension plans would place more than 70 percent of their assets in equity.

Current Issues

The Danish model. When judged by the basic standards of breadth of coverage and adequacy, the Danish employer-provided pension system scores very well. Participation in the second tier is not mandatory but it is quasimandatory and its coverage is surpassed by few other systems. The combined replacement rates it generates, though they depend on the rate of return to participants' contributions, would normally be high. The risk entailed by a defined-contribution system is mitigated by guarantees on the rate of accumulation of assets and the conversion of the balance at retirement, and the current guaranteed rate of interest on contributions of 1.5 percent will at least allow some growth of account balances in real terms.

Implications of the guarantee. The variation in the guarantee has implications for the investment behavior of pension plans. The membership of some plans is relatively young, and a relatively low guarantee rate applies. The average rate for other plans with older memberships is higher. The rate of 1.5 percent encourages plans to invest in shares, while higher rates discourage investment in shares because of the consequences of a down market. The low share of stocks in plans with older memberships has contributed to the growth of unit-linked products, which have no guarantee but can earn a higher rate of return. In 2007, contributions to these products amounted to 21 percent of the total.

How exposed Denmark's pension funds were to the losses incurred on stock and bond markets in 2008–09 is uncertain. The most current data on the asset composition of insurance companies and pension funds date from 2004 (Anderson and Skjodt 2007, 15). The insurance companies held about 65 percent of their assets in Danish and foreign bonds and 18 percent in equities and investment funds. The pension funds were more exposed to the stock market, because their holdings of bonds amounted to 40 percent, and holdings of equities and investment funds to over 40 percent. In 2008–09, the insurance industry apparently hedged its interest risk with swaps and other products, which would have substantially limited its losses.

Germany

Germany's employer-provided pensions are distinguished from those of the other nine countries by the variety of legal forms they can assume and by the modest contribution to retirement income that they have made until now. Although the second tier's coverage in the private sector is estimated to have reached 46 percent by mid-2004 (implying an economy-wide coverage of about 59 percent), it is estimated to account for not much more than 5 percent of the retirement income of the median retiree household, and its assets as of end 2004 amounted to about 18 percent of GDP (Deutsche Bundesbank 2008; Oster 2006). Among today's retirees, coverage is only 20 percent (Callegaro and Wilke 2008). The second tier's modest contribution to retirement security reflects the generosity of the first tier and, to a lesser extent, a culture of voluntary personal saving. It may also reflect in part the strict vesting requirements – ten years for employer contributions to defined-benefit plans – that have prevailed until recently.

The general recognition in Germany that the financial position of its public pension system was unsustainable led to an intense debate in the late 1990s over ways to promote both contractual and personal saving, and thereby reduce the strain created by an aging population on Germany's public finances. This debate culminated in substantial reforms of the first (PAYG-financed) tier, as well as the funded second and third tiers of retirement saving that were introduced between 2001 and 2004. The reform of employer-provided pensions led to the creation of an additional pension vehicle (the so-called pension fund), which is similar in some respects to the Anglo-Saxon pension plan, and is encumbered with less restrictions on its investment policy than other plans. Perhaps even more importantly, the reforms introduced a new type of plan that is legally a defined-benefit plan but one with important defined-contribution features. The reforms also introduced a personal pension known as the Riester pension, after the finance minister with whom it was associated. It has certain features in common with the American IRA, but differs from it in important ways as well. Both the new form of the employer-provided pension and the Riester third-tier pensions benefit from a combination of subsidies and favorable tax treatment.[14]

Basic Structure of the Employer-Provided Tier

Until the recent reforms, German employers could provide pensions to their employees through one of four vehicles: a book-reserve plan, a benefit or support fund, direct insurance, or so-called staff pension insurance.

Book-reserve pensions have traditionally been the most important employer-provided pension in Germany (Table A1.2), accounting for almost 60 percent of employer-provided pension assets in 2004.[15] Book-reserve plans are not a trust or other entity separate from the sponsoring company. Their reserves may be invested externally, but need not be. The companies offering them are expected to employ appropriate actuarial methods in determining their pension liabilities and funding them, but they are not subject to the Federal Financial Supervisory Authority (known more commonly by its German acronym BaFin), and investments backing pension obligations are not subject to restrictions. Employees have no legal claim on the assets of the company, but the employer has a contractual obligation to honor its pension arrangements and must acquire insolvency insurance from an industry-funded pension-guarantee fund, the PSVaG. Because it is a mutual insurance society, the PSVaG is supervised by BaFIN.

Book-reserve pension plans are found in other European countries as well as Germany, but their role in these countries is not nearly so large. Their prominence in Germany reflects the absence of organized capital markets in the early postwar years, and the very strong, contemporary fiscal incentives to charge future pension obligations against corporate profits (Gerke et al. 2006).

---

[14] A contributor receives the higher of a subsidy or the tax relief obtained from a tax exemption. He or she can receive a personal subsidy and a subsidy for each of his or her children, the value of which varies directly and proportionately with the share of income that is "sacrificed" and reaches a maximum value when contributions reach 4 percent of gross salary. Contributions are deductible from gross taxable income up to a maximum of 4 percent of gross salary. Contributions to employer-provided pensions are also exempt from the social insurance payroll tax. For a Riester personal pension to benefit from favorable tax treatment, the contract must specify that at least 70 percent of the balance in the account has to be either annuitized or, if it is not, subject to a fixed annual withdrawal until age 85, when annuitization is compulsory.

[15] This section draws on Deutsche Bundesbank (2001), Oster (2006), and OECD (2008a).

Table A1.2. *Germany: Forms of employer-provided pension plans*

	Book reserve	Support funds	Direct insurance	Pensionskasse	Pension funds
Individual claim or right	N.A.	No	Yes	Yes	Yes
Guaranteed rate of return	No	No	Yes	Yes	Yes
Investment restrictions	None	None	Quantitative restrictions		Very limited (prudent-person rule)
Insolvency Insurance	Yes	Yes	Conditional	No	Yes
Supervision	No	No	Yes	Yes	Yes
Share of industry assets in percent (2004)	58.2	7.8	12.0	21.8	0.2

Source: Deutsche Bundesbank (2001); Oster (2006).

Support funds differ from book-reserve plans in that they are legally autonomous, and may be operated by more than one employer. Employees do not have a legal right to a pension, but can generally make a claim against the enterprise, and support funds must have insolvency coverage (Deutsche Bundesbank 2001). Like book-reserve plans, support funds are free of supervision, and no restrictions apply to their investments.

The *direct-insurance* model entails, as the name suggests, the company providing the pension paying for an insurance policy that covers the plan's obligations to its employees. The key distinction between this vehicle and the others is that the insurance company assumes the investment, longevity, and other risks inherent in a promise to provide a pension. The insurance company is subject to the supervision of the financial authority, and its investments are subject to some quantitative restrictions. Apart from some special cases, direct-insurance arrangements are not covered by the pension-guarantee fund (European Actuarial Consultative Group 2005).

The *Pensionskasse*, or staff-pension insurance, is the second most important type of plan (measured by assets), and is legally autonomous. It operates like insurance companies dedicated to pensions, and may be set up by one or more enterprises.

The fifth type of pension vehicle, *pension funds*, is also the newest, having been introduced in 2001. These funds may offer a pension that can be financed by both employer and employee, and can take the effective if not the legal form of a defined-contribution plan with a guarantee, so that the size of the pension benefit will depend on financial market performance. The direct-insurance and staff-insurance plans are also now allowed to offer this type of plan. Assets held by pension funds have been growing rapidly, but from a tiny base, and stood at €8.3 billion at end 2006.[16] Because

[16] Private communication from Stephanie Siering of BaFin, July 10, 2007.

Table A1.3. *Germany: Summary of pension vehicle taxation*

	Book reserve	Support funds	Direct insurance	Pensionskasse	Pension funds
Employee contributions	Not taxable		Deductible up to 4 percent of social security tax ceiling (about €2,500) with an additional €1800 for new employees		
Employer contributions	Deductible up to certain limits		Deductible as a business expense but taxable as fringe benefits for employees		
Investment income	Taxable	Partly exempt	Exempt	Exempt	Exempt
Benefits	Taxable as personal income for all five vehicles				
Qualification			Contributions of members who joined before 2005 are taxed at lower of 20 percent or income tax rate. Principal component of benefits is not taxed.		

Source: OECD (2008a);Deutsche Bank (2003).

they are a recent development, their accumulated balance is not a good indication of their coverage of the labor force.

The taxation of German pensions varies with the vehicle that provides them. Since 2001, however, direct-insurance, pensionskasse, and pension funds are basically taxed according to the EET model, except that employer contributions, although they are deductible from taxable profits, are taxed as a fringe benefit (see Table A1.3). This is the reverse of the tax treatment of defined-benefit plans in the United States, where employee contributions may not be deducted from personal income subject to tax.

Recent Developments and Issues

Coverage of the second tier. There are signs that the reforms of 2001 are broadening the coverage of the employer-provided pension system, and that the share of non-traditional defined-benefit or hybrid plans is rising, although the data that would permit a more definitive statement about such developments are not readily available (Börsch-Supan et al. 2007). A private survey conducted in 2007 of pension-plan types in Germany and several other European countries found that over 60 percent of the German companies surveyed were offering what the survey termed "defined-contri-bution–like" pensions – despite their legal status as defined-benefit plans – to new employees, and that such arrangements applied to about 50 percent of current employees (Towers Perrin 2007). New pension plans are typically financed by employee rather than employer contributions, a predictable result of the favorable tax treatment of the former. By the end of 2007, the number of personal Riester pension contracts had risen to 10.75 million, or roughly one-fourth of the work force. The coverage of the second tier is estimated to have risen from 38 percent of private-sector employees subject to social security at the end of 2001, to 46 percent at end-2004 (Deutsche Bundesbank 2008, 60–1).

Regulatory developments. In addition to the growing role of hybrid pensions, the main recent development affecting Germany's second tier is the move toward a consolidated and risk-based regulatory framework. A senior BaFin official attributes this move to several influences, including the integration of the country's three regulatory agencies into one, and the need to comply with the introduction of Solvency II, the new supervisory framework for euro area insurance companies (Oster 2006).

The new framework involves the conducting of stress tests and the application of a risk-scoring system (the traffic-light model), which assesses risk in four different areas, as well as the seriousness of the consequences of shocks (which is gauged by plan or company size). The move away from book-reserve plans and the policy of increasing the coverage of pensions offered by a vehicle that is similar to the Anglo-Saxon model have only increased the need for a sound risk-based regulatory framework. The growing role of the second tier has also brought into relief the need for current, comprehensive, and reliable statistics on the coverage and basic characteristics of employer-provided plans, which are now lacking (Deutsche Bundesbank 2008).

Japan

Japan's employer-provided pension system has been radically reformed in the past decade. The financial difficulties Japan endured in the 1990s brought to light weaknesses in the governance and regulation of an important pension form, the tax-qualified pension plan. Laws passed in 2001–02 created new types of pension plans that are closer in structure to the pension plans in other industrial countries than the established plans, and go some way to mitigating the problems of limited vesting and portability that have been a prominent feature of the employer-provided pension system. The regulatory and accounting framework has been revised in much the same way as in other industrial countries, and the oversight of pension plans in general has been enhanced. Given the reform's recent vintage, and its gradualist strategy – the older forms of employer-provided pensions are being phased out and not eliminated outright – it is useful to start with a description of the Japanese system pre-reform.

The System Prior to the Reforms of 2001–02

Prior to the recent reforms, there were three types of employer-provided pension or retirement plans: the lump-sum retirement benefit plan (LSRB), the tax-qualified pension plan (TQPP), and the employee pension fund (EPF). The LSRB dates from the 1930s and predates the other two. As its name suggests, the benefit these plans paid was typically lump sum and estimated to lie in the range of 38 to 45 months of salary, making it relatively generous as severance schemes go. The age of retirement is usually fixed by the sponsoring firm. Currently, more than four out of five employees opt for a pension at age 60 (Japanese Ministry of Health 2009), but perhaps 70 percent of them continue to work, usually for the same company or a subsidiary.

The LSRB system has had very broad coverage. In 1997, 90 percent of Japanese firms offered a retirement package (a benefit under the LSRB, a retirement pension, or both). Of these 90 percent, some 90 percent offered a severance plan, and 52.5 percent offered a pension plan, meaning that about 80 percent of firms offered a severance plan

(National Institute of Population and Social Security Research 2007, 11). The share of employees covered almost certainly exceeded 80 percent, because the proportion of firms offering a retirement benefit of some kind increases with the number of employees a firm has.

LSRBs were popular with employers because they were tax favored, and they have been popular with employees as well. These plans are solely financed by the employer. They typically rely on book reserves and are typically underfunded. They are loosely supervised by local labor standard advisory offices. Their benefits are not vested, although in practice, benefits are paid after three years of employment. Although they undoubtedly contribute to retirement security, they lack essential features of a true pension plan.

TQPPs were established in 1962. They are sponsored mainly by small- and medium-sized enterprises. In 2001, their number exceeded 73,000 (Rajnes 2007, 94). TQPPs are defined-benefit plans, with the benefit being determined by earnings and years of service, or simply by years of service. Retiring workers with at least 20 years of service may choose between an annuity and a lump sum (OECD 2008a, 473). In practice, over 80 percent of retirees have elected a lump sum (Rajnes 2007, 91). A preference for lump-sum distributions is an important feature of Japanese pensioners, and might reflect the long tradition of lump-sum severance payments. Benefits do not vest, although in practice, benefits would be paid to departing employees with at least three years' tenure, as is the case with the LSRB.

According to Sakamoto (2005), TQPPs have tended to be viewed primarily as tax shelters for the plan sponsor because employers' contributions are deductible without limit from their taxable income. In addition, the regulatory demands made of sponsors of TQPPs are far from onerous. For example, provisioning requirements are not strict. More generally, TQPPs lack an adequate delineation of participants' rights and plan sponsors' fiduciary duties.

EPFs were established in 1966. The major motive for their creation was to allow employers to opt out of the earnings-related part of the public system, the Employees' Pension Insurance (EPI).[17] Once a company opts out and establishes an EPF, then all of its employees who are covered by EPI will be members of the EPF plan as well. In return for a reduced payroll tax rate, the employer must agree to fund a pension for each plan member that as of fiscal year 2004 was at least 50 percent higher than the pension the government would have paid.[18] The part of the EPF benefit that substitutes for the EPI benefit is normally paid out as an annuity. The options available to the supplementary component of the EPF depend on an employee's tenure. However, the government is responsible for paying any increases in the pension due to indexation.

[17]   The EPI has a component that varies with the number of years worked (but not with salary), and an earnings-related component. Both components are financed by a payroll tax levied at the rate of 15 percent. The replacement rate for the two components combined for a single worker who has worked for 40 years at the average salary is estimated to be about 43 percent. If the worker has a spouse who does not work outside the home, the replacement rate rises to 59 percent (Rajnes 2007). The increase in replacement rates when a worker is married is also a feature of U.S. Social Security.

[18]   The proportional increase in the pension for which the employer was responsible was 30 percent in fiscal year 2001. It was lowered to 10 percent in fiscal year 2003 before being increased to 50 percent in fiscal year 2004.

EPFs are subject to a more substantial regulatory framework than are TQPPs. In particular, they must be funded through either a trust fund or an insurance contract. There is some limited vesting, and the Pension Fund Association (PFA) facilitates portability by managing the accumulated contributions made on behalf of an employee who has left his or her job before retirement. The PFA also guarantees the supplementary part of the benefit that EPFs pay (although not that part that exceeds the minimum value of the supplement that the government specifies). Benefits paid by other pension plans are not guaranteed. Contributions by the employer to each of the plans are fully tax deductible with no limit. The TQPPs are overseen by the Ministry of Finance, and the EPFs by the Ministry of Health, Labor, and Welfare.

Background to the Reforms of 2001

The stagnation that the Japanese economy endured in the 1990s and early years of the current decade caused a severe deterioration in the financial position of employer-provided pension plans. The difficult financial climate affected both sides of plans' balance sheets. A steep decline in share prices caused a large decline in the value of the assets of both TQPPs and EPFs. The deterioration was initially masked in part by a permissive accounting rule that allowed assets to be recorded at the greater of market or book (acquisition) value.

The valuation of liabilities for plan purposes was initially not affected by the big drop that took place in long-term bond rates as Japanese bond rates fell along with the rate of inflation, because pension plans continued to use the prescribed discount rate of 5.5 percent.[19] In 1997, however, a lower, market-related rate was introduced. The combination of higher liability valuations and declining share prices resulted in underfunding of TQPPs and EPFs amounting, according to one source, to between ¥ 40 and 60 trillion (or roughly $350 and $525 billion) by the late 1990s (Rajnes 2007, 93).

The regulatory framework applying to both the older and the new pension plans had already been revised prior to the promulgation of the new laws. In addition to the adoption of the market-related discount rate already noted, a version of the prudent-person rule was adopted in 1995, replacing quantitative regulation, and in 1997, sponsoring companies were required to recognize plan losses on their balance sheets, to adopt mark-to-market asset valuation, and to apply (in the case of EPFs) a prescribed test for solvency. The concept of fiduciary duty was a part of Japanese pension law before the reforms, although Morito (n.d.) argues that it took on more importance in the late 1990s as investment-allocation rules were liberalized.

On the eve of reform, Japan's second tier had a coverage rate of about 90 percent. The coverage rate for EPFs and TQPPs was about 60 percent. Japanese employers are not obliged to offer their employees a pension plan, but in the past, pensions have been an important item on the collective-bargaining agenda. Plan sponsors are required not to discriminate arbitrarily between groups of full-time employees. EPFs must cover all employees, including part-time employees, who would have been covered by the EPI. Overall, however, coverage rates for part-time employees are lower than those for full-time employees (OECD 2008a, 471).

---

[19] The comparatively large share of lump sums in the benefits that companies paid their workers would have reduced somewhat the impact of declining interest rates on plan liabilities, because the duration of a lump-sum payment is less than that of an annuity.

The Reforms of 2001–02

In 2001, the Japanese employer-provided pension system was substantially reformed with the passage of two laws. The Defined Benefit Corporate Pension Law and subsequent legislation established two new forms of defined-benefit plans: the contract type of defined-benefit plan (DB-C), and the funded type (DB-F). The defined-benefit plans can take the form of a cash-balance plan. The DB-C plan is a more tightly regulated version of the TQPP, which is being phased out by March 31, 2012. In particular, minimum funding rules apply. In addition, the solvency test introduced for EPFs in 1997 was extended to DB-Cs and DB-Fs.[20]

As with the TQPP, the DB-C does not require that the plan sponsor establish a separate legal entity, and there is no substituting. The plan sponsor may contract directly with trustee companies, which are responsible for the management of assets and payment of benefits. DB-C and DB-F plans have bylaws, and the consent of a majority of the employees is required to change them (Morito n.d., sec. 3.2). The benefits accrued by a plan member may be transferred to another DB-C, DB-F, DC-C, or EPF plan (Rajnes 2007).

The DB-F can replace an EPF, although this requires that the sponsors of the EPF make the payroll tax contributions they did not make while they were contracted out of the EPI. The structure of a DB-F is closer to an Anglo-Saxon pension plan or a foundation, in that it must be established as a separate legal entity. It is subject to a minimum funding rule that is the same as the one applying to a DB-C. The benefits paid by the new defined-benefit plans depend on the period of service and are usually based on final salary (OECD 2008a, 474). However, they do not vest. The law requires that some benefit be paid to a plan member with at least three years of service, but the amount can vary with the reason for separation (OECD 2008a, 473).

Cash-balance plans were introduced in 2002. Cash-balance plans may take the legal form of either the DB-C or the DB-F plan. The employer credits a notional account established for each employee with a specified percentage of salary, which accumulates at an interest rate that can be fixed or variable with a guaranteed minimum.

The Defined Contribution Pension Law established two types of defined-contribution plans: the corporate defined-contribution (DC-C) and the individual defined-contribution (DC-I) plans. Morito (n.d.) and other observers maintain that strong support from the business community was behind this law, in part because it was seen as being good for the stock market. The DC-C allows contributions only from employers, but the law is expected to be changed to allow contributions from employees. The upper limit on annual tax-deductible contributions per employee is currently JPY 552,000 when the company offers no other plan and JPY 276,000 if it does, but these limits are expected to be raised shortly to JPY 612,000 and JPY 396,000, respectively.

The DC-I is operated by the National Pension Fund Association, and is aimed at the self-employed and others without access to a corporate pension plan. The DC-C plan vests after three years, and both it and the DC-I forbid withdrawals before age 60. When a participant changes jobs, the plan balances should be transferred to the plan

---

[20] The test as it applied to EPFs requires that if the value of assets is less than 105 percent of the value of contracted-out benefits measured on a termination basis, or 90 percent of total benefits, the shortfall so calculated must be made up in seven years (OECD 2007, 48).

Table A1.4. *Japan: Summary of pension-plan taxation*

	TQPPs	EPFs	DB-F and DB-C	DC-C	DC-I
Employee contributions	Deductible up to JPY 50,000	Deductible with no limit	Deductible up to JPY 50,000	Employee contributions not allowed	Deductible up to JPY 816,000 if self-employed; otherwise JPY 216,000
Employer contributions	Deductible with no limit			Deductible to JPY 552,000 if no other plan; otherwise JPY 276,000	N/A
Investment income	Assets taxed at annual rate of 1.173%				
Benefits	A part of benefits, whether in lump-sum or annuity form, is taxed at a rate between 10–37%. With a lump sum, the tax-free part increases with the number of years of plan membership. With an annuity, the tax-free part depends on a taxpayer's other income and on the number of dependents.				

Source: OECD (2008a); Ministry of Health, Labor, and Welfare (n.d.).
DB-C, contract type of defined-benefit plan; DB-F, funded type of defined-benefit plan; DC-C, corporate defined-contribution plan; DC-I, individual defined-contribution plan; EPF, employee pension fund; TQPP, tax-qualified pension plan.

of the new employer, or to a DC-I if the new employer does not offer a DC-C. Both DC-C and DC-I plans are administered by a third party that is responsible for selecting the investments the plan will offer, managing participants' accounts and benefits, and providing information that will improve financial literacy. Plan participants must have a choice of at least three investment funds, one of which should include a guarantee of return of principal.

The taxation of Japanese pension plans is a little hard to characterize. Contributions are usually exempt up to some limit, but investment income is taxed indirectly and at a variable rate by a proportional tax on assets of 1.173 percent. With a rate of return on assets of 6 percent, this is roughly equivalent to a tax on investment income of 20 percent (Table A1.4).

Current Issues

Changes in coverage and structure. As might be expected given the provisions of the laws, the reforms of 2001 have led to a huge decline in the number of employees covered by TQPPs, from 9.2 million in 2001 to 5.7 million as of March 2006. The decline in the number of employees under EPFs has been even steeper, falling from 10.9 million in 2001 to 5.3 million in March 2006. About 70 percent of this decline of 9.1 million has been compensated by the growth in the number of employees covered by defined-benefit plans (4.5 million as of March 2006) and DC-C plans (2.0 million as of March 2006). Private-sector coverage under all plans excluding severance plans fell from about 60 percent of the private-sector labor force in 2001 to about 50 percent in 2006.

Eight years after the introduction of the new pension plans, the defined-benefit plan retains its dominant position, but its rate of coverage of the employed labor force has fallen substantially. Unlike the United States, the decline that has occurred in the coverage of defined-benefit plans has not been compensated by the increase in coverage of defined-contribution plans. The causes of declining coverage are not obvious. It is possible that workers are giving up pensions in return for more job security or higher wages.

The sluggish start of defined-contribution plans has been attributed to relatively low contribution limits (which increase expense ratios), to the poor performance of the stock market, and to the rule that conversion of an EPF to a DC-C plan requires approval of a union or person representing at least one-half of the work force. Continued long average job tenures would also make the portability of DC-C plans less attractive than it would otherwise be. The minor role that defined-contribution plans are for the moment playing in Japan's second tier means that most plan members continue to work for plans where there is no vesting as such.

The Netherlands

In the Netherlands, the second tier achieves a very broad coverage, and, being integrated with the first tier, also achieves a comfortable replacement ratio for low-, middle-, and high-income earners. The share of defined-benefit plans in labor-force coverage is the highest in the group of five countries with broad coverage, although the dominance of the defined-benefit plan almost certainly depends on the flexibility of the terms of these plans, as discussed in the following section. The Netherlands' risk-management system is one of the most developed in the world, and is discussed at some length in Chapter 4.

Basic Institutional Features and Coverage

Dutch workers have second-tier coverage under one of four institutions: an industry-wide plan, which covers all the workers in a particular sector; a company plan, where coverage is limited to a single company; insurance companies, which manage group contracts for separate and usually small enterprises; and funds set up by professional associations for the self-employed. Most employees are covered by the industry-wide funds, which at the beginning of 2006 were estimated to number 103, compared with 685 company-specific funds and 13 professional associations (Hinz and Van Dam 2008, 53). Among them, about 90 percent of employed persons are covered.

The very broad coverage of the industry funds reflects the fact that pension plans are covered by collective bargaining. Specifically, if an employers' organization covers at least 60 percent of employment in the industry, then it and an employees' organization (no cover ratio is stipulated) can request the government that a pension agreement be binding on all employees of the industry. Individual companies can, however, be exempted from the agreement under certain conditions (OECD 2008a, 267). Pension funds in the Netherlands are legal entities separate from the sponsors, and usually assume the legal form of a foundation. An industry-wide fund must have a governing board consisting of equal numbers of representatives of employer organizations and trade unions.

The Netherlands follows the EET rule in taxing pension plans. The limits that the tax code applies to employer and employee contributions are determined differently from those of other countries. In the case of defined-benefit plans, employee contributions are deductible from taxable income as long as the annual accrual rate of the plan does not exceed 2 percent of final salary or 2.25 percent of career-average salary. In the case of defined-contribution plans, the tax code defines maximum employee contribution rates that vary with the plan member's age and the plan's retirement age in such a way as to provide the same relief as is provided with defined-benefit plans. Similar rules apply to employer contributions.

Almost all covered employees participate in defined-benefit plans – 97 percent as of January 2004. A substantial swing away from final-salary to career-average plans has taken place in just a few years. From the employer's point of view, the benefits payable by career-average plans are less variable from one year to the next than the benefits of final-salary plans. This facilitates the management of the plan's finances and makes employer contributions more predictable. According to one estimate, about 80 percent of contributions are made by employers.

What explains the remarkable staying power of the Dutch defined-benefit plans? The answer may be found in the institution of conditional indexation, which is used as a risk-sharing mechanism and a way of muffling the impact of unfavorable financial developments on a plan's financial position. Conditional indexation works by making projections of contributions from the employer that, given assumptions about interest rates, rates of return, inflation, and plan demography, are sufficient to achieve a target for the funding ratio over a certain period. The plan guarantees a nominal pension, but aims to provide a fully indexed one, which would be reflected in the plan's financial projections. If the actual financial out-turn proved more favorable than assumed, benefits might actually be increased. If, however, the out-turn was less favorable, then benefits might be only partially indexed, and the rate of benefit accrual might even be reduced. In the case of Dutch employer-provided pensions, making adjustments in contributions the sole instrument would pose a heavy burden because plan dependency ratios are high.

The practice of conditional indexation implies that the burden of an adjustment to strained plan finances is not borne entirely by the current working generation, but instead shared across generations. The importance of conditional indexation in the Netherlands reflects the still important social and economic roles played by unions, and their need to represent the interest of active members. Ponds and van Riel (2007) maintain that the unions' concern for social solidarity is broadly shared by Dutch society.

Current Issues

The stock market crash in late 2008 substantially reduced the funding ratios of Dutch plans. The aftermath will test both the system of risk-based supervision and the flexibility of many plans. Two large pension funds, the civil service and the health funds, announced that they would freeze pensions in 2009, and the light engineering fund was to increase contributions by 1 percentage point (Dutch News.nl 2009).

Sweden

The generosity of Sweden's first tier means that the second tier's contribution to retire-ment security in the private sector is less than it is in most of the other nine survey countries. Developments in the second tier have undoubtedly been influenced by the major reform of the public pension system that was implemented in stages beginning in 1995 and is discussed in Chapter 5. It may not be entirely coincidental that the replace-ment of the old defined-benefit public pension by a nonfinancial defined-contribution plan was followed, or even preceded, by a move away from defined-benefit plans to defined-contribution plans among employer-provided plans. Palme (2005) attributes the shift to defined-contribution plans in the private sector to the pressure on employ-ers to get a grip on costs.

Coverage and Structure

The coverage of employer-provided pensions is relatively broad, and has not changed much in recent years. Employer-provided plans cover more than 90 percent of the labor force (Palme 2005). Private-sector employees are automatically covered under plans established under collective agreements if their employer is covered by the agreement, whether or not they are trade union members (OECD 2008a, 304). Two agreements cover the private sector: one for white-collar workers and one for blue-collar workers. Two other agreements cover central-government and county- and local-government employees.

The ITP, the agreement covering white-collar workers, is a defined-benefit plan with a complementary defined-contribution plan (the ITPK), but the defined-benefit plan is being phased out by a defined-contribution plan established in 2007.[21] Blue-collar workers have been covered by a defined-contribution plan since 1999. Even in the public sector, defined-contribution plans are making inroads. The two agreements for public-sector workers combine elements of defined-contribution and defined-benefit plans (OECD 2008a, 304).[22]

The private-sector defined-benefit plans are implemented by each employer indi-vidually through one of three vehicles: a contract with an insurance company, book reserves (like Germany), or an independent pension foundation, overseen by a com-mittee composed of employee and employer representatives in equal numbers. The pri-vate-sector defined-contribution plans are managed by insurance companies, which plan members are free to choose. The pensionable age for all plans is 65, although both early and delayed retirement are possible.

The private-sector defined-contribution plans are funded by employer contributions of 2 percent of salary for white-collar workers and 3.5 percent of wages for blue-collar workers. In the case of the new white-collar plan, at least one-half of the contribution

---

[21] All white-collar employees born in 1979 or later are automatically enrolled in the new plan. In addition, an employer and a local trade union can agree to enroll all employees, even older ones, in the new plans (Invest in Sweden Agency 2009).

[22] Central-government employees are covered by two defined-contribution plans: the indi-vidual old-age pension (IAOP) and the supplementary old-age pension or Kâpan. With the IAOP, investment is self-directed; with the Kâpan it is not. The IAOP benefit is a life annuity; for the Kapân, it is usually a five-year term annuity. The defined-benefit plan, like the two defined-contribution plans, is noncontributory (Wadensjö 2008).

must be devoted to an insurance product with a guarantee feature. Employer contributions for country and local employees are 4.5 percent of salary with a relatively high cap.[23] The designated contribution rate for the central-government employees' individual old-age pension (the first defined-contribution plan) is 2.3 percent. None of the plans provide for employee contributions.

The benefits paid by the two private-sector plans differ. Blue-collar workers normally elect a life annuity but they may also elect a period-certain annuity that must not be shorter than five years. White-collar workers normally use the accumulated balance in the defined-contribution plan to buy an annuity with a term of five years, although it may be longer. There is no automatic indexation for inflation, although ad hoc adjustments are normally made for both public- and private-sector plans (OECD 2008a, 307).

Pensions are portable when the employee's new job classification (blue- or white-collar) is the same as his or her former employment. If that is not the case, his or her benefits are preserved, indexed, and paid at retirement. Vesting is immediate for all plans (OECD 2008a, 307).

Insurance companies are supervised by Sweden's financial authority, *Finansinspektionen* (FI). In the beginning of 2006, the pan-European occupational pension directive became effective, implying the adoption of the prudent-person principle, which FI interprets to include the use, in principle, of a risk-free discount rate to value liabilities (*Finansinspektionen* 2005). The FI adopted a version of the traffic-light supervisory system at the same time. The FI does not supervise pension foundations, although these foundations and any plan sponsors relying on book reserves are required to obtain insolvency insurance from a nonlife mutual insurance company (with the Swedish acronym FPG) dedicated to that purpose. As of the beginning of 2006, the rate was 0.3 percent of accrued benefits for plans financed by book reserves, and 0.1 percent for foundations (OECD 2008(a), 310).

Current Issues

Retirement security. The decline in global equity markets has presumably caused a substantial loss in reserves of the white-collar defined-benefit plan, and has inflicted substantial losses on the account balances of defined-contribution plans, although OECD estimates imply losses were light compared to most other countries (OECD 2008c). Fortunately, the comparative generosity of the mandatory nonfinancial defined-contribution plan, and the fact that many employed persons approaching retirement are still in defined-benefit plans, will cushion its impact on retirement security, but may also prompt questions about the risk employees assume with defined-contribution plans.

Risk management. The FI reportedly carried out a survey of the asset holdings of pension plans in early 2009, and found that holdings of investments such as hedge funds, structured products, CDS, and so on, ranged from 0 to 43 percent of managed assets, with an average of 15 percent (Finansinspektionen 2009). It is not possible to

---

[23] The rate for blue-collar workers applies to incomes less than or equal to 7.5 times the "income base" set by the government. It is being raised in steps to 4.5 percent in 2012. As of the beginning of 2006, the cap applying to county and local employees was set at 30 income bases. The value of the income base was equal to 48,000 Swedish krona, or about $6650 in 2008.

deduce the impact of the financial crisis on funding ratios without more information. The same survey noted a considerable variation in the sophistication of the risk-management techniques of different pension plans. In light of the FI's adoption of risk-based supervision, it appears that risk management is a priority for supervision.

Switzerland

Switzerland and Australia are the only countries in the group of ten whose employer-provided pensions have enjoyed a substantial increase in labor-force coverage in recent decades. The Swiss reform, which was introduced in 1985, required all employers – both public and private sector – to enroll all workers aged 24 years and older and earning more than a stipulated floor in a corporate or multiemployer retirement plan. (Eligibility for other benefits comes earlier.) For various reasons, the reform sparked a big increase in the coverage of defined-contribution plans. However, certain provisions give these plans a strong defined-benefit character.

Coverage and Basic Regulatory Aspects

In 1980, prior to the reform, the employer-provided pension system is estimated to have covered just over 50 percent of the workforce (Queisser and Vittas 2000, 38). The reform entailed a precipitate increase in coverage (as could have been expected), which Queisser and Vittas estimate to have reached 74 percent of the labor force in 1997. Excluding workers whose participation is not required, coverage could be well above 90 percent. As was the case in Australia, the reform also caused a pronounced structural shift in the composition of second-tier plans. The share of plan members in defined-contribution plans has been estimated to be about 57 percent in 1987 and to have risen to 70 percent by 1996. The share of members in defined-contribution plans has undoubtedly risen since then.

Swiss pension plans are normally administered by an independent foundation, with representation from management and membership. Many plans are multiemployer, and cover the employees of a large number of small employers. The self-employed can form their own plans through a professional association. The presumption is that the employer is liable for shortfalls in plan reserves that would prevent the honoring of minimum guarantees. A safety fund at the federal level, which is financed by a levy on wages, exists to ensure the payment of minimum benefits when a plan becomes insolvent and to subsidize the operations of funds burdened by unfavorable demography.

One special feature of the regulatory framework is that pension plans with operations that are concentrated in a particular canton (the regional level of government) are supervised by that canton. This arrangement, which bears some similarity to the Canadian arrangement, has its historical roots in the Swiss federation, although given Switzerland's comparatively small size it may make administration more costly and less effective than it need be.[24]

---

[24] Pension funds of employers that conduct business across the country or internationally are registered with the Federal Office of Social Insurance (FOSI). Life insurance companies, including those that manage pension funds under insurance contracts, are registered with the Federal Office of Private Insurance (FOPI). A recent report from the International Monetary Fund (2006) maintains that neither FOSI nor the cantonal

Switzerland adopted IAS 19 in 1995. Plan assets are marked to market, and plans use a discount rate taken from a range recommended by a professional body, the Chamber of Pension Fund Experts. Funding ratios are to be maintained at 100 percent plus an unspecified cushion to offset volatility. Average ratios were around 110 percent until 2001, when they were pushed down well below 100 percent by the global decline in equity values and interest rates. They have subsequently recovered, but relapsed in the fall of 2008. Plans are expected to take action to reverse underfunding, but are not obliged to eliminate the gap between assets and liabilities at some stipulated rate per year. To this end, plans may request special contributions, reduce the guaranteed rate of return for a period of five years, and even, in particularly difficult periods, reduce pensions (International Monetary Fund 2006, 49).

Switzerland does not as yet rely fully on a prudent-person rule, but instead applies a series of restrictions on asset composition designed to limit the riskiness of the portfolio. These restrictions can, however, be lifted if the plan provides justification. Asset management may be delegated to a specialized institution, and is subject to the goals of achieving a reasonable rate of return, security of investments, and appropriate diversification of risk.

Contribution Rates and Benefits

Swiss pension law defines what are known as contribution credits, which determine minimum pension accruals. Contribution credits are determined by applying rates, which increase with age, to what is called the coordinated salary, which as of January 1, 2009 is that part of a worker's annual salary between CHF 20,520 and CHF 82,080 (from roughly $19,000 to $77,000), with a minimum of CHF 3,420 and a maximum of CHF 58,140.[25] Retirement age is 65 for men and 64 for women. Early retirement is permissible. Actual deductions do not have to equal these rates, but must be sufficient to ensure that the minimum pensions the law requires are fully financed. Employers must pay at least one-half and employees no more than one-half of total contributions. Plan benefits are vested as they accrue, and are fully portable between Swiss pension plans.

The pension benefit normally takes the form of an annuity, with ad hoc indexation at the discretion of the former employer.[26] The minimum payment is calculated by applying a stipulated minimum rate, known as the conversion rate, to the minimum accumulated capital or MAC. The MAC equals the minimum contribution credits accumulated at a stipulated interest rate, which was recently increased from 2.5 percent to 2.75 percent. The conversion rate is currently 7.05 percent for men and 7.0 percent for women, implying that a MAC of CHF 300,000 would give a man a right to

---

offices responsible for pension-plan supervision are equipped to carry out fully adequate supervision.

[25] The maximum value for the coordinated salary equals the upper salary limit (CHF 82,080) minus the sum of the lower limit plus the minimum coordinated salary (CHF 20,520 + CHF 3,420). The credit rates range from 7 percent for someone between 25 and 34 years of age, to 18 percent for men aged 55 to 65 and women aged 55 to 64 (OECD 2008a, 431).

[26] Lump-sum payments are possible if the pension that accumulated contributions would finance falls below a stipulated percentage of the minimum value of the public pension.

a minimum life annuity at retirement of CHF 21,150 per year. Swiss pensions are taxed on the EET principle.

Current Issues

Switzerland's employer-provided pension system has some enviable features. Coverage is broad, there is no problem of adequacy, and the minimum return and maximum premium per Swiss franc of pension income give it some of the most valuable features of a defined-benefit system. One issue to consider is the implication of the guarantees for investment strategy. The guarantees on return and annuity conversion create a firm obligation for pension plans somewhat like the obligation created by a traditional pension plan. In the case of a traditional pension plan, the obligation to pay pensions does not oblige the plan's trustees to follow a conservative strategy, although a poor investment experience could oblige the plan sponsor to make extraordinary contributions over some years to reduce underfunding. Conceivably, the restrictions on asset composition that apply to Swiss plans may be unnecessarily lowering the rate of return to plan assets, and reducing the likelihood of rates of return in excess of the minimum. That said, the ability of funds to index pensions at their discretion would give underfunded plans more leeway to improve their financial position. Another issue, one that is long-standing, is the trade-off between the sensitivities of the cantons and the obvious advantages of nationwide supervision in a small country.

United Kingdom

The pension system in the United Kingdom has no peer in complexity among the other countries the study surveys. The public component of the system includes a basic flat-rate component as well as an earnings-related component known as the State Second Pension or S2P, which is the successor to the State Earnings-Related Pension Scheme (SERPS) introduced in 1978. Both the public pension and the regulatory environment of the private system have undergone considerable change since the late 1970s. In 1979, it became possible to contract out of SERPS to become a member of an employer-provided defined-benefit plan. Subsequently, the types of plans into which an employee could "contract in" were broadened to include defined-contribution plans, and in 1987 personal pensions.[27]

---

[27] The basic condition for contracting out is that the private sector pension must be deemed sufficient to replace 100 percent of the earnings-related pension that would have been payable by National Insurance or NI (the public pension system under SERPS) had the employee not contracted out. When an employee contracts out, the contributions paid by both employer and employee to finance the earnings-related part of the public pension are reduced to allow room for contributions to the private scheme. The conditions under which opting out takes place depend upon whether the private-sector plan is a defined-benefit or a defined-contribution plan. In the case of a defined-benefit plan, the plan's benefits must conform to what is known as the Reference System Test. As of 2008–09, the reductions were: employer's 1.6 percentage points and employee's 3.7 percentage points. In the case of defined-contributions plans, the NI contribution rebate must be paid into a pension fund. (Pensions Commission 2004, 72). The rebates paid to employer and employee increase with age, with the maximum age-related component of the rate set at 7.4 percent as of April 2007. The basic combined employer–employee rebate is 3.0

The role of the British defined-benefit pension, which had already been in decline for two decades, has diminished drastically during the current decade. This trend is especially pronounced in the private sector. These developments reflect influences common to the other Anglo-Saxon countries, but some purely home-grown influences are also at work. The combination of an ungenerous first tier and the erosion of second-tier benefits expected to result from the shift to defined-contribution plans poses a worrisome problem of adequacy.

Coverage and Contributions

The overall coverage of occupational pension schemes in the United Kingdom as of the end of 2007 is estimated to be 30 percent. Coverage in the public sector is much greater than it is in the private sector. Of a private-sector labor force of about 24 million at the end of 2007, only 3.6 million workers were covered by employer-provided schemes. Some 2.7 million of these workers participated in defined-benefit plans, but only 1.3 million were members of plans that remained open. The collapse in the coverage of open defined-benefit plans implies that less than one in ten private-sector workers is actually contributing to an employer-sponsored plan. Public-sector coverage is estimated at 5.2 million of a total public-sector labor force of 5.7 million, implying coverage of about 90 percent. The defined-benefit plan remains dominant in the public sector, especially at the central-government level (see Figure A1.2).

The effective coverage of the United Kingdom's second tier is boosted by membership in group personal pensions (GPPs), which are contracted with an insurance company.[28] GPPs are all defined contribution. The employer may facilitate setting up the contract, and also contribute to the plans. Unlike employer-provided schemes, however, GPPs are not based on a trust arrangement.[29] It is common for an employer to take steps to ensure that these plans are well suited to the needs of its employees, but it has no fiduciary obligation in this regard (The Pensions Regulator 2008). Firms with four or more employees are obliged to make a pension available to them, although participation is voluntary. The obligation to offer these stakeholder pensions is often met through a GPP.

A broader measure of second-tier coverage that includes GPP policyholders and stakeholder pensions would be about 45 percent. Nonetheless, even this adjustment leaves the

percentage points (Department of Work and Pensions 2006b and 2007). Of the accumulated balance in a defined-contribution plan, up to 25 percent may be withdrawn in a lump sum. The rest must be used to purchase a life annuity or a program of phased withdrawals. When a personal pension is chosen (it is known as an appropriate personal pension), rebates are determined in a similar way.

[28] Statistics on the coverage of GPPs are not easy to interpret. The Pensions Commission's estimate of participation in what it calls private pension schemes (defined to include both employer-provided pensions and personal plans) for 2002–03 implies that coverage of GPPs was about 4 million in that period (Pensions Commission 2004, 86). Customs and Excise (2007) tallied a total number of employee-held personal pension accounts receiving contributions in the year ending April 5, 2003 of 4.5 million. This number, which includes individual personal pensions, increases to 5.1 million if stakeholder pensions are also included.

[29] Some insurer-provided schemes are based on a trust, so-called master trusts, but they account for only a small share of the market.

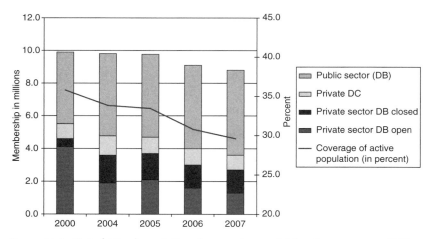

Figure A1.2. United Kingdom: Active plan members and labor-force coverage, 2000 to 2007. *Source*: U.K. Office for National Statistics. Occupational Pension Schemes Annual Report. Various Issues.

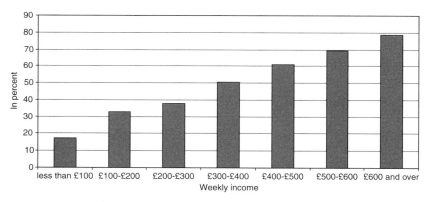

Figure A1.3. United Kingdom: Employer-provided pension coverage by income level, 2007. *Source*: U.K. National Statistical Office. Annual Survey of Hours and Earnings.

rate of coverage of private-sector employees at about 30 percent.[30] As is the case in both Canada and the United States, coverage rates increase substantially with income (see Figure A1.3). They also increase with age, although the disparity between younger and older workers is less marked than that between low- and high-income workers.

The coverage of the United Kindom's private employer-provided pensions has been on the decline since the 1970s, although the pace of decline quickened markedly in the late 1990s and again in the 2000s. The decline in the coverage of defined-benefit plans in the past seven years has been remarkable, particularly the decline in membership of

---

[30] Assuming that GPPs amounted to 4.2 million in 2007, and that no GPP holder was a member of an employer-provided plan, overall coverage would increase by about 15 percent, or somewhat higher if stakeholder pensions were included.

open plans, which has fallen by about 75 percent (see Figure A1.2). However, defined-contribution membership has also fallen, and about one in nine of their membership belongs to a closed plan (U.K. Office for National Statistics 2008). In the private sector, the defined-benefit plan is on the ropes.

The pronounced shift to defined-contribution plans that the 2012 reform will bring about is likely to depress the rate of occupational saving by current members of defined-benefit plans, given the big difference between total contribution rates (weighted by plan size) of the two plan types. For 2007, the combined (employer-employee) rate for defined-benefit plans was 20.5 percent and that for defined-contribution plans 9.1 percent (U.K. Office for National Statistics 2008, 27). It is highly unlikely that the difference in combined rates is entirely attributable to exceptional employer contributions. The overall rate of occupational saving could still increase if the 2012 reform boosts coverage substantially.

The Collapse of the Traditional Plan in the United Kingdom's Private Sector[31]

The drastic decline of defined-benefit plans since the 1980s is the result, quite possibly unintended, of a series of policy acts and a wholesale change in the economic and financial environment in which the plans function. As the first report of the U.K. Pensions Commission (2004) convincingly argues, the 1950s and 1960s were the heyday of the traditional pension. High marginal tax rates made defined-benefit pensions a highly favored form of compensation, especially for senior management (though the same would have been true of defined-contribution plans). Relatively liberal funding rules meant that transfers to a fund could be used to defer taxation when profits were high. In the period before the late 1970s, when incomes polices were still in vogue, fringe benefits like pensions were easier to increase than wages and salaries. In addition, the high inflation rates of the 1970s encouraged a shift to final-salary schemes away from career-average schemes, because the shift served as partial indexation of accrued pension rights. High inflation could also reduce the effective cost of a pension plan when indexation was not mandatory. Finally, before 1987, an employee contracting out of SERPS could only contract out to a defined-benefit plan.

Both the policy framework and financial environment began to change in the 1970s. The Social Security Pension Act of 1975 provided for equal coverage for both women and part-time workers. These measures did not become fully effective until the early 1990s after a series of legal challenges. The Social Security Acts of 1973 and 1985 gave early leavers a right to a refund of contributions if they left with at least five years of plan membership (subsequently reduced to two years), and a right to a "preserved pension," or to the ultimate payment of pension benefits, to former employees with longer tenure. The 1985 Act required pension funds to index preserved pensions.[32] Subsequent legislation stiffened the indexation requirements for defined-benefit pensions and the minimum pension guaranteed when an employee contracts out of the

---

[31] The discussion of this section is drawn largely from the Pensions Commission (2004) and Blake (2006a).

[32] Initially, the indexation applied only to that part of the pension accrued after 1985, but its scope was changed by the SS Act of 1990 to protect the benefits of anyone leaving after the end of 1990.

S2P into a money purchase (defined-contribution) scheme.[33] Finally, the Finance Act of 1986 reduced the leeway companies had to shift excess profits to the accounts of their pension plans.

More recently, the Pension Act of 2004, which introduced some substantial reforms to pension governance and in particular to the responsibilities of trustees, has been criticized for introducing a destructive conflict of interest in the relationships of trustees with the plan sponsor. In particular, it has been argued that trustees who were also employers or officers of the company would find their position untenable. Their absence from pension boards would, it is claimed, deprive the boards of their best financial brains (Byrne et al. 2006). The same Act introduced a new funding standard, replacing the so-called Minimum Funding Standard (MFS) introduced in 1995. Despite the apparent weaknesses of the MFS, some critics point to this part of the legislation as a further example of excessive regulatory rule change.

Most, perhaps all, of these changes can be justified on the grounds that they increased the retirement security of some of British society's more vulnerable groups. Nonetheless, they also increased the cost of providing a traditional pension. In theory, as Chapters 4 and 7 discuss, a plan's parameters can be altered to lower the cost of the pensions earned by long-serving male employees, who would have benefited the most under a traditional pension. In practice, such changes would be contentious.

More recent changes to the accounting and legal frameworks in which traditional plans operate may have also made them less attractive to their sponsors. The accounting standard FRS 17 that took effect in 2005 required both mark-to-market valuation and full recognition of losses in the income statement. Under the subsequently adopted IAS19, losses can be smoothed. Similarly, the move from a discount rate derived from the rate of return on assets to a rate based on what should ideally be the low risk and bond-like character of the plan's liabilities has increased funding requirements. Although, by 2006, funding ratios had recovered from the decline in equity markets at the end of the 1990s, the collapse of international equity markets in the fall of 2008 and a decline in gilt rates have caused a serious degree of underfunding in many companies offering defined-benefit plans, notwithstanding a shift in asset composition back to bonds. The Pension Protection Fund, which provides insurance based on risk adjusted premiums to private-sector defined-benefit plans recorded a net deficit among the almost 7,800 companies it insured of £195 billion at the end of 2008. Nine of ten plans incurred deficits, which totaled about £210 billion (Pension Protection Fund 2009).[34]

Current Issues

Adequacy. The low rate of coverage of the British second tier is not likely to reverse itself, and will probably continue to shrink. Without the reform announced by the

---

[33] In 1988, plan sponsors became responsible for the postretirement indexing of pensions up to a rate of 3 percent. Contracted-out defined-benefit plans have had to index pension benefits accrued up to April 6, 2005 to the retail price index (RPI) up to a rate of 5 percent, and benefits accrued since then up to 2.5 percent. Accrued benefits are not adjusted for a decline in the RPI.

[34] The Pension Protection Fund attempts to estimate what an insurance company would charge to take on a pension plan's liabilities. Its measure is similar to the solvency evaluation used in Canada. Its discount rate is derived from the gilts yield curve, and not the AA corporate bond rate.

government to be introduced in 2012, a serious problem of adequacy could emerge. The reform's main goal is to expand second-tier coverage materially. Its strategy is to rely on default setting or auto enrolment. All employers above a certain size will be required to enroll their employees in a pension plan unless they explicitly opt out. The evidence with default setting, as seen in the United States (Chapter 7), offers some reason for hope that this policy will expand coverage substantially, albeit not universally.[35] However, a problem of adequacy could still emerge, given the low coverage of the second tier and the modest minimum contribution rate the reform will require of employers.

The switch away from defined-benefit plans, as noted, has been associated with a decline in combined employer–employee contribution rates. Unless there is some other funding source, this development means that unless rates of return to these plans are substantially higher than those of defined-benefit plans, average plan benefits will be lower. Because there is no magic way of raising rates of return given the degree of risk, ensuring that the benefits paid by defined contribution plans do not fall short of those of traditional plans will require higher contribution rates.

Financial literacy. The continued growth expected for money purchase plans only magnifies the importance of financial literacy. The City of London's major role in global banking and finance notwithstanding, the available evidence is that U.K. citizens are not particularly sophisticated financially.[36] The government introduced personal financial education into the English schools' curriculum in 2000, and has taken steps to increase opportunities for adult education (U.K. Department for Work and Pensions 2002, 3.5). However, a 2003 survey found that only a small minority of U.K. residents of either sex understood that when interest rates move in one direction, bond prices move in the other. In addition, there was great uncertainty about how much saving was necessary for an adequate income in retirement (Gardner and Orszag 2004). The consequences of this ignorance can be very serious.

Ensuring that the nest egg lasts. The reform, like Australia's, will not require that new pensions be defined contribution, but recent trends suggest that that will be the norm for newly established plans. Except for the restrictions on contracted-out money purchase schemes, no restrictions apply to distributions from defined-contribution plans. The lack of restrictions raises the issue of whether pensioners will obtain adequate longevity insurance. This is one area where default setting – for example, a setting entailing the annuitization of a certain minimum share of the balance of an account subject to certain safeguards on the premium per pound of annuity income and protections for spousal interests – could have a really beneficial effect (for further discussion, see Chapter 7).

The crisis and the appropriate discount rate. Defined-benefit plans now use a discount rate based on high-quality corporate bonds. The increase in the spread between

---

[35] A Department of Work and Pensions official has projected that 6 to 9 million people would either be newly participating or saving more. If private-sector coverage were to increase by as much as 9 million it would increase the coverage rate by about 35 percent (Clark 2008).

[36] Apart from the survey just cited, some indirect but rather painful evidence of the lack of sophistication or its consequences is found in the scandal of mis-selling of schemes in the early 1990s. Over one million people exchanged their SERPS pension rights for a private pension that was worth much less (Guardian.co.uk 2000).

them and gilts means that measured liabilities have declined. Some prominent actors on the pension stage, and notably the head of the United Kingdom's pension regulatory agency argued that this development was perverse (*Financial Times*, October 29, 2008). The level of corporate rates in late 2008 allowed an artificially low level of funding and too high a probability of a shortfall. However, a move to a risk-free rate would entail an unsettlingly large increase in plan liabilities. The impact of financial turbulence on interest rates has intensified the ongoing debate, addressed in Chapter 3, on the appropriate rate of discount.

United States

In the United States, no major reform of the employer-provided pension system has taken place since the passage of the Employee Income Security Retirement Act (ERISA) in 1974. That legislation did not envisage a major change in the structure of the second tier; rather, its architects saw ERISA as addressing various inequities and anomalies with employer-provided pensions as they then were. With the benefit of hindsight, it now appears that ERISA was a good example of the law of unintended consequences. The 1974 Act, despite its efforts to protect plan members, and subsequent legislation right up to the Pension Protection Act (PPA) of 2006 paved the way for the current domination of the 401(k) plan and the decline in the traditional pension. The most important issue facing the United States' employer-provided pension system is how to expand its coverage and ensure adequacy. The spread of the 401(k) plan has mitigated some of the problems with the earlier version of the traditional pension, and notably the latter's lack of portability. It has, however, entailed problems of its own.

Coverage

In the United States, the second tier has covered about one in two workers over the past 40 years, with no discernible trend. The relatively constant coverage rate masks a dramatic decline in the share of defined-benefit plans, most of which occurred before 1995 (Figure A1.4), and an equally pronounced increase in the coverage of 401(k) plans (named after the section of the Internal Revenue Code that sets out the conditions for their favorable tax treatment). As of 2007, defined-benefit plans are estimated to cover 17 percent of the population, and defined-contribution plans [mainly 401(k) plans] 41 percent. [37]

The decline in the coverage of defined-benefit plans actually understates the decline in the traditional pension. Of the many U.S. corporations that closed their traditional plans, some have started a cash-balance plan, which is legally a defined-benefit plan and classified as such.[38] Most companies moved to a 401(k) plan, however.

---

[37] From Mackenzie and Wu (2009). These estimates of coverage include workers who may have both types of plan. The share of workers with only a defined-benefit plan is less than 10 percent, and the share of workers with only a defined-contribution plan is about 33 percent.

[38] The conversion of traditional plans to cash-balance plans has sometimes resulted in costly litigation on behalf of older workers who claimed age discrimination because the conversion had reduced their benefits. The PPA in 2006 established safe-harbor provisions for companies intending to convert their plans that, if observed, would absolve them of liability.

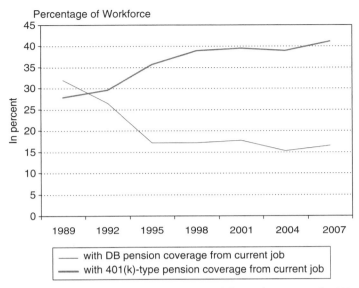

Figure A1.4. United States: Pension coverage by type of plan under current job 1989 to 2007. *Source*: Mackenzie and Wu (2009).

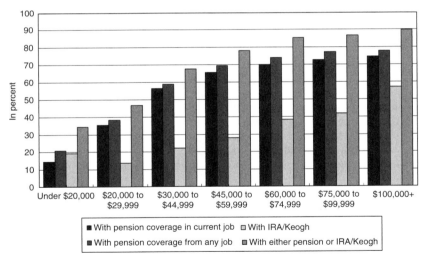

Figure A1.5. United States: Pension/retirement plan coverage by annual salary, 2007. *Source*: Mackenzie and Wu (2009).

The coverage of the second tier varies markedly by age, income, and educational attainment, and also varies systematically with ethnicity (see Figure A1.5 for the relationship between income and coverage). In addition, coverage rates are much higher in large firms than in small ones, and for full-time as opposed to part-time employees. Coverage rates also vary systematically with a worker's tenure (Mackenzie and Wu 2009).

ERISA prescribes some complicated, nondiscrimination rules to prevent pension benefits and coverage from being excessively concentrated on high-income employees. The law does not require a very high rate of coverage of the workforce, but is more concerned with parity of treatment of well- and not-so-well-paid workers. Specifically, a plan can pass the coverage test if the proportion of the employees who are classified as nonhighly compensated (earning less than $110,000 as of 2009 and owning less than 5 percent of company stock) that is covered by the plan is at least 70 percent of the proportion of highly compensated employees who are covered by the plan. However, if the plan satisfies other requirements, including a requirement that the average ratio of pension benefits to compensation for nonhighly compensated workers be at least 70 percent of that of highly compensated employees, the coverage ratio can be less than 70 percent (McGill et al. 2005, 134–6). These requirements do not stipulate that a high share of the workforce must be covered. The overall coverage rate of a plan may be quite small and still respect them.

Other Aspects

As in the other countries with a common law tradition, the standard pension-plan vehicle in the United States is the trust. Plans can and have been established by labor unions, but they are uncommon. Representatives of labor are not entitled to any particular share of the members of administration and investment committees of plans that corporations sponsor, and have no formal say in decisions to close or restructure a plan. The conduct of trustees is guided by the prudent-person rule (see Chapter 1).

In part because of ERISA and IRC requirements, and in part because its inherent complexity, the cost of administering a defined-benefit plan now substantially exceeds the cost of administering a defined-contribution plan. Because the economies of scale with administration and the investment function are considerable, the cost of administering a small defined-benefit plan is prohibitive, as Chapter 6 discussed.

ERISA liberalized the rules for vesting, portability, and preservation of benefits for members of defined-benefit plans, but they still compare unfavorably with most other countries. Under cliff vesting – the policy that applies in most countries – a sponsor of a defined-benefit plan can require that a member participate in a plan for up to five years – which exceeds the average tenure of U.S. workers – before any accrued benefits vest. Once the worker has five years of service, he or she is fully vested. Alternatively, benefits may vest gradually over a period of seven years. The maximum vesting period for 401(k) plans is three years. Employee contributions vest immediately. Some plan sponsors set a vesting period for their defined-benefit plans that is less than the stipulated maximum of five years, but many do not.

The accrued benefits of defined-benefit plans are generally not portable. Vested benefits are preserved, but only in nominal terms. Whatever accrued benefits a separated worker may be entitled to, some workers have a problem locating former employers and claiming their preserved benefits from them (AARP 2009, 4–21). This problem arises because there is no centralized register of preserved benefits.

The United States adheres to the EET tax rule. In particular, plan investment income is not taxed as it is accrued, and distributions are taxed as ordinary income in the hands of plan participants. The tax treatment of contributions depends on the type of plan. With defined-benefit plans, employee contributions are not tax deductible. Employer contributions are deductible, and a complex rule is applied to set a limit that depends on the value of the contribution necessary to maintain a minimum funding requirement. This limit is backstopped by a limit on the annual benefit a plan may pay, currently $195,000.

In contrast with defined-benefit plans, both employer and employee contributions to 401(k) and other defined-contribution plans are deductible up to certain limits. In 2009, a worker could defer tax on up to $16,500 (plus an extra $5,500 if he or she was over the age of 50) by contributing to a plan. These limits, which are indexed annually, are more generous than those that apply to the Individual Retirement Account (IRA), which is a third-tier vehicle. A potentially important difference between the taxation of pensions in the United States as compared with other countries given the spread of 401(k) plans, is that the tax-deferral benefits that upper tax-bracket contributors receive are more obvious to the contributors than the tax deferral that results when an employer funds a defined-benefit plan.[39]

Current Issues

The 401(k) plan: ready to be the foundation of the second tier? The 401(k) plan improves over traditional pension plan in some important respects, given how slow the traditional plans vest, their lack of portability, and their limited preservation. These features mean that many defined-benefit plan members would never receive a pension, or only a very small one, even after years of plan service. With a 401(k) plan, a plan member's contributions, which normally exceed the employer's contribution, are instantly vested.[40] The balance in an account can be rolled over to another 401(k) plan or to an IRA, although amounts below a specified amount can be cashed out.

Nonetheless, the voluntary character of participation in 401(k) plans and the way in which the tax that is deferred by participation increases with income is likely to lower the participation rates of low- to moderate-income earners. The federal tax system provides relief to low-income workers by setting a moderate initial marginal rate of 10 percent and by the Earned Income Tax Credit. The interaction of these two features means that many unskilled workers are not taxed on their last dollar of earned income, and gain no fiscal advantage from contributing to either an employer-sponsored plan or an IRA.

Despite the control that a plan member has over the rate of contribution, a large share – perhaps 25 percent – of workers whose employers sponsor a 401(k) plan do not even participate, let alone contribute. Of those who do, few take advantage of the full tax deferral that the 401(k) offers. Even among those earning $75,000 or more, less

---

[39] Consider an employer choosing between funding a defined-benefit plan and giving an employee a salary increase to put in a 401(k) plan. Tax is deferred in both cases, but the amount of the deferral is clearer in the case of the 401(k) plan, where the taxpayer can see the impact of contributing to a plan on his or her taxable income.

[40] Many employers offer a matching contribution, which varies with an employee's contributions in a way stipulated by the plan. A standard formulation might be: Match an employee's contribution dollar-for-dollar for contributions up to 2 percent of salary, and 50 cents on the dollar up to 3 percent of salary. The matching component of the total employer–employee contribution is sometimes referred to as free money or money on the table. Many contributors do, in fact, leave money on the table. A limit applies to total contributions; for the tax year 2009 it was $49,000. The severe recession of 2008–09 prompted many employers to scrub their matching contribution.

than 10 percent were making the maximum contribution, according to a survey conducted in 2005 (Employee Benefits Research Institute (EBRI) 2008). Finally, although the administrative costs of a 401(k) plan are lower than those of the typical defined-benefit plan, they remain considerable for small employers.

Transparency issues. The transparency of 401(k) plans and specifically of the fees that their participants pay has become an issue in recent years. Typically, plan participants are ignorant not only of the approximate amount of the fees they pay, but of whether they pay fees at all (AARP 2007).[41] A necessary if not sufficient condition for the resolution of this problem is legislation that will require plan service providers (investment advisors, brokerages, record keepers, etc.) to provide adequate information on fees to plan sponsors, and for plan sponsors in return to provide information to plan participants (Mackenzie 2008). Legislation now before Congress addresses these issues.

Pension adequacy of low-income workers. Recent administrations have taken measures to boost the coverage rates or the retirement saving of low-income workers and workers in small businesses, by promoting personal retirement saving accounts and simplified employer plans. The Saver's Credit provides a nonrefundable tax credit for low- and moderate-income taxpayers who contribute to an IRA or 401(k) plan. Eligibility depends on the taxpayer's income and tax filing status (whether filing jointly, singly, etc.). The credit may be as high as $2,000 for taxpayers filing jointly. The SIMPLE IRA, despite its name, is actually an employer-provided plan with simplified provisions and a tax credit feature. Employers are expected to either match contributions up to some stipulated percentage of salary, or make contributions to all employee accounts equal to some specified percent of salary.

Neither of these plans has enjoyed great success in extending coverage or increasing retirement saving. The need to file a tax return and the perceived complexity of the saver's credit may reduce the plan's popularity. In addition, a nonrefundable tax credit cannot benefit taxpayers who have no tax liability. A refundable credit would cost the federal government more in revenues foregone, but would be easier for beneficiaries to understand.

The auto IRA and 401(k) plans may be more successful. Both of these approaches rely on the suggestive power of a plan's default setting. Studies of the default setting for pension plans have shown that changing the initial requirement of potential participants from opting in to opting out greatly increases participation rates. Default settings would apply to participation and to the size of contributions. Specifically, the eligible employees of the company sponsoring the plan would be automatically included in the plan unless they expressly opted out.

Default setting could also be used to increase the rate of saving over time and to improve investment choices. Specifically a default setting that would increase the percentage of salary contributed over time could be part of the plan. Investment choices could also be subject to a default setting – for example, a plan member might have

---

[41] Some 83 percent of 401(k) participants in an AARP-sponsored survey stated that they knew how much they paid in fees. However, 33 of percent of those claiming they knew how much they paid stated that they paid nothing, and 23 percent estimated their fees to amount to 1 percent or less of their account balance (AARP 2007, 4–5). In practice, fees are well above 1 percent of account balances.

his or her contributions automatically invested in a fund where the ratio of equities to fixed-interest securities would decline with age unless he or she expressly chooses other funds. The Pension Protection Act included "safe harbor" provisions regarding default investments so that plan sponsors, if they conformed to them would be relieved of fiduciary liability.

Longevity insurance: making the nest egg last. The typical 401(k) plan distributes its benefits as a lump sum, or at the participant's will. The option of annuitization is not common. Encouraging such an option, along the lines discussed in Chapter 7, could substantially enhance the welfare of older Americans.

APPENDIX 2

Mathematical Treatments and Derivations

Derivation of Certain Conclusions in Chapter 3

*The Cost of a Pension Plan Taking Account of
Vesting and Death Benefits*

The exposition in Box 3.1 assumed that a worker was employed at the same company throughout his or her working life. In what follows, we introduce the possibility of death and separation from the firm, as well as a vesting period.

Specifically, we assume that the plan pays a flat death benefit, B_D, if the participant dies on the job and that plan participants who have vested will be paid their accrued pension benefits once they reach retirement age. We assume the employee is hired in year 1, works to year T (at most), and if still alive, begins receiving a pension in year $T + 1$. The employee has a probability, P_{Dt}, of dying in year t and a probability, P_{Qt}, of separating in year t. The probability that he or she stays with the firm (alive) in year t is $(1 - P_{Dt} - P_{Qt})$. The expected value of the cost of the death benefit (C_{DB}) is given by equation (A2.1):

$$C_{DB} = \sum_{t=1}^{T} P_{Dt}\left(\frac{B_D}{(1+r)^{t-1}}\right) \tag{A2.1}$$

The separation benefit is assumed to equal the accrued pension benefit described in Chapter 3, and the expected cost of the benefit C_{SB} is given by equation (A2.2):

$$C_{SB} = \sum_{t=V}^{T} P_{Qt}\,\alpha W_t \cdot t\ \frac{\ddot{a}_T}{(1+r)^{T-1}}, \ t \geq V \tag{A2.2}$$
$$= 0, \ \ t < V$$

The symbol $\ddot{a}_T$ stands for the cost in year T of a \$1 annuity whose first payment begins in year $T + 1$. The expression (A2.2) for the expected cost of the pension benefit with separation before retirement has a time subscript that begins with year V, reflecting the fact that no benefits vest before that year.

Expressions (A2.1) and (A2.2) are expressions of probability. The actual cost of both the death benefit and the accrued pension benefit could differ substantially from the expected cost in the case of a single employee or a small number of employees.

However, using this approach could give a reasonably good estimate when the work-force is sufficiently large.

The exposition assumes that there is no provision for early retirement. Consequently, the expected cost of a full pension (C_p) as of year 1 depends on the probability that an employee works all T years, and is given by equation (A2.3), where P_R stands for the probability of actually working T years and retiring:

$$EC_p = P_R \cdot \frac{\alpha T W_T \cdot \ddot{a}_T}{(1+r)^{T-1}} \tag{A2.3}$$

The probability of working the full T years and then retiring is given by equation (A2.4):

$$P_R = 1 - \sum_{t=1}^{T}(P_{Dt} + P_{St}) \tag{A2.4}$$

Simulating the Variability of ISA Premiums (Chapter 7)

Deriving a Simple (Unweighted) Measure of the Premium

The premium per dollar for a deferred life-annuity contracted when the annuitant is aged 45 (PPD_{45}), assuming that annuity payments begin at age 66 and no guarantee is provided, can be expressed as shown in equation (A2.5). Equation (A2.5) shows that the value of PPD_{45} depends on the probability of surviving from age 65 to each subsequent age Z ($SP_{65\,to\,Z}$), assuming for convenience that the plan member does not live beyond age 90, on the probability of surviving from age 45 to age 65 ($SP_{45\,to\,65}$), and on the interest rate r, which is assumed to be constant.

$$PPD_{45} = \left(\frac{SP_{45\,to\,65}}{(1+r)^{65-45}}\right)\left(\sum_{Z=66}^{90}\frac{SP_{65\,to\,Z}}{(1+r)^{Z-65}}\right) \tag{A2.5}$$

Equation (A2.5) can be re-expressed to collapse the right-hand side to one term [see equation (A2.6)].

$$PPD_{45} = \left(\sum_{Z=66}^{90}\frac{SP_{45\,to\,Z}}{(1+r)^{Z-45}}\right) \tag{A2.6}$$

However, the formulation of equation (A2.5) is convenient because when the premium per dollar is calculated for subsequent years, only the first term on the right-hand side of equation (A2.5) changes. (The right-hand term is the cost of a life annuity of $1 per year issued at age 65; that is, an immediate and not a deferred annuity). At age 46, for example, the first term becomes $\left(\frac{SP_{46\,to\,65}}{(1+r)^{65-46}}\right)$ or $\left(\frac{SP_{46\,to\,65}}{(1+r)^{19}}\right)$. At age 47, the first term becomes $\left(\frac{SP_{47\,to\,65}}{(1+r)^{18}}\right)$, and so on.

By adding up the premium per dollar calculated at each age from 45 to 65 and dividing by the number of years of contribution (21, in this case), an expression for an average premium per dollar is derived.

The simulations use a single interest rate, the yield on the Treasury ten-year bond.[1] Strictly speaking, the calculation of the premium per dollar should not be based on a single long-term interest rate, but on the term structure of interest rates. If equation (A2.6) were changed to use the term structure it would look like equation (A2.7), where $r_{Z\text{-}45}$ was the interest rate on a bond of maturity $Z - 45$.

$$PPD_{45} = \left(\sum_{Z=66}^{95} \frac{SP_{45\,to\,Z}}{(1+r_{Z-45})^{Z-45}} \right) \tag{A2.7}$$

The simplified approach we adopt is similar to the approach of Blake (2006c, 108–9) and is justifiable on two grounds: It is less demanding computationally, and it is unlikely to result in an appreciable understatement of the variability of premiums, because although short-term rates tend to fluctuate more than long-term rates, the rates on medium and long-term bonds tend to vary in a similar way. Finally, the survival probabilities the simulation uses are taken from a study by the Social Security Administration (SSA 2002).

Calculating the Replacement Ratio

The calculations assume that salary grows at a constant rate, g. The premium per dollar increases from one year to the next for a given rate of interest for the reasons explained in the previous discussion. As before, the estimates assume that the plan member buys a deferred annuity each year that he or she participates in the plan.

The replacement rate is the ratio of pension or annuity income to a measure of working-life income. Here we use a measure of average income during the period of contributions – a kind of career average, except that the period covered does not include the years worked prior to becoming a member of the plan.

Setting first-year income equal to Y_{45}, the contribution rate equal to c, and the growth of salary to g, the numerator of the replacement rate may be expressed as:

$$\frac{cY_{45}}{PPD_{45}} + \frac{cY_{45}(1+g)}{PPD_{46}} + \frac{cY_{45}(1+g)^2}{PPD_{47}} + ... + \frac{cY_{45}(1+g)^{20}}{PPD_{65}} \tag{A2.8}$$

The first term is simply the value of the pension annuity that the plan member buys with his or her contributions when at age 45. The second is the value of the annuity the plan member buys when at age 46, and so on. In like fashion, the denominator equals

$$\left(Y_{45}(1+(1+g)+(1+g)^2+(1+g)^3+...+(1+g)^{20}) \right)/21 \tag{A2.9}$$

Dividing numerator and denominator by Y_{45}, and re-expressing the denominator, the resulting expression for the replacement ratio (RR) is:

$$RR = \left(\frac{c}{PPD_{45}} + \frac{c(1+g)}{PPD_{46}} + \frac{c(1+g)^2}{PPD_{47}} + ... + \frac{c(1+g)^{20}}{PPD_{65}} \right) \bigg/ \frac{(1+g)^{21}-1}{g \cdot 21} \tag{A2.10}$$

Note that the ratio of the standard deviation of the replacement ratio (RR) is not affected by changes in c.

---

[1] The long-term bond yield is assumed to be normally distributed. Its average and standard deviation are based on annual data for 1998–2007, from Morningstar (2008).

Glossary

401(k) plan – A type of employer-provided defined-contribution plan to which a large number of U.S. workers belong. It takes its name from §401(k) of the Internal Revenue Code, which sanctions it. Participation in a 401(k) plan is not a condition of employment. The employer sets the maximum contribution rate, subject to the limits the IRS imposes on contributions. Employers typically provide a matching contribution up to some specified percentage of salary, usually 3 percentage points. Contributions to 401(k) plans may be deducted from taxable income in the year they are made and are taxed in the year in which they are withdrawn. The accumulated balance is almost always withdrawn in a lump sum. The higher the marginal tax rate on a plan participant's income, the greater is the tax advantage from contributing to a 401(k) plan.

Accrual factor – The rate at which a pension increases with the period of service under a defined-benefit plan. For example, a pension might increase by 2 percent of final salary for the first 25 years of plan service, and 1.5 percent up to 35 years of service.

Adverse selection – A phenomenon that affects most insurance markets to some degree. It occurs when the insured have a higher probability than the population at large of experiencing the contingency for which the insurance policy is written. For example, life insurance policy-holders have a higher mortality rate than the general population. Adverse selection implies that insurance rates or premiums will be higher than they would if the insured population was a representative sample of the general population.

Aggregate longevity risk – The risk that a projection of the life expectancy of a particular age cohort will be in error. Aggregate longevity risk cannot be hedged by increasing the size of the insured pool, like individual or select longevity risk.

Bias risk – The risk that a financial instrument used to hedge a particular risk is not well correlated with that risk. The text refers to two examples of bias risk: one that may arise when indexed bonds are used to hedge the impact of salary inflation on the pensionable base if consumer prices are not well correlated with salaries; the other when the index that determines the payments of a longevity bond is based on the mortality experience of a large population, which may not be similar to the experience of a plan's pensioners.

Book reserves – Reserves that are not held in a fund that is separate from the accounts of the company sponsoring a plan, but are instead recorded on the books of the company as a charge against net worth.

Cash-balance plan – A plan that is popular in the United States; technically it is a defined-benefit plan, but with the appearance of a defined-contribution plan. Each member has an account, to which are credited contributions based on pay as well as interest, usually at a fixed rate. This makes the ultimate benefit a function of a participant's salary history, the contribution rate, and the fixed rate of interest, which explains why cash-balance plans are classified as defined benefit.

Cohort life table – A table showing the mortality experience of a particular age cohort.

Conditional life expectancy – The expected number of additional years of life at a given age, or life expectancy conditional on reaching the given age. Life expectancy at birth is often simply referred to as life expectancy.

Conditional rate of return – An expression used to describe the rate of return on an annuity assuming the annuitant lives for the maximum life span.

Defined-benefit pension plan – A pension plan where the benefit paid to plan participants is determined by the terms of the plan. Typically, a defined-benefits plan determines the pension benefit on the basis of the number of years of participation and the participant's salary history. In a typical plan, the pension will be a percentage of the participant's salary over a period of a year or more at the end of the period of service. The percentage will be determined by an accrual factor (see Accrual factor).

Defined-contribution plan – A pension or saving plan that specifies the contributions to be made by plan members and plan sponsors, but not the benefit that members will receive. Defined-contribution plans typically specify the required contribution as a proportion of gross salary or wages. Contributions are invested in the financial markets and the combination of the sum of contributions and investment performance determines the ultimate benefit. With a self-directed plan, the member chooses his or her own asset allocation, typically from a set of mutual funds. A plan may or may not specify the form the benefit takes.

Duration – A measure of the average maturity of a bond or similar fixed-interest instrument; the time between the present and the due date of a payment is weighted by the present discounted value of the payment. The greater the time to maturity of the payments a bond makes, the longer the duration.

Equity risk premium – Because investors are assumed to be risk averse, and stocks are more risky than bonds, investors will require a higher rate of return on stocks than on bonds to be induced to hold equities. The difference in return is known as the equity risk premium. In practice, the difference between stock and bond yields has varied considerably, making it difficult to speak of *the* equity risk premium.

EET – The acronym for "exempt, exempt, taxed," which describes the standard way in which the cycle of contributions, accumulation, and distribution in a pension plan is taxed. Specifically, contributions by employees are usually exempt up to some amount and employer contributions are treated as a cost of doing business; plan income is exempt; and distributions are taxed. Some countries apply variants of the EET rule.

Hybrid plans – Plans that share features of both defined-contribution and defined-benefit plans, like the cash-balance plan. Defined-contribution plans with a guaranteed minimum rate of return can also be considered hybrid plans, because the guarantee reduces the uncertainty surrounding the benefit.

Hyperbolic discounting – The practice of discounting future income at a very high rate, while at the same time not discounting income at two different future dates at a substantially different rate. For example, one dollar ten years hence might be given a present value of only 25 cents, but one dollar 11 years hence might be valued at 24 cents.

Implicit rate of return of a public pension plan – Normally defined as the rate of return that would equalize the discounted value of a particular age cohort's expected benefits with the discounted value of their expected payroll tax contributions and employers' contributions made on their behalf.

Indexed annuity – An annuity with regular payments that are indexed to an indicator of the price level like the consumer price index. The initial nominal payment that an indexed annuity makes must be below the initial payment of a regular or nominal fixed annuity when inflation is positive.

Indifference curves – These are the curves in Figure 1.1 (see Chapter 1). They are usually drawn on a two-dimensional surface, with the consumption of one good, like clothing, measured on one axis and consumption of another, like food, measured on the other. The points on the same indifference curve are all preferred equally: None is inferior or superior to another.

Longevity bond – A bond with a return that varies positively with the difference between the actual survival rates of a population and assumed rates that are part of the terms of the bond.

Moral hazard – A risk thought to infect all insurance markets to some degree, because being insured reduces the disincentive the insured party has to avoid risky behavior. For example, insured drivers are more likely to speed; insured home owners are less cautious about locking their doors. The difference between moral hazard and adverse selection is that adverse selection does not entail a change of behavior.

Noncontributory pension – A pension to which plan members are not obliged to make contributions. All contributions are made by the sponsor.

Notional (nonfinancial) defined-contribution system – A national plan that has the appearance of a cash-balance plan, in that contributions earn a fixed rate of interest. However, the accumulated contributions plus returns are not backed by a pool of assets, but by the government's promise to make good the balance in each contributor's notional account, or to convert it at some usually predetermined rate into an annuity.

Pension wealth – An estimate of the present value of the pension payments a person can expect to receive in the future. The pension wealth of defined-contribution plans would normally be the current balance of the plan.

Period life table – A table showing the mortality experience of a particular year. A period table typically shows this experience by assuming an initial birth cohort of 100,000. The survival rates of each age cohort in one particular year are then applied to this initial figure to generate a series. The series shows the number of the birth cohort who would be alive at different ages assuming that the mortality rates in the chosen year for each age group would be the same as those of the birth cohort.

Projected benefit obligation – An estimate of the cost of a pension based on a projection of a plan member's final salary.

Replacement rate – The ratio of the pension benefit to a measure of income during the working life of the plan member. As Chapter 1 discusses, replacement ratios are sometimes calculated using an average of the last few years of income, and sometimes using an average over a longer period.

Solvency II – The new regulatory framework for European Union insurers. It has been described as having three pillars: quantitative regulation (technical provisions, investment rules and asset-liability management, and capital provisions), supervisory review (based on internal assessments of risks and controls), and disclosure requirements.

Strips – A type of bond created by removing (striping) the coupon payments from a conventional bond. The individual coupons can then become zero-coupon bonds, or a bond with a stream of equal payments.

Tax credit – A reduction in a taxpayer's tax liability that usually depends on the taxpayer satisfying certain conditions (like being a homeowner or being 65 years of age or older). Tax credits may be nonrefundable or refundable. With a nonrefundable tax credit, liability to tax can be reduced only to zero. A refundable tax credit can generate a rebate from the tax authority to the taxpayer.

Tax expenditure – A provision in the tax code that reduces the base or rate of a tax with effects that can be duplicated by an expenditure subsidy. For example, a deduction for mortgage interest could in principle be duplicated by a subsidy, although exact duplication would require that the agency paying the subsidy have information on the marginal rate of taxation of every homeowner.

Underfunded plan – A pension plan where the plan's reserves are not maintained at a level that is sufficient to finance the pensions expected to be paid to current members after taking into account the members' contributions.

Unit credit method – A method of calculating the accrued benefit of a defined-benefit plan that uses current salary rather than a projection of salary at the expected date of retirement.

Vested – The benefits of a plan member are vested when he or she has a claim to them. Defined-benefit plans typically require a period of membership of at least several years before accrued benefits are vested. Benefits derived from employee contributions vest immediately.

Yield curve – The relationship between the interest rate on a bond and its maturity. Typically, the yield curve slopes upward: A ten-year bond pays a higher rate of interest than a two-year bond. The yield curve is said to be inverted when the opposite obtains.

Zero-coupon bonds – Bonds with only one coupon, payable upon maturity. The yield is determined by the ratio between the current price and the value at redemption. For example, a bond with two years to maturity, a price at maturity of $110.25 and a market value of 100 would be paying an interest rate of 5 percent per annum.

References

Aaronson, Stephanie, and Julia Coronado. 2005. Are firms or workers behind the shift away from DB pension plans? Finance and Economics Discussion Series, Federal Reserve Board. 2005–17. http://www.federalreserve.gov/pubs/feds/2005/200517/200517pap.pdf

AARP. 2007. 401(k) Participants' Awareness and Understanding of Fees (July). http://www.aarp.org/research

—— 2009. *The Policy Book*. Washington, D.C.: AARP. http://www.aarp.org/issues/policies/policy_book/

Ambachtsheer, Keith. 2008. The Canada Supplementary Pension Plan (CSPP) – Towards an adequate, affordable pension for *all* Canadians. C. D. Howe Institute Commentary – The Pension Papers. http://www.cdhowe.org/pdf/commentary_265.pdf

American Academy of Actuaries and Society of Actuaries (AAA/SOA). 2006. *Pension Actuary's Guide to Financial Economics*. Joint AAA/SOA Task Force on Financial Economics and the Actuarial Model. http://www.actuary.org/pdf/pension/finguide.pdf

Ameriks, John, Robert Veres, and Mark Warshawsky. 2001. Making retirement income last a lifetime. Journal of Financial Planning (December).

Andersen, Carsten, and Peter Skjodt. 2007. Pension institutions and annuities in Denmark. World Bank. Policy Research Working Paper 4437. (December). http://www-wds.worldbank.org/external/default/WDSContentServer/WDSP/IB/2007/12/12/000158349_20071212140314/Rendered/PDF/wps4437.pdf

Annuity Market News. 2007. A "Match.Com" for SPIA Lovers. 13, 7 (July). http://www.accessmylibrary.com/article-1G1-165901008/match-spia-lovers-hueler.html

Antolin, Pablo. 2007. Longevity risk and private pensions. *OECD Working Papers on Insurance and Private Pensions*. No. 3 OECD Publishing. http://www.oecd.org/dataoecd/38/22/37977228.pdf

Armstrong, Jim. 2004. What is the funding status of corporate defined-benefit plans in Canada? *Financial System Review*. Bank of Canada (June). http://www.bankofcanada.ca/en/fsr/2004/index_0604.html

Association of British Insurers. 2005. The pension annuity market: Further research into supply and constraints. http://www.abi.org.uk

Australian Prudential Regulatory Authority (APRA). 2008. Statistics: Annual Superannuation Bulletin (June 2007; issued March 2008). www.apra.gov.au

2007. Insight: Celebrating Ten Years of Superannuation Data Collection 1996–2006. http://www.apra.gov.au/Insight/APRA-Insight-Issue-2-2007.cfm

Balevich, Igor. 2009. Outsourcing Pension Longevity. Presented at Pension Research Council Conference "Reorienting Retirement Risk Management" (April 30–May 1). http://www.pensionresearchcouncil.org/conferences/conf-2009.php

Barber, Brad M. 2008. Pension fund activism: The double-edged sword. PRC WP2008–13. Pension Research Council Working Paper. Pension Research Council. http://www.pensionresearchcouncil.org/publications/document.php?file=443

Barr, Nicholas. 2001. *The Welfare State as Piggy Bank: Information, Risk, Uncertainty and the Role of the State*. Oxford: Oxford University Press.

Bauer, Roy, Roy Hoevenaars, and Tom Steenkamp. 2006. Asset-liability management. In: *The Oxford Handbook of Pensions and Retirement Income*. Gordon L. Clark, Alicia H. Munnell, and Michael Orszag (Eds). Oxford: Oxford University Press, chapter 21.

BBC News. 2001. It could happen again. http://news.bbc.co.uk/1/hi/business/1251019.stm

Benartzi, Shlomo, and Richard Thaler. 2001. Naïve diversification strategies in defined contribution pension plans. American Economic Review, 91, 79–98.

Berner, Frank. 2006. Reister pensions in Germany: do they substitute or supplement public pensions? Positions in the debate on the new public policy on private pensions. Regina Working Paper No. 13 (December).

Blake, David, and Michael J. Orszag. 1997. The Portability and Preservation of Pension Rights in the U.K. Report of the Director General's Inquiry into Pensions, Volume III. Office of Fair Trading (October).

Blake, David. 2006a. Overregulating your pension out of existence: The long term consequences of British pension policy over the past 30 years. Pensions Institute, Cass Business School. Discussion Paper PI-0616. http://www.pensions-institute.org

2006b. *Pension Economics*. Chichester: John Wiley and Sons.

2006c. *Pension Finance*. Chichester: John Wiley and Sons.

Blake, David, Andrew J. Cairnes, and Kevin Dowd. 2006d. Living with Mortality: Longevity Bonds and Other Mortality-linked Securities. January 16. Presented to Faculty of Actuaries. http://www.ma.hw.ac.uk/~andrewc/papers/baj2006.pdf

Blake, David, Zaki Khorasannee, John Pickles, and David Tyrrall. 2008. An Unreal Number – How Company Pension Accounting Fosters an Illusion of Uncertainty. The Pensions Institute, Cass Business School. http://www.pensions-institute.org/reports/unrealnumber.pdf

Bodie, Zvi, and Michael J. Clowes. 2003. *Worry-free Investing: A Safe Approach to Achievement your Lifetime Financial Goals*. New York: FT-Prentice-Hall.

Boender, Guus C.E., Paul van Aalst and Fred Heemskerk, 2007. Modelling and managing of assets and liabilities of pension plans in the Netherlands. In: *Worldwide Asset and Liability Modelling*. William T. Ziemba and John M. Mulvey (Eds.). New York: Cambridge University Press, chapter 23.

Börsch-Supan, Axel. 2006. What are NDC systems? What do they bring to reform strategies? In: *Pension Reform – Issues and Prospects for Non-financial Defined Contribution (NDC) Schemes*. Robert Holzmann and Edward Palmer (Eds). Washington, D.C.: World Bank, chapter 3.

Börsch-Supan, Axel, and Christina B. Wilke. 2006. The German public pension system: How it will become an NDC look-alike. In: *Pension Reform – Issues and Prospects for Non-financial Defined Contribution (NDC) Schemes*. Robert Holzmann and Edward Palmer (Eds). Washington, D.C.: World Bank, chapter 22.

Börsch-Supan, Axel, Anette Reil-Held, and Daniel Schunk. 2007. The saving behavior of German households: First experiences with state promoted private pensions. Mannheim Research Institute for the Economics of Aging. 136–2007.

Brown, Jeffrey R., and Peter R. Orszag. 2006. The Political Economy of Longevity Bonds. http://www.retirementsecurityproject.org

Brown, Jeffrey R., Olivia S. Mitchell, and James Poterba. 2001. The role of real annuities and indexed bonds in an individual accounts retirement program. In: *The Role of Annuity Markets in Financing Retirement*. Jeffrey R. Brown, Olivia S. Mitchell, James M. Poterba, and Mark J. Warshawsky (Eds). Cambridge, MA: MIT Press, chapter 5.

Brown, Robert L., and Jianxun Liu. 2001. The shift to defined contribution plans: Why did it not happen in Canada? *North American Actuarial Journal* (July). http://www.soa.org/library/journals/north-american-actuarial-journal/2001/july/naaj0107-5.pdf

Brunner, Greg, Richard Hinz, and Roberto Rocha (Eds). 2008. *Risk-Based Supervision of Pension Funds: Emerging Practices and Challenges*. Washington, D.C.: World Bank.

Bunt, Karen, Lorna Adama, Zehra Koroglu, and Eoin O'Donnell. n.d. Pensions and Pension Reform. Department for Work and Pensions – Research Summary. http://www.workandpensions.gov.uk

Byrne, Alisdair, Debbie Harrison, Bill Rhodes, and David Blake. 2006. Pyrrhic victory? The unintended consequence of the Pensions Act of 2004. Pensions Institute, Cass Business School. Discussion Paper PI-0614. http://www.pensions-institute.org

Callegaro, Lisa, and Christina B. Wilke. 2008. Public, occupational and individual pension coverage, In: *Health, Ageing and Retirement in Europe (2004–2007)*. Börsch-Supan, A., A. Brugiavini, H. Jürges, A. Kapteyn, J. Mackenbach, J. Siegrist, G. Weber (Eds). Mannheim: MEA, pp. 220–7.

Campbell, John Y., and Luis M. Viceira. 2006. Strategic asset allocation for pension plans. In: *The Oxford Handbook of Pensions and Retirement Income*. Gordon L. Clark, Alicia H. Munnell, and Michael Orszag (Eds.). Oxford: Oxford University Press, chapter 22.

Catão, Luis, and George A. (Sandy) Mackenzie. 2006. Perspectives on low global interest rates. IMF Working Paper No. 06/76. http://www.imf.org

Chandler, Alfred D., Jr. 1977. *The Visible Hand – The Managerial Revolution in American Business*. Cambridge: Belknap Press.

Clark, Charlotte. 2008. Introduction to UK Pension Systems (presentation to Urban Institute Forum, September 10).

Clark, Gordon L. 2003. Pension Fund Governance: Moral Imperatives, State Regulation, and the Market. Paper presented at World Bank conference: Contractual Savings Conference: Regulatory and Supervisory Issues in Private Pensions. November 3–7. http://info.worldbank.org/etools/docs/library/157491/contractual2003/pdf/pension_fund_governance.pdf

Clark, Gordon L., Alicia H. Munnell, and Michael Orszag (Eds). 2006. *The Oxford Handbook of Pensions and Retirement Income*. Oxford: Oxford University Press.

Clark, Gordon L., and Ashby Monk. 2006. The 'crisis' in defined benefit corporate pension liabilities – Part I: Scope of the problem. Pensions 12(1), 43–54. http://www.palgrave-journals.com/pm/journal/v12/n1/abs/5950041a.html

Clark, Robert L., and Olivia S. Mitchell. 2002. Strengthening employment-based pensions in Japan. NBER Working Paper 8891 (April). http://www.nber.org/papers/w8891

Clark, Robert Lee, A. Craig, and Neveen Ahmed. 2008. The evolution of public sector plans in the United States. PRC WP2008–16. Pension Research Council Research Paper. Pension Research Council. http://www.pensionresearchcouncil.org/publications/document.php?file=448

Copeland, Craig. 2007. Employee tenure, 2006. EBRI Notes 28, 4 (April). http://www.ebri.org

Coronado, Julia Lynn, and Steven A. Sharpe. 2003. Did pension accounting contribute to a stock market bubble? Brookings Papers on Economic Activity, 1, 323–9.

Costa, Dora. 1998. *The Evolution of Retirement: an American Economic History, 1880–1990*. Chicago: University of Chicago Press.

Davis, E. Phillip. 2001. Portfolio regulation of life insurance companies and pension funds. Discussion paper PI-0101. London: The Pensions Institute, Birkbeck College, University of London. http://www.pensions-institute.org/workingpapers/wp0101.pdf

Deloitte. 2006. Securing Retirement: An Overview of the Pension Protection Act of 2006 (August 3). http://www.deloitte.com

De Serres, Alain, and Floria Pelgrin. 2005. The decline in saving rates in the 1990s in OECD countries: How much can be explained by non-wealth determinants? OECD Economic Studies. 36(2003/I), 117–48.

Deutsche Bank. 2003. Deutsche Bank Research. Current issues: More growth for Germany No. 8 (September 5).

Deutsche Bundesbank. 2001. Company pension schemes in Germany. *Monthly Report* (March). http://www.bundesbank.de/download/volkswirtschaft/mba/2001/200103mba_art03_pensionschemes.pdf

    2008. Monthly Report: Outlook for Germany's statutory pension insurance scheme. http://www.bundesbank.de/download/volkswirtschaft/mba/2008/200804mba_en_outlook.pdf

Dutch News.nl. 2009. New debate urged on pension system. (January 30). http://www.dutchnews.nl/news/archives/print/015321.php.

Ellis, Katrina, Alan Tobin, and Belinda Tracey. 2008. Investment performance, asset allocation and expenses of large superannuation funds. APRA Working Paper (October). http://www.apra.gov.au/Research/upload/APRA_WP_LSF_102008-3.pdf

Employee Benefits Research Institute. 2007. EBRI Issue Brief. 311 (November).

    2008a. Notes. 29, 5 (May).

    2008b. Notes. 29, 11 (November).

ERISA: *The Law and the Code*. 2009 edition. Sharon F. Fountain (Ed). Arlington, Virginia: BNA Books.

Escaffre, Lionel, Philippe Foulquier, and Philippe Touron. 2008. The Fair Value Controversy: Ignoring the Real Issue. EDHEC Business School. http://www.edhec-risk.com/site_edhecrisk/public/features/RISKArticle.2008–11–25.0644

European Actuarial Consultative Group. 2005 (revised). Security Standards for Pension Schemes in the European Union. http://www.gcactuaries.org/documents/2005_security_standards.pdf

European Financial Reporting Advisory Group (EFRAG). 2008. Pro-Active Accounting Activities in Europe (PAAinE) Discussion Paper: The Financial Reporting of Pensions. http://www.efrag.org/files/News%20related%20documents/PAAinE%20-%20Pensions%20paper%20-%20Final.pdf

Federal Reserve Board. 2007. Flow of funds accounts of the United States. http://www.federalreserve.gov/releases/z1

Financial Times. 2007. Globalization backlash in rich nations (July 22). http://www.ft.com

2008. How to arrive at fair value during a crisis (July 28). http://www.ft.com

2008. Regulator slams pension rules as bizarre (October 29). http://www.ft.com

Finansinspektionen. 2005. Continuation of FI's work to implement the EU occupational pensions directive (memo dated June 20).

2009. Complicated financial instruments in occupational pension funds. http://www.fi.se/upload/90_English/20_Publications/10_Reports/2009/report_2009_3_eng.pdf

Forman, Jonathan Barry. 2006. *Making America Work*. Washington, D.C.: Urban Institute Press.

Frederick, Shane, George Loewenstein, and Ted O'Donoghue. 2002. Time discounting and time preference: A critical review. Journal of Economic Literature. XL, 351–401.

Friedburg Leora, and Anthony Webb. 2006. Life is cheap: Using mortality bonds to hedge aggregate mortality risk. NBER Working Paper No. 11984. http://www.nber.org/papers/w11894

Friedburg Leora, and Michael T. Owyang. 2005. Explaining the evolution of pension structure and job tenure. Working Paper 2002–022D. Federal Reserve Bank of St. Louis. http://research.stlouisfed.org/wp/2002/2002–022.pdf

Gale, William G., John B. Shoven, and Mark J. Warshawsky. 2005. *The Evolving Pension System: Trends, Effects, and Proposals for Reform*. Washington, D.C.: Brookings Institution Press.

Gale, William, J. Mark Iwry, David C. John, and Lina Walker. 2008. Increasing Annuitization in 401(k) Plans with Automatic Trial Income. Retirement Security Project. http://www.retirementsecurityproject.org/pubs/File/RSP_TrialIncomev4(2).pdf

Gardner, J., and Orszag, J. Michael. 2004. Individual Choice and Financial Education in OECD Countries. Presentation at the OECD/INPRS Conference on Private Pensions, Manila. March 30 – April 1. http://www.oecd.org\dataoecd\37\1331078626.pdf

Gerke, Wolfgang, Ferdinand Mager, Timo Reinschmidt, and Christian Schmieder. 2006. Empirical risk analysis of pension insurance-the case of Germany. *Deutsche Bundesbank*, Series 2: Banking and Financial Studies, Discussion Paper No. 7/2006.

Ghilarducci, Teresa. 2006. Organized labor and pensions. In: *The Oxford Handbook of Pensions and Retirement Income*. Gordon L. Clark, Alicia H. Munnell, and J. Michael Orszag (Eds). Oxford: Oxford University Press, chapter 19.

2008. *When I'm 64: The Plot against Pensions and the Plan to Save Them*. Princeton: Princeton University Press.

Gold, Jeremy, and Gordon Latter. 2008. Marking Public Pension Plan Liabilities to Market. http://www.pensionresearchcouncil.org/conferences/conf-2008.php

Government of Australia. Treasury. n.d. Towards Higher Retirement Incomes for Australians: A History of the Australian Retirement Income System since Federation. http://www.treasury.gov.au

Government of Ontario. 2008. A Fine Balance – Report of the Expert Commission on Pensions. http://www.pensionreview.on.ca/english

Groom, Theodore R., and John B. Shoven. 2005. Deregulating the private pension system. In: *The Evolving Pension System: Trends, Effects, and Proposals for Reform.* William G. Gale, John B. Shoven, and Mark J. Warshawsky (Eds). Washington, D.C.: Brookings Institution Press, chapter 6.

Guardian.co.uk. 2000. Mis-selling bill tops £13 billion (December 2). www.guardian.co.uk/money/2000/dec/02/personalfinancenews.business/print

Guyton, Jonathan T. CFP, and William J. Klinger. 2006. Decision rules and maximum initial withdrawal rates. Journal of Financial Planning (March), 48–58.

Hannah, Leslie. 1986. *Inventing Retirement: The Development of Occupational Pensions in Britain.* Cambridge: Cambridge University Press.

Hinz, Richard, and Rein van Dam. 2008. Risk-based supervision of funds in the Netherlands. In: *Risk-based Supervision of Pension Funds: Emerging Practices and Challenges.* Greg Brunner, Richard Hinz, and Roberto Rocha (Eds). Washington, D.C.: World Bank, Chapter 2.

H.M. Revenue and Customs. 2007. "Pensions." http://www.hmrc.gov.uk/stats/pensions/menu.htm

Hustead, Edwin C. 1998.Trends in retirement income plan administrative expenses. In: *Living with Defined Contribution Plans: Remaking Responsibility for Retirement.* Olivia S. Mitchell, and Silvester J. Schieber (Eds). Philadelphia: University of Pennsylvania Press, pp. 166–77.

International Monetary Fund. 2002. *Global Financial Stability Report.* http://www.imf.org

  2004a. Germany: Selected Issues. http://www.imf.org

  2004b. *Global Financial Stability Report* (April). http://www.imf.org

  2006. Switzerland: Selected Issues. IMF Country Report 6/203. http://www.imf.org

  2007a. *Global Financial Stability Report.* (April). http://www.imf.org

  2007b Denmark: Financial Sector Assessment Program – Detailed Assessment of Observance of the Insurance Core Principles. IMF Country Report No. 07/119. http://www.imf.org

Invest in Sweden Agency. 2009. Social security and pensions. http://www.isa.se/Global/Doing-business/Running-a-business-in-Sweden–an-introduction/Social-security-and-pensions/#

Jagannathan, Ravi, and Narayana R. Kocherlakota. 1996. Why should older people invest less in stocks than younger people? Federal Reserve Bank of Minnesota Quarterly Review. 20, 3 (Summer).

Japanese Ministry of Health, Labor and Welfare. n.d. Overview of the Corporate Pension. Chapter 9 of *Textbook for the Study Program for the Senior Social Insurance Administrators.* http://www.mhlw.go.jp/english/org/policy/p36–37a.html

  2009. "Retirement" (web posting). http://www.mhlw.go.jp/toukei/youran/aramashi/taisyoku.pdf

Keynes, John Maynard. 1973. *The General Theory of Employment, Interest and Money.* Royal Economic Society: London: MacMillan.

Könberg, Bo, Edward Palmer, and Anilka Sundén. 2006. The NDC reform in Sweden: The 1994 legislation to the present. In: *Pension Reform – Issues and Prospects for Non-financial Defined Contribution (NDC) Schemes.* Robert Holzmann and Edward Palmer (Eds). Washington, D.C.: World Bank, chapter 17.

Kotlikoff, Lawrence J. 2008. Economics' approach to financial planning. http://people.bu.edu/kotlikof/New%20Kotlikoff%20Web%20Page/Economics%20Approach%20to%20Fin%20Planning,%20JFP11-08-07%20posted%20Jan%203,%202008.pdf

Laibner, David. 2006. The Importance of Default Options for Retirement Savings Outcomes: Evidence from the United States. Paper presented at The Future of Life-Cycle Saving and Investing Conference held at the Boston University School of Management October 25–27, 2006.http://www.bos.frb.org/economic/conf/lcsi2006/papers/laibson.pdf

Laidler, David, and William B. P. Robson. 2007. The Pension papers: Ill-defined benefits: The uncertain present and brighter future of employee pension plans in Canada. *C.D. Howe Institute Commentary.* No. 250. June. http://www.cdhowe.org/pdf/commentary_250.pdf

Lamb, Charles. 1980. The Superannuated Man. In: *The Portable Charles Lamb.* John Mason Brown (Ed). New York: Penguin, pp. 306–315.

Lewin, C. G. 2003. *Pensions and Insurance before 1800: A Social History.* East Lothian: Tuckwell Press.

Lowenstein, Roger. 2008. *While America Aged: How Pension Debts Ruined General Motors, Stopped the NYC Subways, Bankrupted San Diego, and Loom as the Next Financial Crisis.* New York: Penguin Press.

Mackenzie, George A. (Sandy). 2006. *Annuity Markets and Pension Reform.* Cambridge: Cambridge University Press.

2008. Determining whether 401(k) plan fees are reasonable: Are disclosure requirements adequate? *Insight on the Issues* No. 8 (September). Washington, D.C.: AARP. http://www.aarp.org/research/financial/pensions/i8_fees.html

Mackenzie, Sandy, and Ke Bin Wu. 2009. *Employer-provided Pensions: Less to count on.* Washington, D.C.: AARP. http://assets.aarp.org/rgcenter/ppi/econ-sec/2009-17-pensions.pdf

Mattoon, Richard H. 2007. Issues facing state and local government pensions. *Economic Perspectives,* Federal Reserve Bank of Chicago (Third quarter).

Maurer, Raymond, Olivia S. Mitchell, and Ralph Rogalla. 2008. Reforming German civil service pensions: Funding policy, investment strategy and intertemporal risk budgeting. PRC WP2008-09. Pension Research Council Research Paper. Pension Research Council. http://www.pensionresearchcouncil.org/publications/document.php?file=435

McGill, Dan M., Kyle N. Brown, John J. Haley, and Silvester J. Schieber. 2005. *Fundamentals of Private Pensions,* 8th edition. New York: Oxford University Press.

Mercer. 2006. Pension Scheme Deficits and Trends (December 31). http://www.mercerhr.com

2007a. Pension Scheme Financial Statistics (March 31). http://www.mercerhr.com

2007b. Pension Scheme Commentary (March 31). http://www.mercerhr.com

Milevsky, Moshe A. 2006. *The Calculus of Retirement Income – Financial Models for Pension Annuities and Life Insurance*. Cambridge: Cambridge University Press.

Mina, Jorge. 2005. Risk budgeting for pension plans. Risk Metrics Journal 6, 9–34.

Mitchell. Olivia S. and Stephan Utkus. 2004. Lessons from behavioral finance for retirement plan design. In: *Pension Design and Structure: New Lessons from Behavioral Finance*. O. S. Mitchell and S. P. Utkus (Eds). Oxford: Oxford University Press.

Morito, Hideyuki. n.d. Reconsidering Japanese Corporate and Personal Pensions: From a Legal Point of View. http://www.oecd.org/dataoecd/51/30/2763645.pdf.

Morningstar. 2008. *Ibbotson SBBI Classic Yearbook: Market results for stocks, bonds, bills and inflation 1926–2007*. Chicago: Morningstar.

Munnell, Alicia H. 2006. Employer-sponsored plans: The shift from defined benefit to defined contribution. In: *The Oxford Handbook of Pensions and Retirement Income*. Gordon L. Clark, Alicia H. Munnell, and J. Michael Orszag (Eds). Oxford: Oxford University Press, chapter 18.

Munnell, Alicia H., Kelly Haverstick, and Jean-Pierre Aubry. 2008. Why does funding status vary among state and local plans? Center for Retirement Research, State and local pension plans, No. 6 (May). http://crr.bc.edu/briefs/why_does_funding_status_vary_among_state_and_local_plans__3.html

National Institute of Population and Social Security Research. 2007. Social Security in Japan. http://www.ipss.go.jp/index-e.html

Office of Management and Budget. 2009. *Analytical perspectives. Budget of the U.S. Government. Fiscal Year 2010*. http://www.whitehouse.gov/omb/budget/Analytical_Perspectives

Organization for Economic Cooperation and Development. 2004. *Developments in Pension Fund Risk Management in Selected OECD and Asian Countries*. OECD Secretariat. http://www.oecd.org/dataoecd/38/52/34030924.pdf

2005. *Financial Market Trends – Aging and Pension System reform – Implications for Financial Markets and Economic Policies*. Supplement 1. http://www.oecd.org/document/41/0,3343,en_2649_34849_35620649_1_1_1_37467,00.html

2006. Pension Markets in Focus. Issue 3. (October). http://www.oecd.org

2008a. *Complementary and Private Pensions throughout the World 2008*. Paris: Organization for Economic Cooperation and Development.

2008b. *Private Pensions Outlook 2008*. Paris: Organization for Economic Cooperation and Development.

2008c. Pension Markets in Focus. Issue 5 (December). http://www.oecd.org/dataoecd/42/19/41770561.pdf

Oster, Axel. 2006. Pension Fund Supervision in Germany (Presentation at the conference on Supervision of Pension Systems: Current Trends and Issues, International Experience. Warsaw (17–19 September).

Palme, Joakim. 2005. Features of the Swedish pension reform. The Japanese Journal of Social Security Policy. 4, No. 1 (June).

Panjer, Harry H (Ed). 1998. *Financial Economics – With Applications to Investments, Insurance and Pensions*. Schaumberg: The Actuarial Foundation.

The Pensions Regulator. n.d. Funding Defined Benefits. Regulatory Code of Practice 03. http://www.thepensionsregulator.gov.uk

2007. *Annual Report and Accounts 2006/2007.* http://www.thepensionsregulator.gov.uk

Pension Benefit Guaranty Corporation. 2007. *Pension Insurance Data Book.* http://www.pbgc.gov

Ponds, Eduard H. M., and Bart van Riel. 2007. Sharing risk: The Netherlands' new approach to pensions. Center for Retirement Research. Boston College. No. 7–5 (April). http://crr.bc.edu/briefs/sharing_risk_the_netherlands_new_approach_to_pensions.html

Pozzebon, Silvana. 2008. The outlook for Canada's public sector employee pensions. PRC WP2008–23. Pension Research Council Research Paper. Pension Research Council. http://www.pensionresearchcouncil.org/publications/document.php?file=458

Queisser, Monika, and Dimitri Vittas. 2000. The Swiss multi-pillar pension system: Triumph of common sense? Development Research Group, The World Bank. Policy Research Working Paper, No. 2415 (August). http://econ.worldbank.org/external/default/main?pagePK=64165259&theSitePK=469372&piPK=64165421&menuPK=64166093&entityID=000094946_00092205342254

Rajnes, David. 2007. The evolution of Japanese employer-sponsored retirement plans. Social Security Bulletin 67, 3.

Rappaport, Anna, and John Turner. 2009. How Does Retirement Software Handle Post-retirement Risks? Presented at Pension Research Council Conference "Reorienting Retirement Risk Management" (April 30–May 1).

Rein, Marcus, and John Turner. 2001. Public-private interactions: Mandatory pensions in Australia, the Netherlands and Switzerland. Review of Population and Social Policy. 10, 107–53.

Robertson, Mavis. 2008. Australian Industry Funds. Unpublished manuscript (July).

Ross, Donald, and Lester Wills. 2002. The Shift from defined benefit to defined contribution retirement plans and the provisioning of retirement savings. Pension Institute. Discussion Paper PI-0210 (July). http://www.pensions-institute.org/workingpapers/wp0210.pdf

Sahai, Neeraj. 2006. Securing the promise: Is liability-driven investment the answer to the growing challenge of pension fund deficits? Pensions and Investments (August 22).

Sakamoto, Junichi. 2005. Japan's pension reform. World Bank SP Discussion Paper No. 0541 (December).

Salisbury, Dallas. 2006. Presentation at the Future of Life-cycle Saving and Investing Conference held at the Boston University School of Management (October 25–27, 2006). http://www.bos.frb.org/economic/conf/lcsi2006/presentions/salisbury.pdf

Saas, Stephen. 2006. The development of employer retirement plans: From the 19th century to 1980. In *The Handbook of Pensions and Retirement Income.* 2006. Gordon L. Clark, Alicia H. Munnell, and Michael Orszag (Eds). Oxford: Oxford University Press, chapter 5.

Schieber, Silvester J. 2005. The evolution and implications of federal pension regulation. In: *The Evolving Pension System: Trends, Effects, and Proposals for Reform.* William G. Gale, John B. Shoven, and Mark J Warshawsky. (Eds). Washington, D.C.: Brookings Institution Press, Chapter2.

Schulz, James. 2005. Old-Age Security: Australia Tries a Different Way. AARP. http://assets.aarp.org/rgcenter/econ/2005_21_australia.pdf

Schwartz, Barry. 2004. *The Paradox of Choice*. New York: Harper Collins, Echo.

Sharpe, William. 2001. Budgeting and monitoring the risk of defined benefit pension plans (September). http://stanford.edu/~wfsharpe/art/q2001/q2001.htm

Shiller, Robert. 2000. *Irrational Exuberance*. Princeton: Princeton University Press.

Siemans, AG. 2009. Siemens History Site – Company Development 1865–1890. http://w1.siemens.com/history/en/history/1865_1890_triumph_of_heavy_current_engineering_and_internationalization.htm

Social Security Administration. 2002. Life Tables for the United States: Social Security Area 1900–2100. Actuarial Study No. 116. Office of the Chief Actuary (August).

Soto, Mauricio. 2009. How is the financial crisis affecting retirement savings? (May) http://www.urban.org/publications/411880.html

thestar.com. 2009. Canadian pensions take record hit. (January 23). http://www.thestar.com/article/576105

Statistics Canada.2007. *Canada Year Book 2007*. http://www.statcan.ca.

Statistics Canada. 2009. Statistics Canada. Table 280–0008 – Registered pension plan (RPP) members, by area of employment, sector, type of plan and contributory status, annual (table), CANSIM (database), http://cansim2.statcan.gc.ca/cgi-win/cnsmcgi.exe?Lang=E&CANSIMFile=CII\CII_1_E.htm&RootDir=CII/

Surowiecki, James. 2006. Bitter money and Christmas clubs. Forbes.com. (February 14). http://www.forbes.com/2006/02/11

Thaler, Richard H., and Cass R. Sunstein. 2008, 2009. *Nudge*. New York: Penguin.

theage.com. 2009. Superannuation savings dive 19.7%, and more grief on way. (January 23). http://www.theage.com.au1/23/09

Thompson, Graeme. 2008. Risk-based supervision of pension funds in Australia. In *Risk-Based Supervision of Pension Funds: Emerging Practices and Challenges*. Greg Brunner, Richard Hinz, and Roberto Rocha. (Eds). Washington, D.C.: World Bank, chapter 4.

Towers, Perrin. 2007. Europe's Corporate Pension Mix-2007: European Pension Trends Survey. www.towersperrin.com

Tuer, Eric, and Elizabeth Woodman. 2005. Recent trends in Canadian defined-benefit pension sector investment and risk management. *Bank of Canada Review* (Summer). http://www.bank-banque-canada.ca/en/review

Turner, John A. 2007. The Future of U.S. Defined Benefit Plans: Insights from International Experience. Presentation to the International Brotherhood of Teamsters Benefits Committee, Las Vegas (April 26). http://www.aarp.org/research/ppi/econ-sec/ss/articles/2009_01_socsec.html

    2009. Social Security Financing: Automatic Adjustments to Restore Solvency. Washington D.C.: AARP, Public Policy Institute. http://www.aarp.org/research/ppi/econ-sec/ss/articles/2009_01_socsec.html.

U.K. Department for Work and Pensions. 2002. Simplicity, Security and Choice: Working and Saving for Retirement (December). http://www.dwp.gov.uk

    2006a. Security in Retirement: Towards a New Pension System. (May). http://www.dwp.gov.uk

    2006b. Media Centre. Quinquennial review of contracted out rebate taxes (March 2). http://www.dwp.gov.uk/newsroom/press-releases/20076/mar/pens-049–020306.asp

2007. Media Centre. State pension, pension credit and other rates 2008–2009. http://www.dwp.gov.uk/newsroom/press-releases/2007/october-2007/drc043-181007. shtml

U.K. Government Actuary's Department. 2006. Occupational Pension Schemes 2005 – the thirteenth annual survey by the Government Actuary. http://www.gad.gov.uk

U.K. Office for National Statistics. 2008.Occupational Pension Schemes Annual Report. http://www.statistics.gov.uk/downloads/theme_population/Occ-Pension-2007/ OPSS_Annual_Report_2007.pdf

U.K. Pensions Commission. 2004. *Pensions: Challenges and Choices – First Report of the Pensions Commission.* http://www.intute.ac.uk/cgi-bin/fullrecord.pl?handle= sosig1097587794-25257

U.K. Pension Protection Fund. 2009. PPF 7800 Index. http://www.pensionprotection-fund. org.uk/Pages/PPF7800Index.aspx

Urwin, R. C., S. J. Breban, T. M. Hodgson, and A. Hunt. 2001. Risk budgeting in pension investment. British Actuarial Journal, III.

van Dam, Rein, and Eric Brink Andersen. 2008. Risk-based supervision of pension institutions in Denmark. In *Risk-Based Supervision of Pension Funds: Emerging Practices and Challenges.* Greg Brunner, Richard Hinz and Roberto Rocha (Eds). Washington, D.C.: World Bank, chapter 3.

VanDerhei, Jack. 2006. Measuring retirement income adequacy: Calculating realistic income replacement rates. EBRI Issue Brief No. 297.

Waldensjö, Eshil. 2008. The Swedish Public-Private Mix in Pensions. http://www.reassess.no/asset/3165/1/3165_1.ppt

Wall Street Journal. 2006. Personal Finance Poll. 2, 7 (September 8).

Waring, Barton. 2008. Between Scylla and Charybdis: Improving the cost-effectiveness of public pension retirement plans. PRC WP2008–25. Pension Research Council Working Paper. http://www.pensionresearchcouncil.org/publications/document. php?file=532

Warner, J. T, and S. Pleeter. 2001. The personal discount rate: Evidence from military downsizing programs. American Economic Review, 91, 33–53.

Warren, Diana. 2008. Australia's retirement income system: Historical development and effects of recent reforms. Melbourne Institute Working Paper Series Working Paper No. 23/08. http://www.melbourneinstitute.com/wp/wp2008n23.pdf

Watson Wyatt. 2009. Risk budgeting and the art of good risk taking. http://www.watsonwyatt.com/europe/topics/htrender.asp?ID=16475

Whittington, Geoffrey. 2006. Accounting standards for pension costs. In: *The Oxford Handbook of Pensions and Retirement Income.* Gordon L. Clark, Alicia H. Munnell, and J. Michael Orszag (Eds). Oxford: Oxford University Press, chapter 26.

Wilcox, David. 2006. Reforming the defined benefit pension system. Brookings Papers on Economic Activity 1, 235–304.

Ziemba, William. 2003. *The Stochastic Programming Approach to Asset, Liability and Wealth Management.* Charlottesville: Association of Investment Management and Research.

Index